THE BEST TEST PREPARATION FOR THE
ADVANCED PLACEMENT
EXAMINATION IN

COMPUTER SCIENCE

Ernest Ackermann, Ph.D.
Professor of Computer Science
Mary Washington College
Fredericksburg, Virginia

John Najarian, Ph.D.
Associate Professor
William Patterson College
Wayne, New Jersey

Mohammad Dadashzadeh, Ph.D.
Professor of Decision Sciences
Wichita State University
Wichita, Kansas

Jerry R. Shipman, Ph.D.
Professor and Chairman,
Department of Mathematics
Alabama A&M University
Normal, Alabama

David Hunter, Ph.D.
Professor of Computer Science
Mary Washington College
Fredericksburg, Virginia

Research and Education Association
61 Ethel Road West
Piscataway, New Jersey 08854

The Best Test Preparation for the
ADVANCED PLACEMENT EXAMINATION
IN COMPUTER SCIENCE

Printed in the United States of America

Library of Congress Catalog Card Number 95-68123

International Standard Book Number 0-87891-882-5

Research & Education Association
61 Ethel Road West
Piscataway, New Jersey 08854

REA supports the effort to conserve and
protect environmental resources by
printing on recycled papers.

CONTENTS

AP COMPUTER SCIENCE REVIEW

ABOUT RESEARCH & EDUCATION ASSOCIATION

Research and Education Association (REA) is an organization of educators, scientists, and engineers specializing in various academic fields. Founded in 1959 with the purpose of disseminating the most recently developed scientific information to groups in industry, government, and universities, REA has since become a successful and highly respected publisher of study aids, test preps, handbooks, and reference works.

REA's Test Preparation series includes study guides for all academic levels in almost all disciplines. Research and Education Association publishes test preps for students who have not yet completed high school, as well as high school students preparing to enter college. Students from countries around the world seeking to attend college in the United States will find the assistance they need in REA's publications. For college students seeking advanced degrees, REA publishes test preps for many major graduate school admission examinations in a wide variety of disciplines, including engineering, law, and medical schools. Students at every level, in every field, with every ambition can find what they are looking for among REA's publications.

Unlike most Test Preparation books that present only a few practice tests which bear little resemblance to the actual exams, REA's series presents tests which accurately depict the official exams in both degree of difficulty and types of questions. REA's practice tests are always based upon the most recently administered exams, and include every type of question that can be expected on the actual exams.

REA's publications and educational materials are highly regarded and continually receive an unprecedented amount of praise from professionals, instructors, librarians, parents, and students. Our authors are as diverse as the subjects and fields represented in the books we publish. They are well-known in their respective fields and serve on the faculties of prestigious universities throughout the United States.

In addition to our authors, we wish to thank Bob Motwani for his significant editorial contributions.

PREFACE

This book represents a massive effort to provide you with four complete Advanced Placement Computer Science Exams: two AP Computer Science A and two AP Computer Science AB exams. Each exam is three hours in length, and is composed of every type of question that can be expected on the AP Computer Science Exam. In addition, each exam is followed by an answer key and detailed explanations to every question. By completing the exams which correspond to the test you are taking (A or AB) and by studying the explanations of answers and our Computer Science Review, you can discover your strengths and weaknesses and thereby become well prepared for the actual exam.

ABOUT THE TEST

The Advanced Placement (AP) Computer Science Exam is given each May by the Educational Testing Service under the direction of the Advanced Placement Board. The Advanced Placement program is designed to allow high school students to pursue college-level studies while attending high school. The AP exam is administered to high school students who have completed a year's study in a college-level computer science course. The exam is taken by students in an attempt to earn college credit. At many colleges, if the student scores high enough on the exam, he/she will earn college credits, and will be granted appropriate academic placement. Thus the student may enter the next higher level classes while still a freshman.

There are two AP Computer Science examinations:
- the Computer Science A exam, and
- the Computer Science AB exam

The Computer Science A exam primarily tests programming methodology and procedural abstraction. The study of algorithms, data structures, and data abstraction is also covered, but not as thoroughly as covered in the Computer Science AB exam. The Computer Science AB exam includes all the subjects found on the Computer Science A exam while going into further detail regarding algorithms, data structures, and data abstraction. In addition, any topic covered on both exams will be more fully developed on the Computer Science AB exam.

Each exam consists of two sections.

- Section One

  40 multiple choice questions
  One hour, 15 minutes

- Section Two

  Four to five free response questions
  One hour, 45 minutes

CASE STUDY

Beginning with the May 1995 exam, five to ten of the multiple choice questions and one or two of the free response questions will be based upon a case study. The case study includes a problem, one or more programs to solve the problem, and a description of the path taken by an expert programmer in solving the problem. A copy of the case study will be available from ETS to teachers and students in the fall of the year preceding the exam. Excerpts from the case study will also be provided to the students during the exam. This book includes a case study designed to simulate what students will see in the actual case study.

WHICH EXAM SHOULD YOU TAKE?

There are two ways to determine which exam you should take. 1. If your school is offering the Computer Science A course, then take the A exam. If your school is offering the AP Computer Science AB course, then take the AB exam. 2. If your school only offers a general AP Computer Science course and does not specify if it is A or AB, speak to your teacher regarding which exam you should take. Your teacher will be able to review your abilities and knowledge and help you pick the appropriate exam.

The AB exam is more difficult and requires more knowledge than the A exam, however, a good grade on either exam may result in college credit. Keep in mind that you cannot take both exams, and that you cannot change your mind once you have signed up to take one of the exams, so think carefully about which exam you wish to take.

ABOUT THE REVIEW

Our Computer Science Review provides a comprehensive summary of the main areas tested on the AP Computer Science Exam, and is written to help you understand these concepts. The following topics are discussed.

Computer Systems

Operating Systems, Primary and Secondary Memory, Programs, Computer Languages, and Types of Computer Systems

Programming Methodology

Design, Top Down Approach, Documentation, and Program Correctness

Features of a Block Structured Programming Language: Pascal

Basic Pascal, Program Structure, Identifiers, Standard Data Types, and Constants

Ordinal Data Types, Data Types, Standard Ordinal Data Types, Type Section, Enumerated Data Types, Subrange Data Types, and Sample Programs

Arrays, Array Definition, and One-Dimensional Arrays

Records, Record Definition, Record Processing, Variant Records, and Sample Programs

Sets, Set Definition, Set Constants, Set Assignments, Processing Sets, and Program Examples

Pointer Variables and Dynamic Allocation of Memory, Static Sequential Memory Allocation, Dynamic Allocation of Memory, Pointer Variables, and Sample Programs

Scope of Identifiers

Expressions and Evaluation, Arithmetic Operators, Algebraic Notation, and Standard Functions

Assignment Statement

Control Structures, Sequential Control, Boolean Expressions, Selection, Iteration, Procedural Control Structures, Labels, the Label Section, and the Goto Statement, and Sample Programs

Files and Input/Output Operations, Files, Input Operations on Text Files, Output Operations on Text Files, other Types of Files, and Sample Program

Procedure and Functions

Procedures, Functions, Recursion, and Sample Programs

String Processing

Fundamental Data Structures

Linked Lists, Linear Implementation, Pointer Implementation, Common Operations, and Variations, Stacks, Queues, Arrays and Records, and Trees

Algorithms

Searching, Elementary Sorting, Hashing, Advanced Sorting, and Numerical Integration

Ethical Issues

By studying our review, your chances of scoring well on the actual exam will be greatly increased. After thoroughly studying the material presented in the Computer Science Review, you should go on to take the appropriate practice tests. Used in conjunction, the review and the practice tests will enhance your skills and give you the added confidence needed to obtain a high score.

TAKING THE PRACTICE EXAMS

Make sure to take both practice exams which correspond to the exam you are taking. When taking the practice exams, you should try to make your testing conditions as much like the actual test as possible.

- Work in a quiet place where you will not be interrupted.
- Time yourself!
- Do not use any books, calculators, or similar articles, as these materials will not be permitted into the test center.

By following these tips, you will become accustomed to the time constraints you will face when taking the exam, and you will also be able to develop speed in answering the questions as the test format becomes more familiar.

SCORING THE EXAM

The multiple-choice section of the exam is scored by crediting each correct answer with one point, and by deducting one-fourth of a point for each incorrect answer. Questions omitted receive neither a credit nor a deduction. The free-response section is scored by a group of "chief readers" who read your response and assign it a grade. Then both grades, the raw score on the multiple choice section, and the grade on the free-response section, are combined and converted to the program's five-point scale:

5-extremely qualified

4-well-qualified

3-qualified

2-possibly qualified

1-no recommendation.

Colleges participating in the Advanced Placement Program usually recognize grades of 3 or higher.

ADVANCED PLACEMENT EXAMINATION IN
COMPUTER SCIENCE

Course Review

CHAPTER 1

COMPUTER SYSTEMS

1. INTRODUCTION

Computers and computer systems have grown from single-purpose machines used only for calculation to multi-purpose systems. Changes in the technology used to construct these systems and the increasing spread of applications have characterized four generations of computers. Initially, computers were capable of running only one set of instructions or programs at a given time. Modern systems are capable of serving many users with different applications.

Hardware, software, and firmware are the three components of the modern computer system. Hardware is the machinery that performs the mechanics of operations; software is the prewritten sequence of instructions that direct those operations; firmware is the name for special stored-program instructions which control basic operations such as multiplication, division, etc.

Even though different computers have different features and may include different operational devices, a system typically consists of four types of functional units: the central processing unit, secondary-storage devices, input devices, and output devices. The interrelationships of these units are shown on the diagram below.

The central processing unit (CPU) is the "brain" of the entire system. It contains a control section, an arithmetic/logic unit, and an internal storage unit (also called primary storage or main storage). The control section of the CPU directs and coordinates the operations of the computer system according to a prewritten sequence of instructions (firmware) stored within it. The control section selects instructions, interprets them, and generates signals and commands that cause other system units to perform required operations at appropriate times.

The arithmetic/logic unit performs arithmetic and logical operations. It calculates, shifts numbers to the right or left, sets the algebraic sign of a result, rounds, compares algebraically, and so on.

The internal storage unit can be compared with a post office containing a huge number of numbered mail boxes. Each box, or location, is capable of holding data or instructions. Each such storage location has an assigned address. Using the addresses, the control section of the CPU can locate data and instructions as needed.

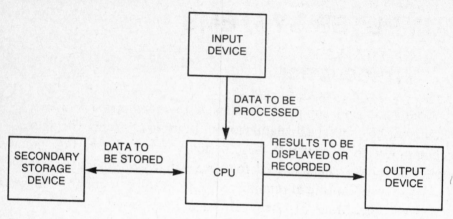

2. OPERATING SYSTEMS

The instructions that manage the system are called the operating system. The operating system must keep track of the status of each resource. It must also decide which process is get how much of each resource and when. Finally, it must allocate and eventually reclaim the resources. Thus the operating system can be viewed as a resource manager. Its functions are classified under four management activities:

I. Memory Management functions:

1) Keep track of memory: what parts are in use and by whom? What parts (of memory) are not in use?

2) If multiprogramming, decide which process gets memory, when it gets it and how much.

3) Allocate the memory when process requests it.

4) Reclaim the resource when the process no longer needs it or has been terminated.

II. Processor Management functions:

1) Keep track of the processor and the status of process. The program that does this has been called the "traffic controller."

2) Decide who will have a chance to use the processor; the "job scheduler" chooses from all the jobs submitted to the system. If multiprogramming, decide which process gets the processor, when, and for how long; this is called the "processor scheduler."

3) Allocate the resource to a process by setting up necessary hardware registers; this is often called "dispatcher."

4) Reclaim processor when process terminates, or exceeds allowed amount of usage.

III. Device Management functions:

1) Keep track of the devices, channels, and control units; this is typically called "I/O traffic controller."

2) Decide what is the most efficient way to allocate the device. If it is to be shared, then decide who gets it and for how long. This is called "I/O scheduling."

3) Allocate the device and initiate I/O operation.

4) Reclaim.

IV. Information Management functions:

1) Keep track of information: its location, use, status, etc. These facilities are often called "file system."

2) Decide who gets to use the file, enforce protection and provide accessing routines.

3) Allocate the file i.e., "open a file."

4) Reallocate the file i.e., "close a file."

3. PRIMARY AND SECONDARY MEMORY

Memory or storage units may be classified as primary or secondary. Primary memory is often a collection of devices or circuits used for the fastest storage and retrieval of information. Secondary memory is often in the form of disks or tape. The methods of accessing the memory are classified by the manner in which the information may be retrieved. These are referred to as direct, random, or sequential access. Input and output devices are used to transmit information to/from the computer to/from an external source. These external sources include terminals, disk drives, and printers.

Instructions are available in either primary or secondary memory. In either case an instruction must be obtained from memory and interpreted by the CPU; then an appropriate action is taken by the computer. Data or information that is manipulated by an instruction is either in storage, comes from an input device, or is sent to an output device.

4.　PROGRAMS

A computer solves problems by executing instructions that people give to it. These instructions are what constitute a program. The instructions are best written or developed in several stages. These stages include defining the problem, determining an algorithm to solve the problem, translating the solution to a computer language, and then testing the solution. The program is written in a specific programming language which is translated into "machine language." We do not directly write our code in this machine language because it is too difficult to understand. Thus, we use languages such as Basic, Pascal, or C which more closely resemble English. Different computers may be constructed differently, each with its own architecture. The machine language consists of the primitive instructions for a specific computer. When a program is executed, each of the machine language instructions is interpreted by the CPU.

5.　COMPUTER LANGUAGES

Computer languages may be classified in a range from "high level" — closest to humans, to "low level" — closest to machines. Machine language programs consist of sequences of zeros and ones, and are difficult for humans to read and write without errors. An assembly language is a language that is unique to a particular computer, and one in which each instruction is translated to a single machine language instruction. While programs written in assembly language are not commonly portable from one type of computer to another, they have the advantage of being symbolic representations of machine instructions. Thus they may be more easily read and understood. Both of these are examples of low level languages. FORTRAN, Pascal, C, or PL/I are examples of high level languages. Most programs are written in high level languages. One instruction in any of these languages often translates into several machine language instructions. The advantage of using these is that a program in a high level language may be used on several different machines.

5.1   Translation

There are two approaches to language translation: **compilation** and **interpretation. A compiler** will translate the entire program from, for example, Pascal, into the machine language. After it translates the entire program, it starts to execute it. On the other hand, an **interpreter** translates the program one statement at a time. The interpreter will translate the first statement, execute it, translate the second statement, execute it, and so on. There are advantages to both approaches. With interpretation, if there is an error in one of the statements the computer can pinpoint which statement caused it, because it is executing each statement as it comes across it. Compilation is useful when there is a task that is repeated several times. The translated version of the task is saved and can be executed directly whenever it is needed without having to translate the same statement over and over again. The compiler is usually more advantageous that an interpreter, and is the approach that is most widely used in translation.

5.2   Language Description

A programming language can be described by its **syntax** and **semantics**. Syntax are the rules that tell us how to put statements together. Semantics are descriptions of how a program is actually written. For example, the syntax of Pascal tells us that

        a := b;

is a correct assignment statement. We use a **grammar** to describe the syntax. The grammar is a set of rules for defining all valid constructs of a language. An example of a grammar is **Backus-Nawr Form (BNF)**. An expression in BNF grammar would be described as:

        expression ::= value operator expression.

Another type of grammar are **syntax diagrams.** Here expression is described as:

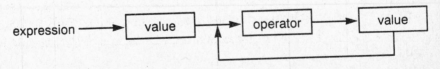

6. TYPES OF COMPUTER SYSTEMS

Computer systems may be single purpose or general purpose. Single purpose systems are designed for specific types of applications such as scientific or business. General purpose systems serve a variety of users. Furthermore, computers may be designed for a single user or may be used simultaneously by several users. If there are several users the system is called a timesharing or multiprogramming system. Most systems have one CPU, thus the needs of several users must be met in a well-managed manner so that it appears that all have appropriate access to system resources. In contrast to a timesharing system, a batch system is one where the computer reads input sequentially. Usually there is a wait of a few hours from the time when the program is submitted until the results are ready. This is much slower than a timesharing system.

CHAPTER 2

PROGRAMMING METHODOLOGY

1.   DESIGN

A computer program is a creative statement of the logical solution of a problem. Program development is the task of creating the program. While not too difficult, efficient programming must be done carefully. It involves more than just simply writing the appropriate code. Several steps must be followed in order to determine the capabilities and constraints of a program. This process is known as **specification.** The steps are:

1. Defining the problem — We must have a clear statement of the goal of our program, of what we want to accomplish. In addition to describing the problem, we must clearly and completely determine our input data and the desired results.

2. Planning a solution algorithm — Deciding on the directions in solving the problem; breaking the task into specific operations that the computer can perform.

3. Coding the solution — Writing a set of instructions for the computer to perform the operations which were identified in the solution algorithm.

4. Checking out the program — Debugging and testing the solution algorithm and its corresponding program to ensure that the desired results are provided in the output. When there are errors in our program, we say that it has "bugs." The process of identifying and correcting the errors is **debugging.**

Logical and design problems are more difficult to identify and are more severe. That is one of the primary reasons for spending the appropriate amount of time and effort in the design phase of program development.

2.   TOP DOWN APPROACH

Problem solving can best be accomplished by dividing the problem into smaller subproblems. This approach is known as the **top down method.** The purpose is to make the problem simple enough so that we can write a program that solves the problem by encoding the subproblems.

The task of breaking the problem down is called **stepwise refinement.** We are refining from the general to the particular, making the problem more specific. Our methodology is to:

    a.   State the problem simply, decomposing it into its logical subproblems

    b.   Develop the code for the subproblems. If you can't produce the code, then

    c.   Refine the subproblems into even smaller subproblems.

We use these techniques to enhance our programming ability. A difficult problem may turn out to be a combination of simple subproblems.

3.   DOCUMENTATION

A good program is one that is easy to read and to understand, detailing exactly what each variable represents and what each procedure does. Documentation explaining these things should always be included.

Furthermore, meaningful names that identify a variable's purpose should be utilized. For example, the declaration

    Var a,b,c: integer;

does not tell us anything about the purpose of these variables. However,

    Var area, base, circumference: integer;

is much clearer.

Documentation is essential to any useful program. Comments throughout the program should explain the purpose of subprograms and how they accomplish their tasks. In addition, indentation, blank lines, spaces, etc. serve to make the program much more readable.

4.   PROGRAM CORRECTNESS

To determine if a program works, we need to do more than just run it. Executing it only tells us that it works for a specific set of data, and is not enough evidence of its reliability. To assure us of a program's correctness, we construct a program proof, a paper analysis of a program that attempts to formally verify that a program will always produce the correct result. This method is akin to a mathematical proof, which is used to justify a mathematical theorem.

4.1 Assertions

The proof of a program is based on a series of **assertions** about the values of program variables and data. It is a statement that we expect to be true. Assertions that come before an action are **preconditions,** while assertions that follow an action are **postconditions.**

An example is

```
{B<>0}
C := A/B;
{A = B*C}
```

Here we want to divide A by B and store the result in C. The closing assertion, the postcondition, is that the answer is correct: A = B * C. In order to do a logical division, B must not equal 0, and thus we have an opening assertion, a precondition that B<>0.

Study this topic especially for 'AB' preparation.

4.2 Invariants

Loops pose a special problem because assertions before and after the loop are not sufficient; the assertions must establish that the loop is not infinite, that it does terminate. An **invariant** assertion is a statement about a loop that is true both before and after each iteration of the loop. Similarly, a variant assertion is one that changes after each iteration. An example is to do integer division by repeated subtraction:

```
remainder := dividend;
quotient := 0;
{invariant assertion: dividend= (divisor*quotient)+remainder}
while remainder >= divisor do begin
```

```
    remainder := remainder – divisor;
    {variant assertion: remainder >= divisor, and remainder declines}
    quotient := quotient + 1;
    {invariant assertion: dividend= (divisor*quotient)+remainder}
    end;
```

Using invariants and assertions helps to simplify the algorithm.

CHAPTER 3

FEATURES OF A BLOCK STRUCTURED PROGRAMMING LANGUAGE: PASCAL

1. INTRODUCTION

Pascal is a modern high-level programming language developed by Niklaus Wirth in the early 1970s and named in honor of the 17th century French mathematician and inventor.

Pascal was designed to be a language to be used in teaching programming. As such it offers a wide range of control structures (if-then-else, case statements, for loops, while loops, repeat-until loops, etc.), the ability to define data types both globally and locally, and allows for subprograms in the form of functions and procedures. These make the language rich enough to use in a variety of applications, and to demonstrate simple and sophisticated programming concepts.

Pascal is a very good language with which to learn programming, because it encourages and enforces the use of modern structured programming techniques. It is available on most systems and is appropriate for developing complex programs.

2. BASIC PASCAL

2.1 Program Structure

The general structure of a Pascal program is illustrated in the following diagram:

program *prg-name (file-list);*

```
label
    { label section }
const
    { constant section }
type
    { type section }
var
    { variable section }

{ subprogram section }

begin
    {executable statements }
end.
```

The general structure of a Pascal program may be divided into three parts: program heading, declaration part, and statement part.

2.1.1 PROGRAM HEADING

The first statement in a Pascal program is the program heading. This statement gives the program name and the kinds of input/output operations that will be performed by the program. The program heading is required for Pascal programs.

Prg-name in the program heading denotes the program name identifier. *File-list* denotes a list of file name identifiers and the type of operations that are permitted on them.

2.1.2 DECLARATION PART

The declaration part of a Pascal program may contain up to five sections. They are the label, constant, type, variable, and subprogram sections. An individual section is required only if an identifier is defined or declared in that particular section. Thus, if a program does not use constant identifiers, the constant section would not appear in the program. The same may be said of the other sections. However, all non-trivial programs will have at least the variable section since all identifiers, including variable identifiers, must be declared before they can be used in a Pascal program.

2.1.3 STATEMENT PART

The statement part of a Pascal program contains the executable statements that manipulate data. The statement part is actually a compound statement which always starts with a **begin** statement and concludes with an **end** statement. It has the form

begin
    statement-1;
    statement-2;
       "
       "
       "
    statement-n;
end.

2.2 Identifiers

Identifiers denote programs, procedures, functions, constants, types, variables, and fields within records. An identifier must begin with a letter followed by any number of letters and/or digits. An identifier may not be one of the Pascal **reserved words** since the latter have special meaning in Pascal. A list of the Pascal reserved words is given in Table 2.2.1. In addition to reserved words, Pascal contains the **standard identifiers** listed in Table 2.2.2.

TABLE 2.2.1
RESERVED WORDS

and	do	forward	mod	procedure	to
array	downto	function	nil	program	type
begin	else	goto	not	record	until
case	end	if	of	repeat	var
const	file	in	or	set	while
div	for	label	packed	then	with

TABLE 2.2.2
STANDARD IDENTIFIERS

abs	eof	in	page	rewrite	text
arctan	eoln	maxint	pred	round	true
boolean	exp	new	put	sin	trunc
char	false	odd	read	sqr	unpack
chr	get	ord	readln	sqrt	write
cos	input	output	real	succ	writeln
dispose	integer	pack	reset		

Standard identifiers are not reserved words and therefore may be redefined by the programmer. However, since standard identifiers have predefined meanings, it is usually not wise to do so.

Pascal is not case sensitive — that is, Pascal makes no distinction between upper case and lower case, with the exception of character and string constants. Therefore, any combination of upper and lower case may be used for user-defined identifiers, standard identifiers, and reserved words. For example, currentyear, CurrentYear, and CURRENTYEAR would denote the same identifier in a Pascal program.

2.3 Standard Data Types

Pascal provides four standard data types. These are **integer, real, char,** and **boolean.** Integer data are the positive and negative counting numbers (e.g., 0, 322, -1476, +91). Real data are the positive and negative numbers that either include decimal points such as 7.6 and -3.91, or are expressed as powers of 10 such as 4.6741E2 and 9.701E-03. The latter two numbers are examples of exponential notation. The "E" should be read as "times ten to the power of." Therefore, 4.6741E2 is 4.6741 times ten to the power of 2 or 467.41, and 9.701E-03 is 9.701 times ten to the power of -3 or .009701.

Character data include all characters — letters, digits, and punctuation marks — that are found on the keyboard. Boolean data are sometimes called logical data. The two possible boolean values are **true** and **false.**

2.4 Constants, Constant Identifiers, and the Constant Section

Constants are quantities whose values cannot be changed during program execution. Examples of constant values were given in Section 2.3. Often, it is useful to name constants in order to make programs more readable and easier to maintain. Constants may be named, or defined, in the constant section. The constant section begins with the reserved word **const**. If present, the constant section has the form

```
const
     identifier-1 = constant-1;
     identifier-2 = constant-2;
         "
         "
```

"
identifier-n = constant-n;

Identifier-1 through *identifier-n* are identifiers and therefore must conform to the rules for forming valid identifiers. The following is an example of a constant section:

```
const
        Pi  = 3.141592654;
  FirstLetter = 'A';
  BaseYear = 1900;
      Cat = 'Felis';
     Okay = true;
```

The name Pi is given, or bound to, the real constant 3.141592654 and BaseYear is bound to the integer constant 1900. Okay is a boolean constant bound to the boolean value **true**. FirstLetter and Cat are character constants. FirstLetter is bound to the single character 'A', while Cat is bound to the string constant 'Felis'. Named constants may be used anywhere in a program where constant values may be used. For example, Pi may be used in place of 3.141592654 anywhere in the program where it is legal to use constant value 3.141592654.

3. ORDINAL DATA TYPES

3.1 Data Types

Pascal supports many data types, both predefined and user-defined, as Figure 3.1 illustrates.

FIGURE 3.1
DATA TYPES SUPPORTED BY PASCAL

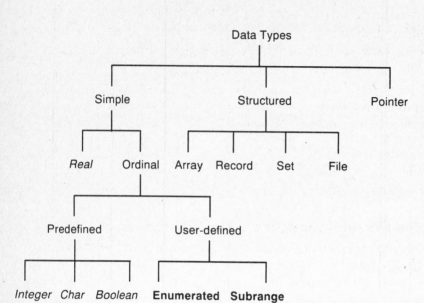

The four standard data types supported by Pascal were introduced in Part Two of this chapter. These include real, integer, char, and boolean. Sometimes they are referred to as **simple** predefined data types. Simple data types are atomic in nature, that is, they cannot be subdivided.

The concept of **ordinal** data types is introduced in the next section. This is followed by a discussion of the two user-defined ordinal types supported by Pascal, namely **enumerated** and **subrange**.

3.2   Standard Ordinal Data Types

An ordinal data type is an ordered set in which every element, except the first element, has an immediate predecessor, and every element, except the last element, has an immediate successor. Integer, char, and boolean types are standard ordinal data types. Real type is not ordinal because a real value has no unique predecessor or successor. By adding additional digits of precision, the predecessor and successor of real values change. For example, is 8.061, 8.0601, 8.06001, or 8.060001 the immediate successor of 8.06? The answer is none of them. Another digit can be added to obtain a more immediate successor — or predecessor.

3.3   Type Section

The general structure of a Pascal program was introduced in Part 2 of this chapter. One of the sections that may be present in the declaration part of a program is the **type** section. If present, the type section has the form

```
type
     identifier-1 = type 1;
     identifier-2 = type 2;
          "
          "
          "
     identifier-3= type-n;
```

Identifier-1 through *identifier-n* are identifiers which conform to the rules for forming valid identifiers. The following example illustrates the use of the **type** section.

```
type
     Status      =   boolean;
     Register    =   integer;

var
     Carry, Zero, Negative: Status;
     AX, BX, CX: Register;
```

In this example, the variables Carry, Zero, and Negative are declared as type Status where Status is type boolean. Likewise, AX, BX, and CX are declared as type Register where the latter is type integer.

3.4   Enumerated Data Types

Enumerated data types comprise one of the two classes of user-defined ordinal data types supported by Pascal. Enumerated data types have the form

```
identifier= (const-ident-1, const-ident-2, ... const-ident-n);
```

An example illustrating the use of enumerated data types is shown below:

```
type
     ExoticColors = (Fuchsia, Magenta, Indigo, Teal, Ecru);
     PrimaryColor = (Red, Blue, Yellow);
```

var
    Paint: Exotic Color;
    Trim: PrimaryColor;

There are a few basic rules regarding the usage of enumerated data types. They are summarized in Table 3.4.1 .

TABLE 3.4.1
RULES GOVERNING USAGE OF ENUMERATED DATA TYPES

Rule 1. A constant identifier cannot appear in more than one enumerated type declaration.

Rule 2. Since enumerated data types are ordinal — an ordered set — relational operators (<, >, =, <=, >=, <>) may be used to compare enumerated type values. This means that enumerated type values may be used in boolean expressions of control structures such as **while, for,** and **repeat** loops, and **if...then...else** statements.

Rule 3. Pred, succ, and ord functions are also applicable with enumerated type values for the reason given in Rule 2.

Rule 4. Values of enumerated data types cannot be read from or written to text files.

The examples that follow demonstrate the implementation of these rules using the declarations given earlier on colors.

EXAMPLE 1

for Paint:= Fuchsia **to** Ecru **do**
    begin
        "
         "
        "
    end;

EXAMPLE 2

Paint:= pred(Indigo);
Paint:= succ(Ecru);

The pred(Indigo) is Magenta. Paint becomes undefined in the second statement since Ecru is the last element in the set and has no successor. This statement will generate a run-time error when it is executed.

EXAMPLE 3.

```
ColorNumber:= ord(Teal);
```

The ord(Teal) is 3. Ord returns the value of the position of the element in the enumerated type. Position numbering begins with zero for the first element.

EXAMPLE 4

```
case Paint of
  Fuchsia:   writeln('Fuchsia');
  Magenta:   writeln('Magenta');
   Indigo:   writeln('Indigo');
     Teal:   writeln('Teal');
     Ecru:   writeln('Ecru');
end;
```

Values of enumerated types cannot be read from or written to text files. This also applies to standard input/output files. This example illustrates one method for outputting text equivalents of enumerated types.

3.5   Subrange Data Types

Ordinal types discussed thus far represent entire ranges of values. It is also possible to define a **subrange type** to be a subrange of an existing ordinal type. The existing ordinal type is known as the base type, which can be one of the standard ordinal types or an enumerated type.

The form of the subrange type is given below:

identifier= lower-bound-value ... upper-bound-value;

where *lower-bound-value* and *higher-bound-value* are values of some ordinal base type and *lower-bound-value* is lower than or equal to *upper-bound-value*. Rules that govern the use of ordinal types apply to a subrange of the ordinal type.

A value of one data type can be assigned to a variable of another data type only if the two data types are compatible. Two data types are compatible if they have the same definition, if they have the same type identifier, if one is a subrange of the other, or if both are subranges of the same base type. An error is generated otherwise.

The major advantage of using subrange types is automatic range checking. By specifying exactly the range of legal values that a variable may take on, the compiler will check to ensure that only values within the specified subrange are assigned to the variable.

Here are two examples of subrange data type definitions followed by the corresponding variable declarations:

```
type
    DayOfWeek = (Monday, Tuesday, Wednesday,
                 Thursday, Friday, Saturday, Sunday);
    WeekDay =   Monday... Friday;
    WeekEnd =   Saturday... Sunday;

var
    WorkDay:    WeekDay;
    PlayDay:    WeekEnd;
```

The subrange type definition and the variable declaration may be combined in one statement.

```
type
    DayOfWeek = (Monday, Tuesday, Wednesday,
                 Thursday, Friday, Saturday, Sunday);

var
    WorkDay:    Monday... Friday;
    PlayDay:    Saturday... Sunday;
```

These two examples are actually identical. However, the first example provides more flexibility for program development since it allows Workday and Playday to be passed as parameters to procedures and functions. If Workday and Playday are declared as they are in the second example, they cannot be passed as parameters to procedures and functions. Procedures and functions are presented in Section 13.

3.6 Sample Program

program EstimateMood(input,output);

```
{   The program reads your mood ratings as rated by other individuals    }
{   from the keyboard until a Ctrl-Z is entered. The Ctrl-Z is interpreted    }
{   as the end-of-file (eof) in the first while loop. After the AverageRating    }
{   of YourRating is calculated, YourMood is assigned the value of    }
{   Melancholy, which is lowest value of type Mood. YourMood is    }
{   incremented as long as its ord value is not equal to the AverageRating    }
{   minus one. The case statement outputs a message based upon the    }
{   value of YourMood.    }

type
    Mood  =   (Melancholy, Gloomy, Sullen, Capricious, Pensive, Sober,
              Humorous, Jubilant, Elated, Ecstatic);

    Rating = 1 . . . 10;

var
    YourMood: Mood;
    YourRating, AverageRating: Rating;
    SumOfRatings, NumberOfRaters: integer;


begin
    SumOfRatings:= 0;
    NumberOfRaters:= 0;
    while not eof do
        begin
            readln(YourRating);
            SumOfRatings:= SumOfRatings + YourRating;
            NumberOfRaters:= succ(NumberOfRaters);
        end;
    writeln;
    AverageRating:= round(SumOfRatings / NumberOfRaters);
    YourMood:= Melancholy;
    while ord(YourMood) <> AverageRating –1 do
        YourMood:= succ(YourMood);
    case YourMood of
        Melancholy: writeln('Make an appointment with your analyst.');
        Gloomy: writeln('Go back to bed.');
        Sullen: writeln('Cheer up. Things could be worse.');
        Capricious: writeln('Don't be so fickle.');
        Pensive: writeln('Enroll in a college course.');
        Sober: writeln('Today you should be mischievous.');
        Humorous: writeln('Get serious. It may mean a promotion.');
        Jubilant: writeln('Go on a shopping spree. You deserve it.');
        Elated: writeln('Ask your boss for a raise.');
```

```
        Ecstatic: writeln('Spread the cheer!');
    end;
        writeln('Your rating is ',AverageRating);
end.
```

4.   ARRAYS

4.1   Array Definition

In addition to simple data types, Pascal provides four structured data types — arrays, files, records, and sets. Files, records and sets are covered in subsequent sections. Arrays are presented in this section.

An array is a data structure that consists of a fixed number of data items, all of the same type. Each item or element in the array is accessed through the array name and a subscript. Arrays are often called subscripted variables.

Although the type of an array may be specified in the variable section of the declaration part of a program, it is preferable to associate it with a type identifier using the following form:

type
    array-type-identifier = **array[***dimensions***] of** *component-type;*

var
    identifier-1, ... identifier-n: array-type–identifier;

Dimensions has the form

    subscript-type-1, subscript-type-2, ... subscript-type-n

where *subscript-type* is any ordinal type. *Component-type* may be a simple type, structured type, or pointer type.[1]

4.2   One-Dimensional Arrays

A one-dimensional array has a single subscript. That is, each element in an array may be accessed through the variable name and one subscript value which uniquely identifies the element. Some example declarations of one-dimensional arrays are given below:

---

(1) Pointer types are presented in Section 7.

```
program declarations;

const
    ArraySize = 100;

type
            ArrayRange    =    -10 . . 10;
               Letter     =    'a' . . 'z';
            MoodTypes     =    (Melancholy, Gloomy, Sullen,
                                Pensive, Sober, Humorous,
                                Jubilant, Elated);
          NameArray       =    array [1. .15] of char;
          ArrayOfReal     =    array [1. .ArraySize] of real;
    LetterFrequencyArray  =    array [Letter] of integer;
          MoodArray       =    array [1. .ArraySize] of MoodTypes;

var
    Name:        NameArray;
    Frequency:   LetterFrequencyArray;
```

5.   RECORDS

5.1   Record Definition

In the previous chapter, an array was shown to be a structured data type that consists of a fixed number of data items, all of the same type. Each element in the array is accessed through an array subscript or index. A **record** is also a structured data type consisting of a fixed number of data items. However, unlike arrays, the data items, or **fields**, of a record may be of different data types. Furthermore, the fields are accessed through **field selector variable names** instead of through subscripts.

Although the record type may be specified in the variable section, it is preferable to associate it with a type identifier. Therefore, a record declaration takes the form

```
type
    record-type-identifier= record
                        record-field-list;
                end;

var
```

identifier-1, ... identifier-n: record-type-identifier;

where record-field–list has the form

fixed-part

or

fixed-part;
variant-part;

or

variant-part;

Only records with a fixed part are dealt with for now. The *fixed-part* of a record has the form

record-list-1: type-1;
record-list-2: type-2;
        "
        "
        "
record-list-n: type-n;

where *record-list-i* has the form

identifier-1, identifier-2, ... identifier-m

The following examples illustrate the preferred method for declaring records:

EXAMPLE 1

const
    StackSize = 30;

type
    StackType = **record**
                        Item: **packed array**[1..StackSize] of **char**;
                        Ptr: 0..StackSize;
            end;

var
    Stack: StackType;

Example 1 illustrates the declaration of a simple record. A stack is an abstract data type sometimes referred to as a FILO (First In Last Out) list. In this example, the stack contains items of type character. Ptr is a pointer that points to the item on top of the stack. Items may be inserted into or removed from the top of the stack only. Ptr equals zero indicates that the stack is empty.

EXAMPLE 2

```
const
    NumberOfLines = 200;

type
    ArrayOfLines = array[1..NumberOfLines] of record
                                    X1, Y1: integer;
                                    X2, Y2: integer;
                             end;

var
    Line: ArrayOfLines;
```

Example 2 illustrates the manner in which an array of records may be declared. Here, Line is an array of 200 lines where each line, specified by an array subscript, is determined by its two endpoints, namely, the pairs $(X1, Y1)$ and $(X2, Y2)$.

EXAMPLE 3

```
type
    Coordinate = record
                    X, Y: integer;
                end;

    TriangleType= record
            Vertex array[1..4] of Coordinate;
        end;

var
    Triangle: TriangleType;
```

The final example is somewhat more complex. It illustrates the declaration of hierarchical or nested records. In this case, a Triangle is a record with one field — the Vertex — which is an array of Coordinate, itself a record. Parenthetically, the reason that Triangle has four Coordinates is that the graphical system used to draw the Triangle requires an enclosed polygon. Therefore, Vertex[4] should be set equal to Vertex[1].

5.2   Record Processing

Each field in a record may be accessed directly by using a field selector variable of the form

record–name.field–name

Some examples of how fields may be accessed using field selectors are given below using the record declarations that were specified in the previous section:

Stack.Item[Ptr]:= Symbol; {where Symbol is type character}

if Line[I].X1 > Line[I].X2 then

Triangle.Vertex[1].X:= 25;
Triangle.Vertex[1].Y:.=100;

Sometimes it is necessary to copy the fields of one record into the fields of another. This can be done by copying the fields one by one using assignment statements. It is more convenient, however, to use a single assignment statement of the form

record–variable–identifier-1:= record–variable–identifier-2;

Assume that Triangle1 and Triangle2 are declared as TriangleType (Example 3). The following assignment statement illustrates this method:

Triangle1:= Triangle2;

5.2.1   THE WITH STATEMENT

Using the field selector variable to access individual fields of a record is tedious. Consider the following declarations for a baseball player's statistics:

```
const
        LastNameLength = 20;
        FirstNameLength = 10;
      TeamNameLength = 20;
type
        LastName = packed array[1..LastNameLength] of char;
        FirstName = packed array[1..FirstNameLength] of char;
        TeamName = packed array[1..TeamNameLength] of char;
        PlayerName = record
                                        Last:       LastName;
                                        First:      FirstName;

            end;
        PlayerStats = record
                                        Name:           PlayerName;
                                        Team:           TeamName;
                                        Year:           integer;
                                        Games:          integer;
                                        AtBats:         integer;
                                        Runs:           integer;
                                        Hits:           integer;
                                        Doubles:        integer;
                                        Triples:        integer;
                                        HomeRuns:       integer;
                                        RunsBattedIn:   integer;
                                        BattingAverage: real;
                end;

var
        Player: Player Stats;
```

Player fields can be assigned values by using their field selector variable names such as

```
Player.Name.Last:= 'Trammell         ';
Player.Name.First:= 'Alan    ';
Player.Team:= 'Tigers          ';
Player.Year:= 1988;
Player.Games:= 128;
        "
        "
        "
```

The **with** statement provides a simpler method for making assignments to record fields. The general form of the **with** statement is given below:

```
with record–variable–identifier do
        statement
```

where *statement* may be a simple statement or a compound statement.

The **with** statement could be used in the following manner to make assignments to the record variable Player:

```
with Player do
    begin
        Year:= 1988;
        Games:= 128;
            "
            "
            "

    end;
```

With statements may also be nested:

```
with Player do
    begin
        with Name do
            begin
                Last:= 'Trammell        ';
                First:= 'Alan      ';
            end;
        Team:= 'Tigers        ';
        Year:= 1988;
        Games:= 128;
    end;
```

5.3   Variant Records

Records may have only a fixed part, or only a variant part, or a fixed part followed by a variant part. The variant part of a record has the form

```
case    tag-field-identifier: type-identifier of
        constant-list-1: (record-field-list-1);
        constant-list-2: (record-field-list-2);
            "
            "
            "

        constant-list-n: (record-field-list-n);
```

where *constant-list-i* has the form

constant-1, constant-2, ... constant-n

and *record-field-list-i* has the same form given earlier for *record-field-list*.

The following record declaration has a variant part but not a fixed part:

type
    ObjectShape = (Square, Rectangle, Circle, Triangle);
    Dimensions = **record**

case Object:		ObjectShape **of**
Square:		(Side: real);
Rectangle:		(Width: real;
		Length: real);
Circle:		(Radius: real;
		Circumference: real);
Triangle:		(A, B, C: real);

        end;

The location used to store a record variant can accommodate any of the variant groups because the latter are overlaid in a single location big enough for the largest group. Object is called the **tag field** in this record. When a value is assigned to the tag field, the fields associated with that value are activated. For example, if Object has the value Circle, it activates the fields associated with that value, in this case, Radius and Circumference. If Object is undefined, then the variant part of the record is undefined.

Each variant's fields must be unique identifiers. No field identifier may appear in more than one group. However, the tag field is shared by all of the variant groups.

Variant structure gives records considerable flexibility. By using the variant record structure, one record may be used where several record structures might, otherwise, have to be used.

The Player record that was presented earlier is modified in the example below so that it includes a fixed part and a variant part. The fixed part of a record always comes before the variant part.

const
            LastNameLength = 20;
            FirstNameLength = 10;
        TeamNameLength = 20;

```
type
    PlayerPosition = (Pitcher, Catcher, Infielder, Outfielder);
        LastName = packed array[1..LastNameLength] of char;
        FirstName = packed array[1..FirstNameLength] of char;
      TeamName = packed array[1..TeamNameLength] of char;
      PlayerName = record
                                    Last:       LastName;
                                    First:      FirstName;
            end;
            PlayerStats = record
                                    Name:       PlayerName;
                                    Team:       TeamName;
                                    Year:       integer;
                                    Games:      integer;
                                case Position of
            Pitcher:    (InningsPitched:        integer;
                                    Won:        integer;
                                    Lost:       integer;
                            EarnedRuns:         integer;
                            EarnedRunAve:       real);
            Catcher,
            Infielder,
            Outfielder:         (AtBats:        integer;
                                    Runs:       integer;
                                    Hits:       integer;
                                Doubles:        integer;
                                Triples:        integer;
                            HomeRuns:           integer;
                        RunsBattedIn:           integer;
                    BattingAverage:             real);
            end;

var
    Player: PlayerStats;
```

The fields Name, Team, Year, and Games make up the fixed part of the record. All Player records contain these fields, as well as the tag field Position. If the value of Position is Pitcher, then those fields associated with that value are activated. If the value of Position is Catcher, Infielder, or Outfielder, then the fields associated with these values are activated.

5.4   Sample Program

The program in this section simulates the arithmetic checksum technique used to detect transmission errors through a computer network. Checksum is the sum of the collating (i.e., ASCII) values of the data bytes or characters in a data packet.

A selected number of random character strings of specified length are generated. Each string is subjected to a set of random errors during transmission. The checksum for the transmitted string is compared to the checksum for the received string to determine whether the error was detected. For more details, the reader is referred to the program's documentation.

```pascal
program CheckSum(Input, Output);

{   CheckSum simulates one technique used to detect errors when data   }
{   packets are transmitted over a computer network.                   }

const
          MaxBlockSize = 75;
               Space = 32;
          RangeOfChars = 95;
             MaxErrors = 10;

type
          Location = (Origin, Transmitted, Destination);
    PacketOfData = packed array[1..MaxBlockSize]of char;
       DataBlock = record
                          Blocksize:        0..MaxBlockSize;
                               Data:        PacketOfData;
                     OriginCheckSum:        integer;
                  case DataLocation:        Location of
                             Origin:        ( );
                       Transmitted::        (ErrorCount: integer);
                       Destination:         (Error: boolean;
                                             DestinationCheckSum: integer);
                  end;

var
    OriginalDataBlock,
    TransmittedDataBlock,

    ReceivedDataBlock: DataBlock;
    I, NumberOfBlocks: integer;
```

```
procedure InputNumberOfBlocksAndBlockSize(var NumberOfBlocks:
                                                  integer;
                         var OriginalDataBlock: DataBlock);

{    InputNumberOfBlocksAndBlockSize receives input from the        }
{    user which specifies the number of blocks to be transmitted    }
{    and the size of the blocks.                                    }

begin { InputNumberOfBlocksAndBlockSize }
    ClrScr;
    repeat
        write('Enter Number of Blocks (8-128) to be Transmitted: ');
        readln(NumberofBlocks);
    until (NumberofBlocks >= 8) and (NumberofBlocks <= 128);
    repeat
        write('Enter the Block Size (16 – 128 bytes) >> ');
        readln(OriginalDataBlock. BlockSize);
    until    (OriginalDataBlock.BlockSize >= 16) and
             (OriginalDataBlock.BlockSize <= MaxBlockSize);
end;    { InputNumberOfBlocksAndBlockSize }

procedure InitializeAllDataBlocks(var OriginalDataBlock,
                              TransmittedDataBlock,
                              ReceivedDataBlock: DataBlock);
{    InitializeAllDataBlocks initializes appropriate fields in the three data   }
{    blocks. Note that this includes the tag field for the three data blocks    }
{    which will activate the appropriate variant part of their records.         }

var
    I: integer;

begin { InitializeAllDataBlocks }
    with OriginalDataBlock do
        begin { with }
            OriginCheckSum:= 0;
            DataLocation:= Origin;
            for I:= 1 to MaxBlockSize do
                Data[ I ]:= ' ';
        end;    { with }
    TransmittedDataBlock.DataLocation:= Transmitted;
    with ReceivedDataBlock do
        begin { with }
            DataLocation:= Destination;
            for I:= 1 to MaxBlockSize do
                Data[ I ]:= ' ';
```

```
     end;   { with }
end;   { InitializeAllDataBlocks }

procedure GenerateRandomSetOfData(var OriginalDataBlock:
                                          DataBlock);

{   GenerateRandomSetOfData generates a random data block which is  }
{   to be transmitted. The reason for using Space is that in the implemen-  }
{   tation of Pascal used to generate this program many of the characters  }
{   with ASCII values below that of a blank space are unprintable. Like-  }
{   wise, many of the characters with an ASCII value greater than 126 are  }
{   also unprintable. The procedure could be modified to read a text tile  }
{   one block at a time which could be transmitted.  }

var
    I: integer;

begin { GenerateRandomSetOfData }
    for I:= 1 to OriginalDataBlock.BlockSize do
         OriginalDataBlock.Data[ I ]:= chr(random(RangeOfChars) + Space);
end;   { GenerateRandomSetOfData }

procedure TransmitData(var TransmittedDataBlock: DataBlock;
                           OriginalDataBlock: DataBlock);
{   For the most part, TransmitData should be viewed as a black box. As  }
{   the data is transmitted errors are randomly inflicted on the block of  }
{   data. Checksums for the transmitted and received data are generated.  }

    var
        I: integer;

    procedure InflictErrorsOnData(var TransmittedDataBlock: DataBlock);

{   InflictErrorsOnData randomly inflicts errors on the transmitted data.  }
{   This procedure ensures that errors are inflicted on all transmitted  }
{   data blocks.  }

    var
        I, Local: integer;
            Ch: char;

    begin { InflictErrorsOnData }
        TransmittedDataBlock.ErrorCount:=Random(MaxErrors) + 1;
        for I:= 1 to TransmittedDataBlock.ErrorCount do
            begin { for }
```

```
                    Local:= Random(TransmittedDataBlock.BlockSize) + 1;
                    repeat
                        Ch:= Chr(Random(RangeOfChars) + Space);
                        until Ch <> TransmittedDataBlock.Data[ I ];
                    TransmittedDataBlock.Data[Local]: Ch;
                end; { for }
            end; { InflictErrorsOnData }


begin { TransmitData }
    TransmittedDataBlock.BlockSize:= OriginalDataBlock.Blocksize;
    with OriginalDataBlock do
        for I:= 1 to BlockSize do
            begin { for }
                OriginCheckSum:= OriginCheckSum + Ord(Data[ I ]);
                TransmittedDataBlock.Data[ I ]:= Data[ I ];
            end; { for }
    TransmittedDataBlock.OriginCheckSum:=
                                    OriginalDataBlock.OriginCheckSum;
    InflictErrorsOnData(TransminedDataBlock);
    ReceivedDataBlock.BlockSize:= TransmittedDataBlock.BlockSize;
    with ReceivedDataBlock do
        for I:= 1 to BlockSize do
            begin { for }
                Data[ I ]:= TransmittedDataBlock.Data[ I ];
                DestinationCheckSum:=
                                DestinationCheckSum + Ord(Data[ I ]);
        end; { for }
    ReceivedDataBlock.OriginCheckSum:=
                            TransmittedDataBlock.OriginCheckSum;
end;    { TransmitData }


procedure CheckSumErrorDetection(var ReceivedDataBlock: DataBlock);

{   CheckSumErrorDetection determines whether the checksum method   }
{   detected the transmission error. At least one error is always inflicted   }
{   on the transmitted data block, so an error should be detected.   }
{   However, it is possible for checksum to miss an error depending upon   }
{   the combination of errors that occur.   }

begin { CheckSumErrorDetection }
    with ReceivedDataBlock do
    if OriginCheckSum <> DestinationCheckSum then
        ReceivedDataBlock.Error:=True
    else
        ReceivedDataBlock.Error:=False;
```

```pascal
end;   { CheckSumErrorDetection }

procedure OutputResults(OriginalDataBlock,
                TransmittedDataBlock, ReceivedDataBlock: DataBlock);

{   OutputResults writes the results out to the terminal. The program     }
{   could be modified to write the results to a data file.                }

var
    I: Integer;

begin {OutputResults}
    writeln;
    writeln('Block Size =   ',OriginalDataBlock. BlockSize);
    writeln;
    with OriginalDataBlock do
        writeln(Data);
    with ReceivedDataBlock do
        writeln(Data);
    writeln;
    if ReceivedDataBlock.Error = True then
        writeln('CheckSum Detected Transmission Error')
    else
        writeln('CheckSum Failed to Detect Transmission Error');
end; { OutputResults }

begin {Main Program}
    InputNumberOfBlocksAndBlockSize(NumberOfBlocks,OriginalDataBlock);
    for I:=1 to NumberOfBlocks do
        begin
            InitializeAllDataBlocks(OriginalDataBlock,TransmittedDataBlock,
                                        ReceivedDataBlock);

            Randomize { Initialize Random Number Generator };
            GenerateRandomSetOfData(OriginalDataBlock);
            TransmitData(TransmittedDataBlock,OriginalDataBlock);
            CheckSumErrorDetection(ReceivedDataBlock);
            OutputResults(OriginalDataBlock,TransmittedDataBlock,
                                        ReceivedDataBlock);

        end;
    end.   { Main Program }
```

6. SETS

6.1 Set Definition

Sets are the last structured data type to be presented. A set may be defined as an unordered collection of objects called elements or members of the set. Members of a set must be of the same type, known as the component or base type. The component type must be ordinal in nature.

Since the members of a set are unordered, there is no first element or second element or third element. Therefore, a set member cannot be accessed directly in Pascal. This characteristic distinguishes sets from arrays. Since the elements of an array are ordered, they can be accessed by their location or subscript. A set differs from a record in two ways. First, the items in a record may be of different types, and second, items in a record may be accessed directly.

Like the declaration of items of other structured data types, sets may be declared in the variable section of the declaration section of a program. Nevertheless, as always, it is preferable to associate a set type with a type identifier in the type section. Therefore, a set declaration takes the form:

type
    set-type-identifier = **set of** *component-type;*

var
    identifier-1, ... identifier-n: set-type-identifier;

The following examples illustrate a few methods of declaring sets in Pascal:

type
    SetOfDigits = **set of** 0 . . 9;

var
    Digits: SetOfDigits;

type
    Letters = 'A' . . 'Z';
    SetOfLetters = **set of** Letters;

var
    Vowels, Constants: SetOfLetters;

```
type
    Fruit = (Orange, Banana, Pear, Raspberry, Apricot);
    FruitSalad = set of Fruit;

var
    Salad: FruitSalad;
```

Most Pascal compilers limit the size of sets. Therefore, the following set declarations often are not permitted:

```
type
    SetOfIntegers = set of integers;
    SetOfChars = set of char;
```

6.2   Set Constants

Set constants take the form

[*element-list*]

where *element-list* is

constant-1, constant-2, ... constant-n

Examples of set constants are given below:

[1,   3,   5,   7,   9]

[8,   2,   4,   0,   6]

6.3   Set Assignments, Operations, and Relations

Set constants, set variables, or set expressions may be assigned to set variables assuming that they are of the same component type. The following assignments demonstrate valid set assignments:

```
Vowels:= ['A', 'E', 'I', 'O', 'U'];
Consonants:= ['A' . . 'Z'] – Vowels;

ThisSet:= ThatSet;

Operators:= Operators + ['*'];
```

Salad:= [ ];

The **empty set** is denoted by [ ] in Pascal.

6.3.1 THE RELATIONAL OPERATOR 'IN'

Determining whether an object is a member of a particular set is an important operation. **Set inclusion** may be determined with the **in** relational operator. The following two examples illustrate the usefulness of the **in** operator:

EXAMPLE 1

```
Even:= [0, 2, 4, 6, 8];
        "
        "
        "
if Number in Even then
    case Number of
        0:  statement–1;
        2:  statement–2;
        4:  statement–3;
        6:  statement–4;
        8:  statement–5;
    end;
```

Standard Pascal will generate an error if the value of Number is not equal to one of the values listed as case labels. The use of the **in** relational operator in the **if** statement ensures that the **case** statement is executed only if Number is one of the case label values.

EXAMPLE 2.

```
X:= 0;
while Digits <> [ ] do
    begin
        while not (X in Digits) do
            X:= succ(X);
        writeln X;
            Digits:= Digits – [X];
    end;
```

This example illustrates a method of writing the members of a set. Digits is a set of digits. X is assigned to the first possible value that might be a member of Digits. While Digits is not an empty set and while X is not a member of Digits, X is incremented. When X is a member of Digits, it is written and then removed from the set. This process is repeated until Digits is empty.

6.3.2 SET EQUALITY, SET INEQUALITY, SUBSETS AND SUPERSETS

Set equality is denoted by the relational operator '=' in Pascal. Two sets are equal if they contain exactly the same elements. Set inequality is denoted by '<>'. The subset relationship is denoted by the relational operator '<=' in Pascal, while the **superset** relationship is denoted by '>='. Consider the following sets:

```
A:= [7,  3,  4,  9,  5,  1];
B:= [3,  9];
C:= [2,  4,  9];
D:= [4,  2,  9];
```

The following relationships hold:

```
B <= A

C = D

C <> A

A >= B
```

6.3.3 SET UNION, INTERSECTION, AND DIFFERENCE

In addition to the relational operators, Pascal supports three binary operators — union, intersection, and difference. Union is denoted by +, intersection by *, and difference by –. The following examples elucidate these operations:

```
[3, 5, 9, 1]  +  [2, 4, 1]  =  [2, 3, 4, 5, 9, 1]

[3, 5, 9, 1]  *  [2, 4, 1]  =  [1]

[3, 5, 9, 1]  -  [2, 4, 1]  =  [3, 5, 9]
```

Precedence levels for set operators combined with boolean operators to form compound boolean expressions are given in Table 6.3.3.1.

TABLE 6.3.3.1 PRECEDENCE LEVELS FOR SET OPERATIONS. GIVEN FROM HIGHEST PRIORITY TO LOWEST

Operator	Priority
not	Highest
*, div, mod, and	
+, −, or	
=, <>, <=, >=, in	Lowest

6.4 Processing Sets

Sets may not appear in output lists of write and writeln statements. Therefore, some other method must be found to display the members of a set. An example of how set members may be displayed is given in Section 6.3.1. Likewise, sets may not appear in input lists of read and readln statements. Rather, sets must be built. Each member must be read and then added to the set. The following example illustrates this method:

```
Digits:= [   ];
while not eof(infile) do
    begin
        readln(X);
        Digits:= Digits + [X];
    end;
```

6.5 Program Example

Sets are probably the most underused structured data type in Pascal. This may be due, in part, to the fact that sets are sometimes difficult to use with large applications, or with applications having a large set of data. Most implementations of Pascal drastically limit the size of sets. The implementation used for the program SieveOfErathosthenes limits the size of the sets to 256 elements. Since the author wants to find all prime numbers between 2 and some large number N, a convenient way of using an array of sets to simulate a single set, 2 .. N, must be found.

The size of N may range from 2 to MaxInt. MaxInt is an integer constant identifier provided by Pascal and differs in value from implementation to implementation and from computer to computer. Some implementations of Pascal, including the one used here, provide a long integer that may be used instead of MaxInt. This allows the size of N to be considerably larger.

One question that immediately arises is how should the sets be declared. For example, should Sieve0 be declared as a set of 0 .. 255 and Sieve1 as a set of 256 .. 511, and so on? Obviously, this will not work since a thousand arrays may be required. Instead, Sieve is defined as an array [0 .. 999] of set of 0 .. 255. Therefore, the Ith value in the set Sieve[J] represents an integer K in the range 2 .. N which is determined by the following equation:

$$K = J * StSz + I \bmod StSz$$

StSz is the maximum number of elements in each set: 256 in SieveOfErathosthenes.

After N has been entered, the program initializes Sieve[0] through Sieve[N div StSz] with values representing integers in the range 2 .. N. For example, if N = 300, Sieve[0] = [2 .. 255] and Sieve[1] = [0 .. 54].

The procedure FindPrimeNumbers removes all of the nonprime numbers from the Sieve. It starts with the smallest prime number in the Sieve, which is 2. It then removes all multiples of 2 from the Sieve. It then finds the next smallest prime number in the Sieve, this time 3, and removes all multiples of 3 from the Sieve. It repeats this process until the working prime number is greater than the square root of N. At this point, only prime numbers remain in the Sieve.

The final procedure, WritePrimeNumbers, outputs the prime numbers from the Sieve. It works by beginning with the potential prime number, Num = 2. It determines whether its equivalent value remains in the appropriate Sieve set. If it does, it is removed from the set and written out. Num is incremented until its equivalent is found in the appropriate Sieve set. It is removed and written out. This process continues until the last Sieve set is empty.

```
program SieveOf Erathosthenes(input, output);

{    SieveOfErathosthenes finds all prime numbers between 2 and N     }
{    where N is a value entered by the user.                          }

const
        MaxSizeOfN = MaxInt;
```

```
          StSz = 256;

type
        SetRange = 0 .. 999;
        SetValues = 0 .. 255;
     SetOfValues = Set of SetValues;
       SieveArray = array[SetRange] of SetOfValues;
          NValue = 2 .. MaxSizeOfN;

var
    N:      NValue;
    Sieve:  SieveArray;

procedure GetN(var N: NValue);

{   GetN prompts user for a value N.                                           }

begin { GetN }
    write('Enter value of N (2 .. ', MaxSizeOfN:6,') : ');
    readln(N);
end;   { GetN }

procedure InitializeSieve(N: NValue; var Sieve: SieveArray);

{   Sieve Sets 0 through N div StSz are initialized in initialize              }
{   Sieve. First, the Sets are initialized to empty. Then they are             }
{   filled with appropriate values representing the integers 2                 }
{   through N. Note that InitializeSieve and FindPrimeNumbers                  }
{   write a short message to the terminal followed by a slow                   }
{   stream of dots (' . '). If the value of N is quite large, it could         }
{   take some time for the program to initialize the array Sieve and           }
{   then to find the prime numbers. The stream of dots lets the                }
{   user know that the program is still working.                               }

var
    I: NValue;
    J: SetRange;
    K: SetValues;

begin { InitializeSieve }
    writeln;
    write('Initializing Sieve');
    for J:= 0 to N div StSz do
        Sieve[J]:= [  ];
    for I:= 2 to N do
```

```pascal
            begin { for }
                J:= I div StSz;
                K:= I mod StSz;
                if K = 0 then
                    write (' . ');
                Sieve[J]:= Sieve[J] + [K];
            end;    { for }
        writeln;
    end; { InitializeSieve }

    procedure FindPrimeNumbers(N: Nvalue; var Sieve: SieveArray);

    {   FindPrimeNumbers finds all prime numbers between 2 and N      }
    {   by starting with 2, the first prime number in the Sieve array of  }
    {   sets. All multiples of 2 are removed from their respective sets.   }
    {   The next prime number remaining in the 'Sieve' is found and    }
    {   its multiples are removed. This process is repeated until the  }
    {   prime number is greater than the square root of N. At this point  }
    {   all non-prime numbers have been removed from the set.         }

    var
        P, I: NValue;
            J: SetRange;

    begin { FindPrimeNumbers }
        writeln;
        write('Finding Primes');
        P:= 2;
        while P <= sqrt(N) do
            begin { while }
                write(' . ');
                for I:= 2 to N div P do
                    begin { for }
                        J:= P * I div StSz;
                        Sieve[J]:= Sieve[J] - [P * I mod StSz];
                    end; { for }
                repeat
                    P:= Succ(P);
                until (P mod StSz) in Sieve[P div StSz];
            end; { while }
        writeln;
    end; { FindPrimeNumbers }

    procedure WritePrimeNumbers(N: Nvalue; var Sieve: SieveArray);
```

```
{   WritePrimeNumbers outputs all the numbers remaining in the    }
{   Sieve of sets. The values in these sets are converted to their    }
{   prime number equivalents. Note: Notice that Sieve is passed    }
{   by reference, as opposed to being passed by value. Is this    }
{   necessary? The answer is no. However, passing Sieve by    }
{   reference makes the program more efficient since passing by    }
{   reference passes only the starting address of the array. if    }
{   Sieve were passed by value, all of the values in the array    }
{   would have to be copied.    }

var
        P: NValue;
     Count: integer;
        I: SetRange;

begin { WritePrimeNumbers }
    writeln;
    Count:= 0;
    P:= 2;
        for I:= 0 to (N div StSz) do
            while Sieve[ I ] <> [  ] do
        begin { while }
            while not ((P mod StSz) in Sieve[P div StSz]) do
                P:= succ(P);
            Count:= succ(Count);
            write(P:7);
            if (Count mod 10) = 0 then
                writeln;
                Sieve[P div StSz]:= Sieve[P div StSz] – [P mod StSz];
            end;    { while }
    writeln;
end;    { WritePrimeNumbers }

begin  { SieveOfErathosthenes }
    GetN(N);
    InitializeSieve(N, Sieve);
    FindPrimeNumbers(N, Sieve);
    WritePrimeNumbers(N, Sieve);
end.    {SieveOfErathosthenes}
```

7. POINTER VARIABLES AND DYNAMIC ALLOCATION OF MEMORY

> Study the entire section as preparation for the 'AB' exam.

7.1 Static Sequential Memory Allocation

One of the jobs of the compiler is to allocate memory for data structures declared in the variable section of a program. Pascal compilers use **static memory allocation** to allocate space for variables declared as simple data types — real or ordinal — or as structured data types — array, record, or set. When memory is allocated statically, the contents of data structures may vary, but the amount of memory allocated is fixed and cannot change during program execution. The reader might argue that the variant record is an exception. However, the programmer must spell out, in advance, variations in a variant record. In effect, the variant record is simply the union of static data structures. Variation comes from the selection of predeclared objects, not from the construction of undeclared ones.

Memory allocated for components of structured data types, such as arrays, is not only fixed, but is also allocated sequentially. In other words, successive components of structured data types are stored in successive memory locations. This is known as **sequential memory allocation.**

The advantage of **static sequential memory allocation** is that the job of the compiler is straightforward. It is also easy for programmers to keep track of data and to access and manipulate data.

Static sequential memory allocation does have limitations, however. Arrays must be created large enough to meet every possible case that a program may encounter. For example, if 99% of the time a program needs an array with 1000 elements, but 1% of the time it needs 10,000 elements, then the array must be declared large enough to meet the latter case.

Another limitation of static sequential memory allocation is that it is impossible for data structures of different types and/or sizes to share the same space. In the previous example, this implies that, 99% of the time, most of the space set aside for the array is wasted.

Finally, an array's structure is fixed by static associations among its components. A[1] always precedes A[2], A[2] precedes A[3], ..., and A[N–1] precedes A[N]. It is not possible, for example, to change the structure to A[K], A[K + 1], ... A[N], A[1], A[2], ..., A[K–1]. All of the values in the array could be exchanged so that A[1] is assigned the value of A[K] and so on. This is much more involved than the original intent, however, which was to make the substructure A[K .. N] precede the substructure A[1 .. K–1].

7.2 Dynamic Allocation of Memory

Pascal also provides a means for allocating and deallocating memory for data structures during program execution. An area of memory known as the Pascal heap is used for **dynamic memory allocation.** A program can allocate memory from the Pascal heap when it is needed to construct or expand a data structure. When the program is finished processing data in an element or **node** of the data structure, the node's memory can be freed so that it may be re-used as needed.

The advantage of using dynamic allocation of memory is that memory utilization can be very efficient. Memory is allocated only when needed and then deallocated when processing has been completed. The disadvantage is that memory management is more complex and becomes the responsibility of the programmer. For example, the nodes of a data structure might not be allocated in consecutive memory locations. Therefore, a method of tracking nodes of a data structure must be implemented. The Pascal pointer variable, the last data type to be presented, is used for this purpose.

7.3 Pointer Variables

The first eight chapters of this text dealt with ordinary variables — variables of all data types except pointer type. The reader will recall that when the compiler generates machine language code from Pascal source code, it also allocates memory for ordinary variables. In fact, for all practical purposes a variable identifier is synonymous with its memory location. An assignment to an ordinary variable changes the value stored in its location. Therefore, an assignment to an ordinary variable identifier is known as **direct access** of a memory location.

In contrast, a **pointer variable** — the subject of this chapter — references, or points to, a storage location. An assignment to a pointer variable does not change the contents of the location referenced, but rather, changes the location referenced. This type of memory access is known as **indirect access.** The contents of the referenced location can be examined or changed through the pointer variable via special notation.

Pointer variables will be presented here by examining a typical pointer definition:

```
type
    Vehicle = record
                Make: packed array[1..15] of char;
                Model: packed array[1..15] of char;
                          "
                          "
                          "

            end;
    AutoPointer = ^Automobile;
    Automobile= record
                            Info:       Vehicle;
                            Next:       AutoPointer;
            end;

var
    AutoList, CE: AutoPointer;
    Item: Vehicle;
```

AutoPointer is a pointer to a location of type Automobile. Automobile is called the reference type. A circumflex (^) or upward arrow (↑) precedes the name of the reference type. A pointer type may be defined before its reference type, as is the case in this example. This example also illustrates the reason why. AutoPointer is defined as type Automobile, while Automobile's Next field is defined as type AutoPointer. This situation creates a set of cyclic definitions. In such situations, either the pointer must be defined before its reference type, or the reference type must be defined before the pointer. The former method is correct.

7.3.1   STANDARD PROCEDURE 'NEW'

AutoList and CE (Current Entry) are pointer variables which are declared as type AutoPointer. Like ordinary variables, pointer variables are undefined when they are declared. In addition, memory for the location that a pointer references must be allocated dynamically during program execution with the standard procedure **new**. For example, the statement

```
new(CE);
```

dynamically allocates memory for a node of type Automobile. The value of pointer CE is the memory location where the node is located. When the node is created, its fields are undefined. This includes the data field Info and the pointer field Next. The diagram in Figure 9.3.1.1 illustrates the relationship between CE and the node.

FIGURE 7.3.1.1
POINTER VARIABLE AND NODE

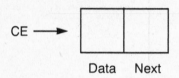

Data   Next

7.3.2   POINTER ASSIGNMENTS

AutoList has not yet been assigned a value so it is still undefined. By assigning AutoList the value **nil** — a reserved word — AutoList has a null address:

AutoList:= **nil**;

AutoList is now defined although it does not point to a storage location.

The location referenced by one pointer may be assigned to another pointer as the following example illustrates:

AutoList:= CE;

The Info and Next fields that are in the node referenced by CE are not affected by this assignment. The diagram in Figure 7.3.2.1 illustrates the new relationship among CE, AutoList, and the node.

FIGURE 7.3.2.1
TWO POINTER VARIABLES REFERENCING THE SAME NODE

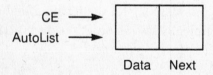

Data   Next

7.3.3   COMPARING POINTERS

Pointer variables may be compared using the "=" and "<>" relational operators in order to determine whether they reference the same location.

After the assignment

    AutoList:= CE;

the boolean expression

    AutoList = CE

is true, while the boolean expression

    AutoList <> CE

is false. These boolean expressions may be used in control structures such as the following statements illustrate:

    if AutoList = CE **then**
        "
        "
        "

    while CE <> AutoList **do**
        "
        "
        "

It is permissible for a pointer variable with a **nil** value to appear in a boolean expression. However, an error will occur if an undefined pointer is used.

7.3.4 ASSIGNING VALUES TO NODE ELEMENTS

Special notation must be used to assign values to the fields within a node. The following example illustrates how values may be assigned to data and pointer fields within a node:

    CE^.Info.Make:= 'Chevrolet   ';
    CE^.Info.Model:= 'Astro   ';
    CE^.Next:= nil;

7.3.5 BUILDING LINKED LISTS

Suppose that more nodes are created. How can they all be tracked? The answer is by the Next pointer. The Next pointer is used to link nodes together to form a structure known as a **linked list**. The following text illustrates how this might be done. Diagrams accompany each step to help clarify the process.

The process of building a linked list begins with the creation of a new node:

new(CE);

Assuming that one node already exists with AutoList referencing it, Figure 7.3.5.1 illustrates the new situation.

FIGURE 7.3.5.1
SECOND NODE CREATED

(a) new (CE)

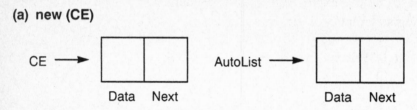

After the following assignments are made to the fields in the new node, the new node may be linked to the linked list.

```
CE^.Info.Make:= 'Toyota      ';
CE^.Info.Model:= 'Corolla     ';
CE^.Next:= nil;
```

There are several approaches that may be used to add a node to a linked list. The method presented here adds nodes to the front of a linked list. The pointer assignments are made in the following manner:

```
CE^.Next:= AutoList;
AutoList:= CE;
```

Figure 7.3.5.2 illustrates this process. The order in which the above two assignments are executed is important. For example, if CE is assigned to AutoList before AutoList is assigned to CE^.Next, the node pointed to by AutoList will be "lost" since there is no longer a pointer referencing that node. Instead of pointing to the next node in the linked list, CE^.Next will point to its own node (Figure 7.3.5.3).

FIGURE 7.3.5.2
LINKING NEW NODE TO LINKED LIST

(a) CE^.Next:= AutoList;

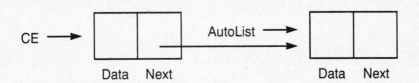

(b) AutoList:= CE;

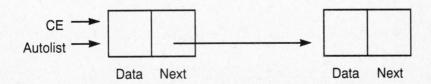

FIGURE 7.3.5.3
IMPROPER METHOD OF LINKING NEW NODE TO LINKED LIST

(a) AutoList:= CE;

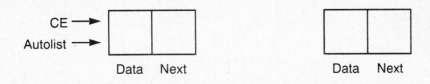

(b) CE^.Next:= AutoList;

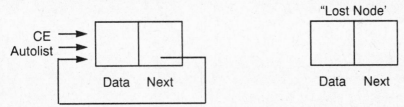

New nodes may be created and added to the linked list as long as there is sufficient free memory in the Pascal heap. The following procedure formalizes the previous discussion on adding nodes to a linked list:

procedure AddNode(**var** AutoList: AutoPointer; Item: Vehicle);

var
    CE: AutoPointer;

begin

```
      new(CE);                { Create new node. }
      CE^.Info:= Item;        { Get information for data fields. }
      CE^.Next:= AutoList;    { Link new node to front of list. }
                              { This works even if AutoList=nil. }
      AutoList:= CE;          { Reset AutoList to the new front node. }
end;
```

7.3.6   STANDARD PROCEDURE 'DISPOSE'

When a node is no longer needed, its space may be freed so that it might be re-used. The standard procedure dispose is used for this purpose. The node in Figure 7.3.6.1 may be disposed of with the following statement:

dispose(CE);

FIGURE 7.3.6.1
DISPOSING OF A NODE

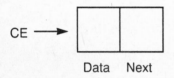

Data   Next

(a) **dispose(CE);**

CE ⟶ { Undefined }

Disposing of a node that is part of a linked list is a little more complicated. Consider the linked list in Figure 7.3.6.1. How can the first node in the linked list be disposed of? If the statement

dispose(AutoList);

is executed without proper preparation, the entire linked list will be lost to the program. A node must be deleted from a linked list before it can be disposed of. The following set of statements should be executed in order to properly delete the first node (Figure 7.3.6.2).

```
CE:= AutoList;
AutoList:= CE^.Next;
dispose(CE);
```

FIGURE 7.3.6.1
LINKED LIST

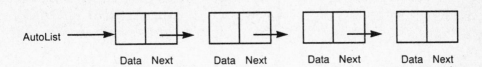

FIGURE 7.3.6.2
DELETING THE FIRST NODE IN A LINKED LIST

(a)   CE:= AutoList;

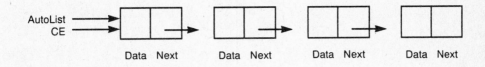

(b) AutoList := AutoList^.Next;

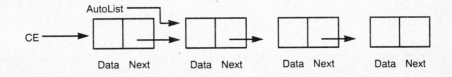

(c)   dispose(CE);

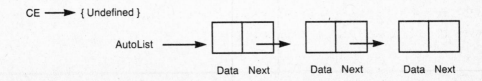

Deleting a node other than the first node is somewhat more complicated since it requires an additional pointer. Figure 7.3.6.3 illustrates the steps required to delete the third node in the linked list. It is assumed here that CE already references the node to be deleted. Likewise, TP (Temporary Pointer) references the node that points to the node that is to be deleted. Now the node can be deleted by doing the following:

```
TP^.Next:= CE^.Next;
dispose(CE);
```

FIGURE 7.3.6.3
DELETING NODE FROM WITHIN A LINKED LIST

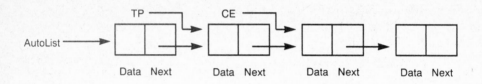

(a) TP^.Next:= CE^.Next;

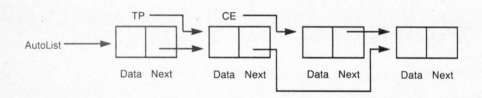

(b) dispose(CE);

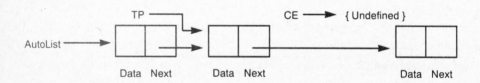

The following procedure formalizes the previous discussion on deleting nodes from a linked list:

```
procedure DeleteNode(var AutoList: AutoPointer;
                          var Item: Vehicle);
```

```
var
    TP, CE: AutoPointer;

begin
    if Item = AutoList^. Info then          { Delete first node? }
    begin
        TP:= AutoList;
        AutoList:= AutoList^.Next;
    end
else
    begin
        CE:= AutoList;
        while CE^.Next^.Info <> Item do      { Find target Node }
            CE:= CE^.Next;                    { Retrieve info from list }
            TP:= CE^.Next;                    { target node. }
            CE^.Next:= TP^.Next;              { Remove node from list }
        end;
        dispose(TP);                          { Dispose of node }
end;
```

7.4   Sample Program

The preceding discussion on linked lists is cursory in nature. Linked lists may be used to implement and process ordered lists, stacks, queues, trees, and many other abstract data types.

The following program illustrates the use of linked lists. It reads an infix expression from a file and converts it to its corresponding postfix expression. In an infix expression, the operator is placed between its two operands. If A and B are operands, then A + B is an infix expression. The same addition operation may be represented using two other forms of notation. If the operator precedes the two operands, as with +AB, the expression is referred to as a prefix expression. The operator may follow the two operands as is the case in a postfix expression. AB+ is a postfix expression. The prefixes "in," "pre," and "post" refer to the relative position of the operator with respect to the two operands.

In the program, Opstk is a stack (First In Last Out List), and is implemented as a linked list, as are Infix and Postfix, which are lists that represent the Infix and Postfix expressions. Since this program is the last one to be presented in the text, it incorporates many features of Pascal. The reader should be able to identify (1) enumerated data types, (2) two-dimensional arrays, (3) records, (4) sets, (5) text files, (6) procedures and functions, and (7) dynamically allocated linked lists.

program Infix_To_Postfix(PrecedenceTableFile,InfixFile);

{   Program Infix_To_Postfix reads infix expressions from the   }
{   InfixFile and converts them to their equivalent postfix expres-   }
{   sions. For processing convenience, each infix expression is   }
{   terminated with a '$'. A precedence table is built from the   }
{   PrecedenceTableFile. The precedence table is used to com-   }
{   pare the precedence between two operators. Based upon the   }
{   precedence relationship between two operators, the program   }
{   is able to determine whether an operator should be written to }
{   the postfix expression or the other operator should be pushed }
{   onto a stack.   }

type

        OperatorType = (Left, Mul, Divide, Add, Sub, Terminator, Right);
      SetOfOperators = **set** of char;
   TableOfPrecValues = **array**[Left..Terminator] **of**
                      packed array[Left..Right] **of** boolean;

var

     PrecedenceTable: TableOfPrecValues;
  PrecedenceTableFile,
          InfixFile: text;
       OperatorSet: SetOfOperators;

procedure InitializePrecedenceTable(**var** PrecedenceTableFile:text;
                         var PrecedenceTable: TableOfPrecValues);

{   Procedure InitializePrecedenceTable initializes the Precedence Table }
{   with boolean equivalents of the contents of the PrecedenceTableFile. }

var

   I, J: OperatorType;
   P: char;

begin { InitializePrecedenceTable }
     reset(PrecedenceTableFile);
     for I:= Left **to** Terminator **do**
        begin { for }
           for J:= Left **to** Right **do**
              begin { for }
                 read(PrecedenceTableFile, P);
                 If P = 'T' **then**
                     PrecedenceTable[I, J]:= true
                 else

```
                        PrecedenceTable[ I, J]:= false;
                end; { for }
            readln(PrecedenceTableFile);
        end; {for}
end;    { InitializePrecedenceTable }

procedure InitializeOperatorSet(var OperatorSet: SetOfOperators);

{    InitializeOperatorSet initializes OperatorSet with the legal           }
{    arithmetic operators.                                                  }

begin  { InitializeOperatorSet )
    OperatorSet:= [ '(', '*', '/', '+' '–', ')', '$'];
end;    { InitializeOperatorSet }

procedure ConvertInfixToPostfix(var InfixFile: text; OperatorSet:
                    SetOfOperators; PrecedenceTable: TableOfPrecValues);

{ ConvertInfixToPostFix converts an infix expression to its equivalent     }
{ postfix expression. It determines whether the current infix symbol is an }
{ operand or an operator. If the symbol is an operand, it is written to the }
{ postfix expression. If the symbol is an operator, it is compared to the   }
{ symbol on top of the stack. If the stack is empty or the symbol has       }
{ greater precedence than the symbol on the top of the stack, the          }
{ symbol is pushed onto the stack. If the symbol on the stack has           }
{ precedence over the current symbol, it is popped off the stack and        }
{ written to the postfix expression.                                        }

type
            ItemType = char;
            StackPtr = ^StackType;
        StackType = record
                            Item:    ItemType;
                            Next:    StackPtr;

        end;
            StringPtr = ^StringType;
        StringType = record
                            Symbol:    ItemType;
                            Next:      StringPtr;

        end;

var
        Opstk: StackPtr;
        StackSymbol, Infix, Postfix: StringPtr;
        Symbol, TopSymbol: ItemType;
```

```
{   Five routines make up the interface to the Opstk. The Opstk is     }
{   accessed through these routines only. The routines making up        }
{   the stack interface are:                                            }
{   ResetStack — Resets the Opstk so that a new infix expres-           }
{                sion may be processed. A '$' is the first              }
{                symbol placed into the stack.                          }
{   EmptyStack —Returns true if the stack is empty, false               }
{                otherwise.                                             }
{   PopStack —   Pops a symbol off the top of the stack. An             }
{                error message is generated if the stack is             }
{                empty.                                                 }
{   PushStack — Pushes a symbol onto the top of the stack.              }
{   StackTop —   Returns the top symbol on the stack without            }
{                removing it from the stack.                            }

procedure ResetStack(var Opstk: StackPtr);

begin { ResetStack }
    new(Opstk);
    Opstk^. Item:= '$';
    Opstk^.Next:= nil;
end; { ResetStack }

function EmptyStack(var Opstk: StackPtr): boolean;

begin  { EmptyStack }
    EmptyStack:= Opstk = nil;
end;   { EmptyStack }

function PopStack(var Opstk: StackPtr): ItemType;

const
    Underflow = 'stack underflow';

var
    CE: StackPtr;

begin { PopStack }
    if EmptyStack(Opstk) then
        writeln(underflow)
    else
        begin { else }
            CE:= Opstk;
            Opstk:= Opstk^.Next;
```

```pascal
                PopStack:= CE^.Item;
                dispose(CE);
        end; { else }
end; { PopStack }

procedure PushStack(var Opstk: StackPtr; symbol: ItemType);

var
    CE: StackPtr;

begin { PushStack }
    new(CE);
    CE^.Item:= Symbol;
    CE^.Next:= Opstk;
    Opstk:= CE;
end; { PushStack }
function StackTop(Opstk: StackPtr): ItemType;

begin { StackTop }
    StackTop:=Opstk^. Item;
end; { StackTop }

function Precedence(TopStack, Symbol: ItemType; PrecedenceTable:
                                    TableOfPrecValues): boolean;

{   Precedence returns a boolean value that represents the precedence    }
{   relationship between the operator on top of the stack and the        }
{   operator currently being examined from the infix expression. If the  }
{   operator on the stack has greater precedence, it is written to the   }
{   postfix expression. Otherwise, the operator currently being examined }
{   from the infix expression is pushed onto the top of the stack.       }

var
    Top, NewOperation: OperatorType;

    function TableIndex(Symbol: ItemType): OperatorType;

{   TableIndex returns an index for the PrecedenceTable that corresponds }
{   to Symbol.                                                           }

    begin { TableIndex }
        case Symbol of
            '(':        TableIndex:= Left;
            '*':        TableIndex:= Mul;
            '/':        TableIndex:= Divide;
```

```
            '+':     TableIndex:= Add;
            '–':     TableIndex:= Sub;
            ')':     TableIndex:= Right;
            '$':     TableIndex:= Terminator;
        end; { case }
    end; { TableIndex }
    begin { Precedence }
        Top:= TableIndex(TopStack);
        NewOperation:= TableIndex(Symbol);
        Precedence:= PrecedenceTable[Top, NewOperation];
    end; { Precedence }
```

```
{    ReadInfixExpression reads an InfixExpression from the InfixFile.          }
```

```
    procedure ReadInfixExpression(var InfixFile: text; var Infix: StringPtr);

    var
        CE, BP: StringPtr;

    begin { ReadInfixExpression }
        new(CE);
        read(InfixFile, CE^.Symbol);
        CE^.Next:= nil;
        Infix:= CE;
        while not(eoln(InfixFile)) do
            begin { while }
                BP:= CE;
                new(CE);
                read(InfixFile, CE^.Symbol);
                CE^.Next:= nil;
                BP^.Next:= CE;
            end; { while }
            readln(InfixFile);
    end; { ReadInfixExpression }
```

```
    procedure RetrieveInfixSymbol (var CE: StringPtr; var Symbol: ItemType);
```

```
{    RetrieveInfixSymbol returns the next symbol to be processed from the   }
{    infix expression.                                                       }
```

```
    begin { RetrieveInfixSymbol }
        if CE = nil then
            begin { if }
                CE:= Infix;
                Symbol:= CE^.Symbol
```

```
            end { if }
        else
            begin { else }
                CE:= CE^.Next;
                Symbol:= CE^.Symbol;
            end; { else }
    end; { RetrieveInfixSymbol }

        procedure ResetString(var PostFix: StringPtr);
```

{   ResetString resets the Postfix expression to nil in preparation   }
{   for processing the next infix expression.   }

```
        begin { ResetString }
            Postfix:= nil;
        end; { ResetString }

    procedure AddSymbolToPostfixExpression(var Postfix: StringPtr;
                                            var Symbol: ItemType);
```

{   AddSymbolToPostfixExpression adds the next symbol to the   }
{   Postfix expression. In order to do this, the procedure must   }
{   search for the end of the list.   }

```
        var
            NP, CE: StringPtr;

        begin { AddSymbolToPostfixExpression }
            new(CE);
            CE^.Symbol:= Symbol;
            CE^.Next:= nil;
            if PostFix = nil then
                PostFix:= CE
            else
                begin { else }
                    NP:= PostFix;
                    while NP^.Next <> nil do
                        NP:= NP^.Next;
                    NP^.Next:= CE;
                end; { else }
        end; { AddSymbolToPostfixExpression }

    procedure WriteOutput(Infix, Postfix: StringPtr);
```

{   WriteOutput displays the infix expression and its equivalent postfix   }

```
{    expression.                                                    }

    var
        CE: StringPtr;

    begin { WriteOutput }
        CE:= Infix:
        while CE^.Symbol <> '$' do
            begin { while }
                write(CE^.symbol);
                CE:= CE^.Next;
            end; ( while }
        write('  =  ');
        CE:= Postfix;
        while CE <> nil do
            begin { while }
                write(CE^.Symbol);
                CE:= CE^.Next;
            end; { while }
        writeln;
    end; { WriteOutput }

    begin { ConvertInfixToPostfix }
        ResetStack(Opstk);
        ResetString(Postfix);
        ReadInfixExpression(InfixFile, Infix);
        StackSymbol:= Infix;
        repeat
            RetrieveInfixSymbol(StackSymbol, Symbol);
            if not(Symbol in OperatorSet) then
                AddSymbolToPostfixExpression(PostFix, Symbol)
            else
                if Symbol <> ')' then
                    while (not EmptyStack(Opstk)) and
                        precedence(StackTop(Opstk),
                                        Symbol, PrecedenceTable) do
                            begin { while }
                                TopSymbol:= PopStack(Opstk);
                                AddSymbolToPostfixExpression
                                    (PostFix, TopSymbol);
                            end { while }
                    else
                        begin { else }
                            TopSymbol:= PopStack(Opstk);
                            while TopSymbol <> '(' do
```

```
                        begin { while }
                            AddSymbolToPostfixExpression
                                            (PostFix, TopSymbol);
                            TopSymbol:= PopStack(Opstk);
                    end; { while }
                    end; { else }
                if Symbol in (OperatorSet − [ ')', '$' ]) then
                    PushStack(Opstk, Symbol);
            until Symbol = '$';
            WriteOutput(Infix, Postfix);
    end; { ConvertInfixToPostfix }

begin { Infix_To_Postfix )
        reset(InfixFile);
        InitializePrecedenceTable(PrecedenceTableFile, PrecedenceTable);
        InitializeOperatorSet(OperatorSet);
        while not eof(InfixFile) do
            ConvertInfixToPostfix(InfixFile, OperatorSet, PrecedenceTable);
        close(PrecedenceTableFile);
        close(InfixFile);
    end. { Infix_To_Postfix }
```

8.   SCOPE OF IDENTIFIERS

The scope of an identifier refers to those parts of the program — known as blocks — in which the identifier is active. A block consists of a definition part, declaration part and statement part.

There are two situations that are considered here regarding the scope of identifiers. First, suppose that two variables, each called Number, are declared in a program and one of its procedures. When the main program has program control, the identifier Number refers to the program variable. When the procedure has program control, the identifier Number refers to the procedure variable.

Now let's consider the more general situation. What is the scope of an identifier when duplicate identifier names have not been declared? The scope of a global identifier — an identifier declared in the main program — is the entire program. The scope of a local identifier is the subprogram in which it is declared along with other subprograms declared within that subprogram. The example on the following page illustrates some possibilities.

TABLE 8.1
SCOPE OF IDENTIFIERS

Identifiers defined in:	Their scope is blocks:
Program A	A, B, C, D, E, F
Procedure B	B, C, D
Procedure C	C
Procedure D	D
Procedure E	E, F
Procedure F	F

```
program A
    procedure B
        procedure C
            begin {C}
                "
                "
                "
            end; {C}
        procedure D
            begin {D}
                "
                "
                "
            end {D}
        begin {B}
            "
            "
            "
        end; {B}
    procedure E
        procedure F
            begin {F}
                "
                "
                "
            end {F}
        begin {E}
            "
            "
            "
        end {E}
    begin {A}
        "
        "
```

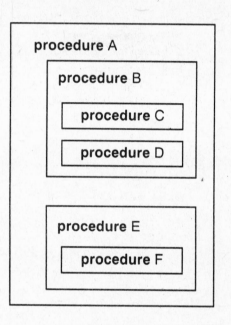

"

end. {A}

9. EXPRESSIONS AND EVALUATION

9.1 Arithmetic Operators

There are six arithmetic operators in Pascal. The operators, operand types, and type of result are shown in Table 9.1.1.

TABLE 9.1.1
ARITHMETIC OPERATORS

Operator	Operation	Operands	Result
+	addition, unary plus	integer/real	integer/real
–	subtraction, unary minus	integer/real	integer/real
*	multiplication	integer/real	integer/real
/	real division	integer/real	real
div	integer division	integer	integer
mod	remainder in integer div.	integer	integer

A few examples of simple arithmetic expressions are given here. Assume that the variables I and J have been declared as integer type and X and Y have been declared as real.

1.	X * I	4.	X /(–Y)
2.	I + J	5.	I **mod** J
3.	– I	6.	I **div** J

The first expression illustrates the use of the multiplication operator. The '*' operator must always be used for multiplication. Although XI denotes multiplication in an algebraic expression, it has an entirely different meaning in Pascal. In Pascal, XI would be interpreted as a single identifier name.

Unary operators are illustrated in the third and fourth examples. Note the use of parentheses in the fourth example. The parentheses are necessary because no two operators may appear next to each other in an expression. For example, I * –J is illegal. However, I * (–J) is legal.

Operands may be integer and/or real for addition, subtraction, multiplication, and real division. For addition, subtraction, and multiplication, the result is integer if both operands are integer. The result is real if either operand is real. Real division produces real results regardless of the type of the two operands. Only integer operands are allowed for the **div** and **mod** operators. The results generated are always integer.

9.1.1 OPERATOR PRECEDENCE

Operator precedence refers to the order in which arithmetic operations are performed in an expression. Arithmetic operators are divided into two levels of precedence in Pascal — high and low. The operators '*', '/', **div**, and **mod** have high precedence, while '+' and '−' have low precedence.

When arithmetic expressions have more than one operator, high precedence operators are evaluated first, in order, from left to right. Next, low precedence operators are evaluated, in order, from left to right. The use of parentheses in arithmetic expressions can alter the order in which operators are evaluated. If an expression contains a subexpression enclosed within parentheses, the subexpression is evaluated first using the rules of precedence just described. If the parentheses are nested, the innermost subexpression is evaluated first. The following algorithm may be used to evaluate arithmetic expressions by applying each rule in order beginning with Rule 1:

Rule 1. If an expression contains subexpressions (parentheses), evaluate the subexpressions first, beginning with the innermost subexpression.

Rule 2. Evaluate high precedence operators, in order from left to right.

Rule 3. Evaluate low precedence operators, in order from left to right. Return to Rule 1, if necessary.

Five examples are given to illustrate the use of these rules to evaluate an arithmetic expression. The order in which operators in an expression are evaluated is given beneath the expression. Assume that all operands have been properly declared.

```
A   –   B   *   C   +   D  div  E
    3       1       4       2

(A   –   B)   *   (C   +   D)   /   E
     1         3        2        4
```

```
(A   –   B)   *   ((C   +   D) mod E)
  1          4      2         3

A   +   B   /   (-C   *   D)   +   E
  4       3    2    1       5

A   *   (((B   –   C)   *   D)   –   E   *   F)   +   G
  5        1      2         4       3       6
```

9.2   Algebraic Notation

> Study Section 9.2 for the 'AB' exam.

9.2.1   ALGEBRAIC ORDERS AND TREE TRAVERSALS

When writing an algebraic expression consisting of a binary operator applied to its two operands (i.e., arguments), three standard orders of operators and operands are used. The names of these three orders are related to the placement of the operator relative to the two operands.

		Example:
PREFIX	**operator** first-operand second-operand	+ a b
POSTFIX	first-operand second-operand operator	a b +
INFIX	first-operand operator second-operand	a + b

These three orders are also related to tree traversal orders seen in Section D.6.2. The second tree shown in Section D.6.2 has operators as the information stored in the interior nodes. The tree traversals listed there correspond to the three orders listed in this section. Thus, the preorder traversal of that tree gives an algebraic expression in prefix order, and so on.

COMMENTS

1) PREFIX order is "functional notation" — the mathematical order used when writing functions of two variables, e.g., $f(a,b) = a + b$ could also be written $+(a, b)$.

2) INFIX order is the standard arithmetic notation order, e.g., $a + b$.

3) POSTFIX order is also called RPN order, e.g., a, b, +. RPN is the abbreviation for *R*everse *P*olish *N*otation, developed by the Polish mathematician Jan Lukasiewicz. It is also the order used by certain types of

calculators. In these machines, a stack is used to store the operands (i.e., numbers) and these are combined when an operator is indicated. These types of calculators are recognized by the absence of an equals key.

9.2.2 GENERAL CONVERSION RULES

Conversion between the various algebraic orders is usually accomplished by first fully parenthesizing the expression. In other words, parentheses are inserted so that there is one set of each operator. For example,

| #1 | normal algebraic: | A+B*C |
| | fully parenthesized: | (A+(B*C)) |

| #2 | normal algebraic: | (A+B)*C |
| | fully parenthesized: | ((A+B)*C) |

To convert from infix to postfix (prefix),

1) fully parenthesize the expression,

2) move operator to the right (left) parenthesis that corresponds to it,

3) and then remove all parentheses.

Continuing the previous examples:

| #1 | fully parenthesized: | (A+(B*C)) |
| | RPN | (A(B C*)+) = ABC*+ |

| #2 | fully parenthesized: | ((A+B) *C) |
| | RPN | ((A B+) C*) = AB+C* |

Conversion from postfix (prefix) to infix is done in a similar way, but "fully parenthesizing" a postfix or prefix expression is significantly more complicated.

Starting with a postfix (prefix) expression, a set of parentheses is included around the outside and a right (left) parenthesis after (before) each operator. Then the expression is scanned from the center toward the other side, inserting a matching parenthesis every time two operands have been identified corresponding to each operator. The process is illustrated in the following example which fully parenthesizes A B C + D * +.

(A B C + D * +)   Outer parentheses inserted.

(A B C +)D *) +)   Right parenthesis next to each operator.
(A B C +)D *) +)   First pair of operands identified.
    ^1 2 0^
(A(B C +)D) +)   First left parenthesis inserted.
(A (B C +)D *)+)   Next pair of operands identified.
  ^   1 2 0^

           (Note the first operand is an entire
           expression: (B C +).)
(A((B C +)D *)+)   Second left parenthesis inserted.

The expression is now fully parenthesized.

To convert from postfix (prefix) to infix,

1) fully parenthesize the expression,

2) move the operator of each group in between its operands,

3) and then remove unnecessary parentheses.

Continuing the example above,

fully parenthesized:	(A((B C +)D *)+)
with moved operators:	(A+((B+C)* D))
unnecessary parentheses removed:	A + (B+C)*D

NOTES

1) With infix expressions, all parentheses may not always be able to be removed.

2) When converting from one order to another order, the order of the operands (arguments) always stays the same.

3) The changes in the expression include the order of the operators, the presence or absence of parentheses, and the position of the operators relative to their own operands.

9.3   Standard Functions

Pascal provides several built-in or **standard functions.** In Pascal, a function is a subprogram that computes and returns a value. Standard functions are predefined for the programmer. They may be classified into three groups — arithmetic, ordering, and boolean. Pascal's standard functions are listed in Table 9.3.1 through Table 9.3.3 with a description of each function, type of argument, and type of value returned by each function.

TABLE 9.3.1
ARITHMETIC FUNCTIONS

Function	Description	Type of Argument	Type of Value
abs(x)	absolute value of x	integer/real	same as argument
arctan(x)	inverse tangent of x[1]	integer/real	real
cos(x)	cosine of x[2]	integer/real	real
exp(x)	e to the x power	integer/real	real
ln(x)	natural logarithm of x	integer/real	real
round(x)	x rounded	real	integer
sin(x)	sine of x[2]	integer/real	real
sqr(x)	x squared	integer/real	same as argument
sqrt(x)	square root of x	integer/real	real
trunc(x)	x truncated	real	integer

(1) Value returned is in radians.
(2) Value of argument x is in radians.

ex: abs(–5) = abs(5) = 5
trunc(7.98) = 7, trunc(3.005) = 3
round(7.98) = 8, round(3.005) = 3
Note that for non-negative values of x, round(x) = trunc(x + . 5)
For negative values, round(x) = trunc(x – 0.5)

TABLE 9.3.2
ORDERING FUNCTIONS

Function	Description	Type of Argument	Type of Value
chr(x)	character whose ordinal value is x	integer	character
ord(x)	ordinal number of x	ordinal[3]	integer
pred(x)	predecessor of x	ordinal[3]	ordinal[3]
succ(x)	successor of x	ordinal[3]	ordinal[3]

(3) Ordinal data types are discussed in Chapter 3.

ex: Suppose we have the following declaration:

type
      DAYS = (sun, mon, tue, wed, thu, fri, sat)

The ord values of such user-defined type are ordered starting with 0.

Therefore

ord (sun) = 0; ord (mon) = 1; .... ord (sat) = 6

ex. pred (6) = 5, pred (tue) = mon
   pred (true) = false, pred (sun) = undefined

ex. succ (7) = 8, succ (tue) = wed
   succ (false) = true, succ (sat) = undefined

TABLE 9.3.3
BOOLEAN FUNCTIONS

Function	Description	Type of Argument	Type of Value
eof(f)	true if end-of-file, false otherwise	file[4]	boolean
eoln(f)	true if end-of-line, false otherwise	file[4]	boolean
odd(x)	true if x is odd, false otherwise	integer	boolean

(4) Text files, input, and output are presented in Chapter 4.

9.3.1   INVOKING A PASCAL FUNCTION

A Pascal function is used by making a function call. A function call usually has two parts — the function name followed by an argument contained within parentheses.

9.4   Sample Program

program Circle(input, output);

```
{   Program Circle reads the radius of a circle and calculates the circum-  }
{   ference and area of the circle and then displays the radius,            }
{   circumference, and area.                                                }
```

const
    Pi = 3.141592654;
    Filler = '   ';

var
    Radius,

```
      AreaOfCircle,
      Circumference: real;
```

begin
```
      write('Enter radius of circle >> ');
      readln(Radius);
      AreaOfCircle:= Pi * sqr(Radius);
      Circumference:= 2 * Pi * Radius;
      writeln;
      writeln('      Radius      Circumference      Area ');
      writeln(Radius, Filler, Circumference, Filler, AreaOfCircle);
```
end.

Readln, write, and writeln are Pascal statements for input and output. [5]

----

(5) Input/output and files are covered in Section 12

10.   ASSIGNMENT STATEMENT

The assignment statement is used to assign a value to a variable. It has the form

variable–identifier: = expression

Variable-identifier must be declared in the variable section of the program. *Expression* may be a constant, another variable, or a formula that must be evaluated before the value is assigned to the variable. Some examples of assignment statements are given here. Assume that all variables have been appropriately declared.

```
      Percent:= 0.115;
      SaveX:= X;
      Sum:= Sum + Amount;
      Ch:= chr(60);
      C:= sqrt(sqr (A) + sqr(B));
```

In the first example, the constant, 0.115, is assigned to the variable, Percent – that is, 0.115 is stored in the memory location with which Percent has been associated.

In the second example, the value of X is copied to SaveX. A problem arises, however, if a value has not been assigned to X previously. When a variable is first declared, its value is undefined. Therefore, it is crucial that a value is assigned to a variable before it is used on the right-hand side of an assignment statement. Otherwise, whatever random value that happens to be stored in the variable's memory location will be used, which probably not what the programmer intended.

The third example is interesting because it illustrates a difference between Pascal assignment statements and algebraic equations. The algebraic equation, Sum = Sum + Amount, is true only if Amount equals zero. However, the Pascal assignment statement, Sum:= Sum + Amount, is interpreted differently to mean add the value currently stored in Amount's memory location to the value currently stored in Sum's memory location and store the new value in Sum's memory location.

The last two examples of assignment statements illustrate the use of function calls. The last one contains function calls nested within a function call. In this example, the function sqr(A) is evaluated first, followed by the sqr(B). The results of these calculations are summed, and the square root of this value is calculated and assigned to C.

11.   CONTROL STRUCTURES

11.1 Control Structures

Five control structures govern the logical flow of Pascal programs. Three of these — **sequential, iteration (repetition),** and **selection** — are often associated with structured programming. A fourth, **procedural**, should also be added to this list, although few computer science educators or computer science textbook authors are inclined to do so.

The fifth control structure, the **goto statement,** is often considered a taboo programming structure and rightfully so. The **goto** statement decidedly is not a canon of structured programming and usually is not covered in Pascal programming courses. Nevertheless, there are a few occasions when the judicial use of the **goto** statement is warranted.

11.2 Sequential Control

Sequential control of program execution refers to the sequential execution of program statements, one after another, in the order in which they appear in the program. Sequential control of Pascal programs is governed by the compound statement. A compound statement starts with the reserved word **begin** and terminates with the reserved word **end**. Compound statements have the form:

```
begin
    statement-1;
    statement-2;
        "
        "
        "
    statement-n
end
```

11.3 Boolean Expressions

Recall that Boolean data types may be assigned one of two values, either true or false. **Boolean expressions** are assertions that have a boolean result. Selection and iteration structures, as well as other structures, incorporate boolean expressions.

A **simple boolean expression** may consist of a boolean variable, a boolean constant, a reference to a boolean-valued function, or an expression of the form

expression-1 relational-operator expression-2

where *expression-1* and *expression-2* are of the same type. **Relational-operator** is one of the operators shown in Table 11.3.1.

TABLE 11.3.1
RELATIONAL OPERATORS

<	less than
>	greater than
=	equal to
<=	less than or equal to
>=	greater than or equal to
<>	not equal to

Consider the assignment statement

Num1Greater:= Num1 > Num2

where Num1Greater is declared as boolean and Num1 and Num2 as real. 'Num1 > Num2' is a boolean expression. If the value of Num1 is greater than the value of Num2, then the value true is assigned to Num1Greater. Otherwise, false is assigned to Num1Greater.

Additional examples of boolean expressions are given here.

```
Side >= 10
Ch = 'Q'
X< 14.27
OddNum = odd(Num)
Rotate = Y>X+ 10
```

Three boolean operators — **and, or,** and **not** — may be used to combine boolean expressions to form **compound boolean expressions.** Compound boolean expressions have the form

boolean-expression-1 boolean-operator
boolean-expression-2

where *boolean-expression* is a boolean expression of the form already described. The three boolean operators are defined in Table 11.3.2 where **p** and **q** represent boolean expressions which have one of the truth values, true or false.

TABLE 11.3.2
BOOLEAN OPERATORS

Boolean Operator	Boolean Expression	Definition
not	not p	negation of p
and	p and q	conjunction of p and q
or	p or q	disjunction of p or q

The negation of p is true if p is false; it is false if p is true. The conjunction of p and q is true if both p and q are true, otherwise it is false. The disjunction of p or q is false if both p and q are false, otherwise it is true. These rules are summarized by the truth table in Table 11.3.3.

TABLE 11.3.3
TRUTH TABLE ILLUSTRATING NEGATION, CONJUNCTION, AND DISJUNCTION

p	q	not p	p and q	p or q
T	T	F	T	T
T	F	F	F	T
F	T	T	F	T
F	F	T	F	F

The following precedence table illustrates the order in which operators are evaluated in boolean expressions that have combinations of relational operators, boolean operators, and/or arithmetic operators.

TABLE 11.3.4
OPERATOR PRECEDENCE

Operator	Priority
not	highest
/, *, div, mod, and	
+, –, or	
<, >, =, <=, >=, <>	lowest

Operators with the highest precedence in a boolean expression are evaluated first, in order, from left to right. Operators with the next highest precedence are evaluated next, and so on until all operators have been evaluated. As with arithmetic expressions, the use of parentheses can alter the order in which operators are evaluated. Five examples of boolean expressions are shown below. The order in which operators in the expressions are evaluated is given below each expression. Assume that A, B, and C are declared as integer; X, Y, and Z as real; and P and Q as boolean.

```
X    +    10   <=   Y/Z
     2         3    1
(0   >    X)   and  (X    <=   10)
     1         3          2
(X   <    Y)   or   (A    >    B)   and  (B    <    C)
     1         5          2         4          3
(X   +    10   <    Y)   and  (A    div   B    <    C)
     1         2         5          3         4
```

(A	+	B	**mod**	C	>	0)	**and**	**not**	(p	or	q)
	2		1		3		6	5		4	

Although logical in nature, boolean expressions can be tricky. In light of this, two cautionary notes are made here. First, the expressions that are connected by boolean operators must, themselves, be boolean. This seems obvious, but consider the following expression:

0 > X **and** X <=10

In this example, **and** has the highest priority and is evaluated first. This is clearly an illegal expression since **and** cannot be applied to numeric operands. This may be more evident when parentheses are added for clarity:

0 > (X **and** X) <= 10

The addition of parentheses does not change the order of evaluation. They do, however, show more clearly that the operands for the **and** operator are numeric, not boolean, as is required. The second cautionary note pertains to boolean expressions containing real data type. It should be remembered that most real values cannot be represented exactly in computer memory. Therefore, it is possible that unexpected results may occur when using the '=' or '<>' operators to compare real values. Consider the following expression:

1.0 = X * (1.0/X)

Although this expression is always algebraically true for X <> 0, it is possible for a computer to evaluate it as false. For example, if X equals 0.1, the value calculated by a computer for the right-hand side of the expression would not be exactly 1.0. Thus, the boolean expression would be false.

11.4 Selection

The **selection**, or **branching**, **control structure** introduces decision points in programs. It is used when a program must choose between two or more possible courses of action. The computer's ability to make decisions and to execute different sequences of instructions is what enables the computer to solve a variety of problems by responding to different situations in different ways. Pascal provides two selection control structures, the **if** statement and the **case** statement.

11.4.1 THE IF STATEMENT

The **if** statement has the following forms in Pascal:

> **if** *boolean-expression* **then**
>   *statement*

and

> **if** *boolean-expression* **then**
>   *statement-1*
> **else**
>   *statement-2*

In the first form of the **if** statement, the *statement* portion is executed only if the boolean expression is true, otherwise it is skipped. In the second form, *statement-1* is executed if the boolean expression is true, otherwise *statement-2* is executed.

Examples of both forms of the **if** statement are given below:

```
if not EndFlag then
    Value:= Value * 10 + ord(NextDigit);

if Object = 'Circle' then
    begin
        Circumference:= 2 * Pi * Radius;
        Area: = Pi * sqr(Radius)
    end
else {Object is a Square}
    begin
        Circumference:= 4 * Side;
        Area:= sqr(Side)
    end;
```

In the first example, the value of the variable Value is recomputed if EndFlag is false, otherwise the statement is skipped. In the second example, it is assumed that Object can be a 'Circle' or a 'Square' only. However, the strict interpretation of the second example is that if Object equals 'Circle', the **if** clause is executed; if Object is not equal to 'Circle' the **else** clause is executed. Therefore, the **else** clause is executed if Object equals 'Triangle', even though this might not be what the programmer intended.

11.4.1.1   Nested 'If' Statements

The statement part of an **if** statement may itself be an **if** statement. In this case, the **if** statements are said to be nested. Nested **if** statements may take many forms. Several examples are given here with appropriate commentary:

EXAMPLE 1

> if *boolean-expression-1* **then**
>> if *boolean-expression-2* **then**
>>> *statement*

This form is equivalent to

> if *(boolean-expression-1)* **and** *(boolean-expression-2)* **then** *statement*

EXAMPLE 2

> if *boolean-expression-1* **then**
>> if *boolean-expression-2* **then**
>>> *statement-1*
>> **else**
>>> *statement-2*

In this form of nested **if** statements, there are two **if** clauses and only one **else** clause. In such situations the **else** clause is always associated with the last unpaired **if** clause. In this case, the **else** is paired with the second **if** clause. Therefore, if *boolean-expression-1* is false the entire if block is skipped. If *boolean-expression-1* is true and *boolean-expression-2* is true, then *statement-1* is executed. If *boolean-expression-1* is true and *boolean-expression-2* is false, then *statement-2* is executed.

The question arises as to how the last example could be modified so that the single **else** clause is paired with the first **if** clause instead of the second. The following example demonstrates how this can be done.

EXAMPLE 3

> if *boolean-expression-1* **then**
>> **begin**
>>> if *boolean-expression-2* **then**
>>>> *statement-1*
>> **end**
> **else**

statement-2

If statements may be nested in such a way that a selection may be made from many alternatives, as in the next example.

EXAMPLE 4

if *boolean-expression-1* **then**
    statement-1
else
    if *boolean-expression-2* **then**
        statement-2
    else
        if *boolean-expression-3* **then**
            statement-3
        else
          "
          "
          "

          statement-n

If there are many alternatives to choose from, Pascal provides another selection control structure to use — the **case** statement.

11.4.2 THE CASE STATEMENT

The **case** statement has the following form

case *selector* **of**
    case-label-list-1: statement-1;
    case-label-list-2: statement-2;
        "
        "
        "
    case-label-list-n: statement-n
end;

where *selector* is a variable or expression whose type is either integer, character, boolean, enumerated, or subrange[6]. The selector may not be real. The *case-label-list* is a list of values of the same type as the **case** *selector*. When the **case** statement is executed the **case** *selector* is evaluated. The statement that is associated with the *case-label-list* with a value equal to the

---

(6) Enumerated and subrange types are covered in Section 3.

case *selector's* value is then executed. Execution then continues with the statement following the **end**.

In standard implementations of Pascal, a run-time error will occur if the value of the **case** *selector* is not found in the *case-label* list. To avoid this problem many implementations of Pascal have added an **otherwise** clause or an **else** clause to catch all **case** *selector* values not found in the *case-label* list. The following example illustrates one possible form:

```
case selector of
    case-label-list-1: statement-1;
    case-label-list-2: statement-2;
        "
        "
        "
    case-label-list-n: statement-n
otherwise {or else}
    statement
end;
```

Note that the **case** statement does not have a **begin,** but it is always terminated with an **end.**

An example of a standard implementation of the **case** statement is shown below:

```
case ErrorCode of
        1: writeln('**** File not found ****');
        2: writeln('**** File already exists ****');
        3: writeln('**** Illegal file type ****');
        4: writeln('**** Illegal file name ****');
        5: writeln('**** Insufficient disk space ****');
        6: writeln('**** Invalid directory ****');
        7: writeln('**** Disk not formatted ****');
        8: writeln('**** Error writing to device ****');
        9: writeln('**** Invalid parameter ****');
       10: writeln('**** Check printer ****');
end;
```

11.5 Iteration

Iteration — or **repetition** — **control structures** make it possible to repeat the execution of one or more statements. Iteration control structures are often called **loops** for this reason. Pascal provides three iteration control structures — the **for** loop, the **while** loop, and the **repeat** loop.

11.5.1 THE FOR STATEMENT

The **for** statement has two forms:

> **for** *control-variable:= initial-value* **to** *final-value* **do** *statement*

and

> **for** *control-variable:= initial-value* **downto** *final-value* **do** *statement*

where *control-variable* is of type integer, character, boolean, enumerated, or subrange[7]. *Initial-value* and *final-value* may be any legal Pascal expression, but they must be of the same type as the *control-variable*. Also note that, as always, *statement* may be either a simple Pascal statement or a compound statement.

When the **for** statement in the **to** form is executed, the *control-variable* is assigned the initial value and the **body** of the **for** statement is executed provided that the initial value is not larger than the final value. The *control-variable* is incremented by one and if it is still less than or equal to the final value, the body of the **for** statement is executed again. This process continues until the *control-variable* is greater than the final value. In the **downto** form of the **for** statement, the *control-variable* is decremented until its value is less than the final value. The *control-variable,* the *initial-value*, and the *final-value* may not be altered by the body of the **for** loop.

The **for** statement should be used whenever the loop can be controlled by a simple counter that can be incremented or decremented by one. The **for** statement cannot be used if the loop is event driven. A loop is event driven if the number of times that the loop executes is determined by an event — one or more statements — in the body of the loop.

Two examples of the **for** statement are shown below:

---

(7) Enumerated and subrange types are covered in Section 3.

```
for Ch:= 'A' to 'Z' do
    writeln(Ch, Space, ord(Ch));

readln(Num2);
for := 1 to Num2 do
    begin
        readln(Num2);
        if odd(Num2) then
            Sum:= Sum + 1
        else
            Sum:= Sum + Num2 div 2
    end
writeln(sum);
```

11.5.2 THE WHILE STATEMENT

The **while** statement has the form

while *boolean-expression* **do**
    statement

The **while** statement is sometimes called a **pretest loop** since the boolean expression is evaluated before the body of the loop is executed. If the expression is false, the body of the loop is not executed at all. If the boolean expression is true, the body of the loop is executed. The boolean expression is reevaluated and if true the body of the loop is executed again. This process is repeated until the boolean expression becomes false.

The **while** statement is event-driven since the body of the loop must affect the boolean expression in such a way that the boolean expression eventually becomes false. If it doesn't, the program enters an infinite loop — the **while** statement is executed *ad infinitum*.

The **while** statement should be used if the loop is event-controlled and nothing is known about the loop's first execution — that is the programmer may not know in advance whether the body of the **while** statement will be executed at least once.

An example of the **while** statement is shown below:

```
CharCount:= 0;
while not eof(infile) do
    begin
            read(infile,Ch);
```

```
        if ch <> BlankSpace then
            CharCount:= succ(CharCount)
    end;
```

11.5.3 THE REPEAT STATEMENT

The **repeat** statement is a **post-test loop.** The boolean expression controlling its execution is tested after the statements in the body of the loop have been executed. The **repeat** statement has the form

```
repeat
    statement-1;
    statement-2;
        "
        "
        "
    statement-n
until boolean-expression
```

When the **repeat** statement is executed, *statement-1* through *statement-n* are executed. Next the boolean expression is evaluated. If it is false the body of the **repeat** statement is executed again. Then the boolean expression is re-evaluated. This process continues until the boolean expression is true.

Like the **while** statement, the **repeat** statement is event-driven. That is, the statements in the body of the **repeat** must affect the evaluation of the boolean expression in such a way that the latter eventually becomes true. Otherwise, the program becomes locked in an infinite loop. Unlike the **while** statement, whose body may never be executed, the body of the **repeat** statement is always executed at least once. Therefore, the **repeat** statement may be selected only if the loop is event-driven and only if the loop will be executed at least once no matter what conditions exist when the loop is first encountered.

Both the **while** statement and the **repeat** statement are appropriate in many circumstances in which the loop will be executed at least once. In such situations, choose the one that better reflects the semantics of the problem associated with the boolean expression. If the problem is stated in terms of when to keep looping, select the **while** statement. If the problem is stated in terms of when to stop looping, select the **repeat** statement.

An example of the **repeat** statement follows:

```
Sum:= 0;
Num:= 0;
repeat
    Sum:= Sum + Num;
    read(Num)
until Num < 0;
writeln(Sum);
```

11.6 Procedural Control Structures

It is not uncommon to find identical segments of code or near identical segments of code repeated two or more times in large programs. In Pascal, it is possible to replace redundant segments of code with single statements which invoke a **procedure** or a **function** containing the displaced code.[8] Clearly, one of the advantages of this feature is that redundant code is removed from a program. Another advantage is that the program is more readable.

11.7 Labels, the Label Section, and the Goto Statement

Ninety-nine programs out of 100 should be written with only the four control structures already presented — sequential, selection, iteration, and procedural. These control structures lend themselves to modular, well-structured, and easily readable and maintainable programs.

There are rare situations in which the use of only these four control structures is awkward or inefficient. For example, an error or other exceptional situation arises during a process that requires the suspension of the process. In such situations, the **goto** statement may be used.

The **goto** statement is used to transfer program control to a statement that is prefixed by a **label.** The **label** must be declared in the label declaration section immediately following the program heading. The label section has the following form:

label
    label-1, label-2, ... label-n;

---

(8) Procedures and functions are covered in Section 13.

Each *label* is a positive integer from one to four digits. A label may be used to label only one statement. The label appears as a prefix to a statement as follows:

label: statement

Program control can be transferred to the labeled statement by using a **goto** statement:

goto *label*

The general rule for using **goto**s is to use them only when absolutely necessary. Use only sequential, selection, iteration, and procedural control structures whenever it is reasonably possible. Careless use of **goto**s may lead to unreadable and difficult to maintain programs.

An example of **label** declarations and the use of **goto** statements is illustrated below:

```
label 100;
    "
    "
    "
begin
    "
    "
    "
    if token <> 'Program' then
        begin
            writeln('*** Error: "Program" expected ***');
            goto 100
        end
    "
    "
    "

100: end;
```

11.8 Sample Program

The following program illustrates some of the structures that were presented in this Section.

program Calcpower(input,output);

```
{    Program Calcpower finds X raised to the Nth Power. The algorithm    }
{    used in the program works only for values of X greater than zero.   }
{    Therefore, the repeat loop checks the value of X to ensure that it is }
{    greater than zero. Note that the writeln formats the values of X, N  }
{    and Power. In the case of X and Power which are real numbers,        }
{    the output  will be written in decimal form with a total of six positions }
{    (including the decimal) with two decimal places. The value of N      }
{    will be formatted as a two digit integer.                            }

var
    X,
    Power: real;
    I,
    N: integer;
begin
    repeat
        write('Enter X and N: ');
        read(X,N);
        writeln
    until X > 0;
    Power:= 1;
    for I:= 1 to abs(N) do
        Power:= Power * X;
    if N < 0 then
    Power:= 1/Power;
    writeln(X:6:2,'^',N:2,' = ', Power:6:2);
end.
```

12. FILES AND INPUT/OUTPUT OPERATIONS

12.1 Files

The advantage of writing computer programs is that they can be used with different sets of data. To achieve this flexibility, data must be kept separate from the program. When data values have been stored in variables, a program can manipulate the data values producing sought-after results. New values can be stored in the variables without changing the program and the program can be executed again. To accomplish this flexibility, data are stored separately from the program in a file. A **file** is a collection of data items, usually stored in secondary memory, that is, input to or output by a program.

12.1.1 STANDARD SYSTEM FILES — INPUT/OUTPUT FILES

Pascal provides two standard system files, one called **input** and one called **output**. Generally, these files are associated with the terminal device and are used for interactive processing. The input and output files do not have to be opened by the program. They are opened automatically for the programmer.

Pascal often has difficulties with interactive processing. Consider, for example, the following program segment:

```
      "
      "
      "
while not eof do
    begin
        write('Enter value: ');
        readln(num);
    end;
      "
      "
      "
```

A potential problem exists with the eof in the **while** statement. Eof returns true if the end of the input file has been reached. Otherwise, it returns false. In this case, however, the program may be unable to determine the status of the input file if the boolean check is made before any read operations have been performed on the file. Generally, the program will appear to hang until some value is entered and then the prompt will appear. To overcome this problem, many implementations of Pascal provide a special interface or set of procedures to handle interactive processing.

12.1.2 TEXT FILES

Like the standard system file input, text files consist of a sequence of characters. Each line of text contains data items separated by spaces and terminated with an end-of-line mark. The file is terminated with an end-of-file mark. Pascal provides two standard functions that detect these marks, namely, **eoln** and **eof**.

Text files are accessed through file variables which are declared as **type text**. The following example demonstrates the declaration of a file variable:

```
var
    RatingInfo: text;
```

In addition, the file name must appear in the program heading such as

program EstimateMood(output, RatingInfo);

12.2 Input Operations on Text Files

Before a text file can be read it must be opened. The **reset statement** is used to open a text file for input. It has the form:

reset(*file-variable)*

Therefore, to open the file RatingInfo for input the statement becomes

reset(RatingInfo);

Many implementations of Pascal use a modified form of this method to open a file for input that associates the logical file name used in the program with the actual physical file name that is used by the computer. One method used is to modify the reset statement as follows

reset(*file-variable, file-name)*

where *file-variable* is the program variable that is associated with the actual *file-name* used by the computer.

Another common method is to use a separate statement called **assign** that performs the binding between the logical file name used by the program and the actual physical file name. In such implementations the standard form of the reset statement is used to open the file.

Two Pascal statements may be used to input information once a text file is opened. However, before covering these statements, the reader must first understand the concept of a file marker. A file marker may be thought of as a pointer that points to the next data item in the file that is available for processing. When a file is opened with the reset statement the file marker is set to the beginning of the file. As the file is processed, the file marker is automatically advanced as data items are read from the file.

Two statements — the **read statement** and the **readln statement** — are used to input information from a text file into a program. The read statement has the form

```
read(file-variable, parameter-1, parameter-2, ... parameter-n)
```

where *file-variable* refers to the file to be read. The file's data are read into the program variables specified in the parameter list *parameter-1* through *parameter-n*. The reason that the items are referred to as parameters is that the read and readln statements, as well as the write and writeln statements, are actually standard Pascal procedures. An example of a read statement is shown below:

```
read(StudentFile, Grade1, Grade2, Grade3, Average);
```

where StudentFile is the *file-variable*, and Grade1, Grade2, Grade3, and Average make up the parameter list.

Data values that are read from the file must be of the same type as the variables into which the data values are placed. For example, assume that Grade1, Grade2, and Grade3 have been declared as type integer and Average has been declared as type real. Then the three data values that are read from the file StudentFile into the three variables Grade1, Grade2, and Grade3 must be of type integer. Likewise, the data value read from the file into the variable Average must be of type real. Otherwise, an error is generated.

The single read statement above could have been written as two, three, or four separate statements. For example, the read statement shown previously is equivalent to the following:

```
read(StudentFile, Grade1, Grade2, Grade3);
read(StudentFile, Average);
```

The readln statement has the same form as the read statement:

readln(file-variable, parameter-1, parameter-2, ... parameter-n)

The difference between the read statement and the readln statement is that the readln statement advances the file marker to the beginning of the next line in the file after the data have been read into the program. The read statement does not advance the file marker to the next line. This means that the readln statement may be used to skip remaining data on a line. Another difference between the two statements is that the readln statement may be used without a parameter list while the read statement may not.

12.2.1 EOF AND EOLN FUNCTIONS

Eof is a standard boolean function that may be used to detect the end of a file. It is often necessary to make this check because attempting to read beyond the end-of-file mark will generate an error. A call to eof has the form:

eof(file-variable)

The standard file input is assumed if the *file-variable* and parentheses are omitted. Eof returns the value true if the file marker is positioned at the end-of-file mark. Otherwise, it returns the value false.

Likewise, the function **eoln** may be used to detect the end-of-line mark. Eoln returns true if the file marker is positioned at an end-of-line mark. Otherwise, it returns the value false. A call to eoln has the form

eoln(file-variable)

If the *file-variable* and parentheses are omitted, the standard system file input is assumed.

Most implementations of Pascal provide a **close** procedure to close a text file when the processing of the file has been completed. When an implementation of Pascal provides a close procedure, it is always wise to use it to close a text file when processing of the file has been completed. This is particularly true if the text file has been used for output. Failure to close a file that has been written to could result in lost data.

12.3 Output Operations on Text Files

Just as with input, a text file must be opened before information can be written to it. The **rewrite statement** is used to open a text file for output. It has the form

rewrite(*file-variable*)

The implementation dependent variations for opening input text files also apply to opening output text files. Furthermore, as before, the *file-variable* must be declared as type text and must appear in the program heading.

When a file is opened with the rewrite statement, the file marker is set to the beginning of the file. If the file already exists, this action will effectively erase all data in the file. Therefore, programmers always want to be careful that they do not accidentally open an input file with the rewrite statement. Otherwise, they will have to restore their input file.

Two statements may be used to output data to a file once the file has been opened with the rewrite statement. They are **write** and **writeln.** In their simplest form they have the form

write(*file-variable, parameter-1, parameter-2, ... parameter-n*)

and

writeln(*file-variable, parameter-l, parameter-2, ... parameter-n*)

The standard system file output is assumed if the *file-variable* is omitted. The difference between the write and writeln statements is that the latter will advance the file marker to a new line after output is completed, while the former will not. Therefore, several consecutive write statements may be used to write data to the same line in the file.

Both the write and writeln statements may be used to output literals — constant values — as well as a combination of literals and parameter values. Two examples are shown below:

EXAMPLE 1

writeln('Your monthly payment will be ', MonthlyPayment);

EXAMPLE 2

```
write(OutFile,'Score 1 = ', Score1);
write(OutFile,'     Score 2 = ', Score2);
writeln(OutFile);
```

In example one, output is directed to the standard system file output. In example two, two write statements are used to output information to one line of the file OutFile. The writeln is used to advance the file marker to a new line in the file.

In both examples, the output might appear somewhat awkward. There probably will be several blank spaces between the literal that is being output and the variable value that follows the literal. Or in the case of example 1, MonthlyPayment may be output in exponential form (scientific notation). This can be corrected in most implementations of Pascal by formatting the variable value that is output. Assuming that MonthlyPayment is type real and Score1 and Score2 are type integer, the output can be modified as follows:

EXAMPLE 3

```
writeln('Your monthly payment will be ', MonthlyPayment:7:2);
```

EXAMPLE 4

```
write(OutFile,'Score 1 = ', Score1:3);
write(OutFile,'     Score 2 = ', Score2:3);
writeln(OutFile);
```

The output for Example 3 will look something like

Your monthly payment will be 1345.32

For example 4, the output will look like the following:

Score 1 = 245 Score 2 = 266

Study Section 12.4 for the "AB" exam.

12.4 Other Types of Files

Elements in a text file are always of type **char**. It is possible for the elements of a file to be of any predefined or user-defined data type except for another file type. This includes files of enumerated types, files of type integer, files of record types, and more. Examples of several file declarations are shown below:

```
type
    Colors = (Red, Blue, Yellow, Orange, Purple, Green);
    Rating = 1..10;
    FileOfColors = file of Colors;
    FileOfNumbers = file of integer;
    FileOfRating = file of Rating;

var
    ColorFile: FileOfColors;
    NumFile: FileOfNumbers;
    RatingFile: FileOfRating;
    Color: Colors;
    CurrentRating: Rating;
```

The statements reset, rewrite, read, and write may be used on nontext files. So may the functions eof and eoln. Assume the type definitions and variable declarations given above. The following program segment illustrates some of these principles.

```
        "
        "
        "
    rewrite(ColorFile);
    Color:= Red;
    write(ColorFile,Color);
    Color:= Blue;
    write(ColorFile,Color);
        "
        "
        "
    reset(RatingFile);
    while not eof(RatingFile) do
```

```
begin
    read(RatingFile, CurrentRating);
    writeln(CurrentRating);
end;
    "
        "
            "
close(ColorFile);
close(RatingFile);
    "
        "
            "
```

Note that in this implementation, a close statement is used to close both files.

Output to a file actually takes place in two steps. In the first step, the value stored in the variable is transferred to a special variable called a file buffer variable. The file buffer variable is created automatically when a file is opened. In the example above the statement

```
rewrite(ColorFile);
```

creates the file buffer variable which is denoted by ColorFile^.

Once data have been transferred to the file buffer variable the data are written to the file by a **put procedure.** Therefore,

```
write(ColorFile, Color);
```

is equivalent to

```
ColorFile^:= Color;
put(ColorFile);
```

Input from a file is analogous to output to a file. When a file is opened with the reset statement two actions are carried out. First, the file buffer variable is created, and second, the first set of data in the file is copied from the file into the file buffer variable. Third, the data are transferred from the file buffer variable to the program variable. Therefore,

```
read(RatingFile, CurrentRating);
```

is equivalent to

```
    CurrentRating:= RatingFile^;
    get(RatingFile);
```

There are some advantages to using the get statement instead of the read statement. Many applications required look-ahead capability. The use of the file buffer variable and the get statement not only makes this possible but easy to do.

Before closing this section, it is important to note that some implementations of Pascal do not support the file buffer variable, the put statement, and the get statement. In such cases, the programmer must use the read and write statements for input from and output to a nontext file.

12.5 Sample Program

```
program EstimateMood(RatingFile, Output);

{   This program is a modified version of the program given in Section 3.4. }
{   It reads ratings from a file of type Rating. Note that this implementation }
{   uses a close statement to close the file when processing is done.        }

type
    Mood = (Melancholy, Gloomy, Sullen, Capricious, Pensive, Sober,
                    Humorous, Jubilant, Elated, Ecstatic);
    Rating = 1 ...10;
    FileOfRating = file of Rating;

var
    YourMood: Mood;
    YourRating, AverageRating: Rating;
    SumOfRatings, NumberOfRaters: integer;
    RatingFile: FileOfRating;

begin
    reset(RatingFile);
    SumOfRatings:= 0;
    NumberOfRaters:= 0;
    while not eof (RatingFile) do
        begin
            read(RatingFile, YourRating);
            SumOfRatings:= SumOfRatings + YourRating;
            NumberOfRaters:= succ(NumberOfRaters);
        end;
    writeln;
```

```
AverageRating:= round(SumOfRatings/NumberOfRaters);
YourMood:= Melancholy;
while ord(YourMood) <> AverageRating – 1 do
    YourMood:= succ(YourMood);
case YourMood of
    Melancholy: writeln ('Make an appointment with your analyst.');
    Gloomy: writeln('Go back to bed.');
    Sullen: writeln('Cheer up. Things could be worse.');
    Capricious: writeln('Don't be so fickle.');
    Pensive: writeln('Enroll in a college course on Greek Mythology.');
    Sober: writeln('Today you should be mischievous.');
    Humorous: writeln('Be serious today. It may mean a promotion.');
    Jubilant: writeln('Go on a shopping spree. You deserve it.');
    Elated: writeln('Ask your boss for a raise.');
    Ecstatic: writeln('Spread the cheer!');
end;
writeln('Your rating is ',AverageRating);
close(RatingFile);
end.
```

13.   PROCEDURES AND FUNCTIONS

13.1 Procedures

The programs that were presented in previous chapters are monolithic in nature. Most problems requiring the application of a computer, however, are too complex to be solved with such a brute force approach. Therefore, a **top-down** approach that employs a **divide-and-conquer** strategy is used to solve complex problems. This strategy calls for the programmer to divide the problem repeatedly into simpler subproblems until each subproblem can be solved easily. Separate algorithms, which are developed for each subproblem, are translated into subprograms or modules. Finally, these modules are combined into a single program in such a way that the program solves the original problem. Pascal supports top-down strategy and modular programming by providing subprogram structures known as procedures and functions.

A **procedure** is a subprogram that usually performs a single task. Information is passed between a procedure and the calling module via parameters. A Pascal **procedure definition** is nearly identical to a program. However, a **procedure heading** contains an optional **parameter list,** and the procedure definition is terminated with a semicolon instead of a period. A procedure definition is placed in the subprogram section immediately following the variable **(var)** section. The reader is referred to Section 2 for a review of program structure and organization.

13.1.1 PROCEDURE HEADING

The procedure heading has the form:

procedure *identifier;*

or

procedure *identifier(formal-parameter-list);*

where *formal-parameter-list* has the form

parameter-group-1; parameter-group-2; ...
parameter-group-n

A *parameter-group* has the form

identifier-1, identifier-2, ... identifier-m: identifier-type

or

var *identifier-1, identifier-2, ... identifier-m: identifier-type*

Several examples of procedure headings are given below in order to illustrate the varied possibilities:

procedure DisplayMenu;

procedure WriteRecord(OutRecord: RecordType);

procedure ReadRecord(**var** InFile: text; **var** InRecord: RecordType);

procedure Rotate(**var** X, Y, Z: integer);

procedure NextGeneration(**var** Cell, Copy: Automaton; Rule: Rules);

procedure PushStack(**var** S: Stack; I: Item);

The first procedure heading does not have the optional *formal-parameter-list*. The next five examples do. Some of the *parameter-groups* in these examples begin with the reserved word **var** while others do not. The presence or absence of **var** determines the manner in which information is passed to procedures. Its implications on parameter passing will be explained in a moment. The fourth and fifth examples show how more than one formal parameter may be declared with the same type.

Let's consider an example in more detail. In Chapter 3 two methods of declaring WorkDay were presented which use the following type definitions:

type
     DayOfWeek = (Monday, Tuesday, Wednesday, Thursday, Friday,
                   Saturday, Sunday);
     WeekDay = Monday . . Friday;

WorkDay may be declared as a formal parameter in a procedure heading using the following method:

     procedure GetDailySchedule(**var** Infile: Calendar;
                                     var Workday: Weekday);

However, Workday could not be declared as a formal parameter using the following method:

     procedure GetDailySchedule(**var** Infile: Calendar;
                                     var Workday: Monday . . Friday);

13.1.2 PROCEDURE INVOCATION

A procedure may be invoked or called by a **procedure reference statement** containing the procedure name followed by an optional list of **actual parameters.** It has the form

identifier(actual-parameter-list)

The **actual-parameter-list** is a list of actual parameters that are associated with the formal parameters in the procedure heading. The number of actual parameters must be the same as the number of parameters in the formal parameter list of the procedure heading. Likewise, each actual parameter must have the same type as the formal parameter in the same position.

Consider the **procedure** Swap given below:

procedure Swap(**var** X, Y: integer);

var
    Temp: integer;

begin
    Temp:= X;
        X:= Y;
        Y:= Temp;
end;

Swap may be invoked by the following procedure reference statement:

    Swap(A, B);

where A and B are declared as type integer. In this example, the actual parameter A is associated with the formal parameter X, and B is associated with Y.

13.1.3 PARAMETER TYPES

There are two methods of passing parameters in Pascal — **pass-by-reference** and **pass-by-value.** When parameters are passed by reference, the formal parameters in a parameter group of the procedure heading are preceded by the reserved word **var** and therefore are called **variable parameters.** Parameters are passed by value when formal parameters in a parameter group are not preceded with the reserved word **var**. They are called **value parameters.**

When parameters are passed by reference, information may be transferred into and out of a procedure via the variable parameters. This is because the **location** (address in memory) of the actual parameters are passed to the formal parameters and not their values. There is only one copy of information, which is used by both the calling routine and the procedure. When the procedure is called, the formal parameters and actual parameters become synonyms for the same locations in memory. Any change made to the value of a formal parameter will be found in the actual parameter when control is returned to the calling routine.

Consider the **procedure** Swap from above. If Swap is called with A = 10 and B = 20, X becomes synonymous with A and Y with B. The values of X and Y are exchanged by Swap so that when control is returned to the calling routine, A will have the value 20 and B will have the value 10.

When parameters are passed by value, information may be transferred into a procedure but not out of the procedure. In this case, another copy of the information is made and passed to the procedure. Consider the following procedure:

```
procedure CalculateAbsoluteDifference(var Diff: NonNegInt;
                                      X, Y: NonNegInt);


begin
    If X > Y then
        Swap(X,Y);
    Diff:= Y – X;
end;
```

Suppose that CalculateAbsoluteDifference is invoked with the following procedure reference statement:

```
CalculateAbsoluteDifference(Difference,A,B);
```

with A = 20 and B = 10. The starting value of Difference is not of any consequence in this case. The value of A is copied and passed to X and the value of B is copied and passed to Y. Since X is greater than Y, the values of X and Y will be exchanged. However, since the values of A and B were passed to the procedure and not their addresses, A will still have the value 20 and B will still have the value 10 when control is returned to the calling routine.

In Pascal, if parameter arrays are not declared *VAR*, new memory is allocated whenever a subprogram is involved that can (needlessly) use up large amounts of memory. In extreme cases, in recursive routines, a run-time error may occur because of no more available memory.

13.1.4 NESTED SUBPROGRAM DEFINITIONS

Procedures may be defined within procedures. Swap, for example, could be defined within CalculateAbsoluteDifference:

```
procedure CalculateAbsoluteDifference(var Diff: NonNegInt;
                                       X, Y: NonNegInt);

    procedure Swap(var X, Y: integer);

    var Temp: integer;

    begin {procedure Swap}
        Temp: = X;
        X:= Y;
        Y:= Temp;
    end; {procedure Swap}

begin {procedure   CalculateAbsoluteDifference}
    If X > Y then
        Swap(X,Y);
    Diff:= Y – X;
end; {procedure   CalculateAbsoluteDifference}
```

13.1.5 FORWARD DECLARATION OF SUBPROGRAMS

A basic Pascal maxim regarding subprograms is that they must be declared before they are invoked. Occasionally, this maxim creates a dilemma for the programmer. Consider, for example, two procedures each calling the other. Which procedure should the programmer declare first? Regardless of the choice, one of the two procedures will be invoked before it has been declared.

This dilemma is actually created by the compiler. The compiler, which makes two passes through the source code, enters all constant, variable, and subprogram identifiers into a symbol table on its first pass. If the compiler encounters an identifier which has not been declared, such as a procedure identifier in a procedure reference statement, it will generate an error message. How then can the programmer's dilemma be overcome?

Pascal provides the **forward** declaration which tells the compiler that a subprogram identifier is valid. The **forward** declaration has the form

procedure *identifier(formal-parameter-list);* **forward**;

The procedure must be declared later within the subprogram declaration section. A partially coded example follows:

procedure DeclaredLater*(parameter list);* **forward**

```
procedure DeclaredHere(parameter list);

local declarations

begin
        "
        "
        "
    DeclaredLater(argument list);
        "
        "
        "

end;

procedure DeclaredLater; {Omit parameter list}

local declarations

begin
        "
        "
        "
    DeclaredHere(argument list);
        "
        "
        "

end;
```

Although the formal parameter list is omitted when the **procedure** DeclaredLater actually declared, it is wise to include a comment statement listing them for documentation purposes.

13.2 Functions

A **function** is a subprogram that is called from within an expression, and ordinarily computes and returns a single value to the calling routine via the function name. Pascal provides several predefined functions which were presented in section 1.8. Pascal also provides the means for programmers to define their own functions.

Like procedures, user-defined functions are declared in the subprogram section. The declaration and statement parts of a function declaration also have the same form as for procedures. The function heading is different, however, and has the following form:

function *identifier: identifier-type;*

or

function *identifier(formal-parameter-list): identifier-type;*

Another feature of functions is that at least one of the statements in the statement part must assign a value to the identifier that names the function. Two examples of a function definition are shown below:

function Cube(X: real): real;

begin
    Cube:=(X*X*X);
end;

function Power(X: real; Y: integer): real;

var
    Z: real:

begin
    Z:= 1.0;
    while Y > 0 do
        begin
            if odd(Y) **then**
                Z:= Z * X;
            I:= I **div** 2;
            x:= sqr(X);
        end;
    Power:= Z;
end;

Note that both functions have a statement that assigns a value to the name of the function.

13.2.1 FUNCTION CALL

A function may be called from within an expression. The two examples shown here call the functions Power and Cube:

```
Z2:= Power(X2, Y2);

If Volume = Cube(W) then
    "
    "
    "
```

Like procedures, the number and type of actual parameters must be the same as the number and type of corresponding formal parameters. Functions may be defined within procedures and other functions. Although Pascal permits variable parameters to be passed to functions, it is general practice not to use them. Functions are usually defined as returning a single value. Therefore, if it is necessary to return more than one value, a procedure should be written instead of a function.

13.3 Recursion

A recursive definition is a definition in which something (i.e. a set or function) is defined in terms of a simpler version of itself. There are two parts to a recursive definition — the basis clause and the general or inductive clause. The basis clause presents the case for which the solution can be stated nonrecursively. The inductive clause presents the case for which the solution is expressed in terms of a simpler version of itself.

In Pascal, recursion is a process whereby a function or procedure references itself. Direct recursion is when a function or procedure invokes itself. Indirect recursion is when a function or procedure invokes another subprogram or series of subprograms which eventually invokes the first subprogram. The following recursive function returns the greatest common factor:

```
function GCF(M, N: NonNegInt): NonNegInt;

begin
    if N = 0 then
        GCF:= M
    else
        GCF:= GCF(N, M mod N);
end;
```

The statement

    GCF:= M

corresponds to the basis clause in a recursive definition, while the statement

    GCF:= GCF(N, M **mod** N)

corresponds to the inductive clause.

The next recursive function is somewhat more complex. It is known as Ackerman's function:

    function Ackerman (M, N: NonNegInt): NonNegInt;

    begin
       If M = 0 **then**
           Ackerman:= N + 1
       else if (M <> 0) **and** (N = 0) **then**
           Ackerman:= Ackerman(M – 1,1)
       else
           Ackerman:= Ackerman(M – 1, Ackerman(M, N – 1))
    end;

Note that in this example there are two statements that make up the inductive clause. The second of these

    Ackerman:= Ackerman(M – 1, Ackerman(M, N – 1))

invokes itself twice. Also note that the second reference to the function Ackerman is actually the second parameter to the first reference.

13.3.1 RECURSIVE CALLS AND THE STACK

Whenever a procedure or function is called recursively, a new set of value parameters and local variables is allocated. Only the new set may be referenced within that call. This set is known as an **activation record**. When a return from the procedure or function takes place, the most recent activation record is freed and the previous copy is reactivated.

Pascal uses a **stack** to keep track of activation records. A stack is a FILO (first-in-last-out) data structure. Whenever a new activation record is activated, it is pushed onto the stack. Whenever an activation record is freed, it is popped off the stack.

Now, what happens when the recursive function GCF presented earlier is first called with M = 196 and N = 36? The series of stack figures in Figure

13.3.2 show the changes that take place in the stack contents each time the GCF is invoked. Understanding how Pascal handles the stack with recursive calls will help the reader understand how recursion works.

FIGURE 13.3.2

CHANGES IN STACK CONTENTS WHEN GCF IS INITIALLY INVOKED WITH GCF(196, 36)

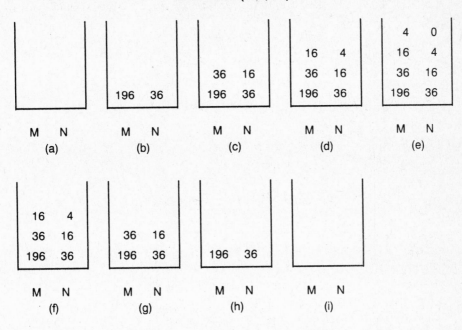

In Figure 13.3.2, each row in a stack figure represents an activation record. The current activation record is on top of the stack. When GCF is called for the first time, an activation record is created with M = 196 and N = 36 which is pushed onto the stack (Figure 13.3.2.b). Since N <> 0, GCF is called recursively by the statement **GCF:= GCF(N, M mod N)** where N = 36 and (M mod N) = 16. A new activation record is created with M = 36 and N = 16 (Figure 13.3.2.c). Keep in mind that the actual parameters are matched up with the formal parameters according to their relative positions. Therefore, the actual parameter N is matched with the formal parameter M, while the actual parameter M mod N is matched with the formal parameter N.

GCF is called again recursively with N = 16 and M mod N = 4 (Figure 13.3.2.d) and then with N = 4 and M mod N = 0 (Figure 13.3.2.e). Since the value of the formal parameter N in the last activation record is now equal to zero (Figure 13.3.2.e), GCF returns a value of 4 with the execution of the statement **GCF:= M.** As a part of this process, an activation record is deallocated and popped off the stack resulting in Figure 13.3.2.f.

Remember that when GCF called itself recursively with the statement **GCF:= GCF(N, M MOD N)** an activation record was created and the execution of GCF started anew. When an activation record is deallocated and the stack is popped, program execution continues with the statement following **GCF:= GCF(N, M MOD N).** In this case, the next statement is the **end** statement that terminates the procedure. When the **end** statement is reached, another activation record is deallocated and the stack is popped again. This procedure continues until there are no more activation records and the stack is empty.

The Fibonacci sequence of numbers can easily be translated into a Pascal recursive function as follows:

```
FUNCTION fibon(n:INTEGER):INTEGER;
BEGIN
    IF n <= 1 THEN
        fibon := 1
    ELSE
        fibon := fibon(n-1) + fibon(n-2)
END;
```

In Figure 13.3.3, each row in a stack figure represents an activation record. The current activation record is on top of the stack. When Fibonacci is called for the first time an activation record is created with N = 5, and is pushed onto the stack (Figure 13.3.3.a). Since N <> 1, Fibonacci is called recursively by the statement **X:= Fibonacci(N – 1)** where N – 1 = 4. A new activation record is created with N now equal to four (Figure 13.3.3.b). This process continues until N = 1 (Figure 13.3.3.e).

FIGURE 13.3.3
CHANGES IN STACK CONTENTS WHEN FIBONACCI IS
INITIALLY INVOLED WITH A VALUE OF 5.

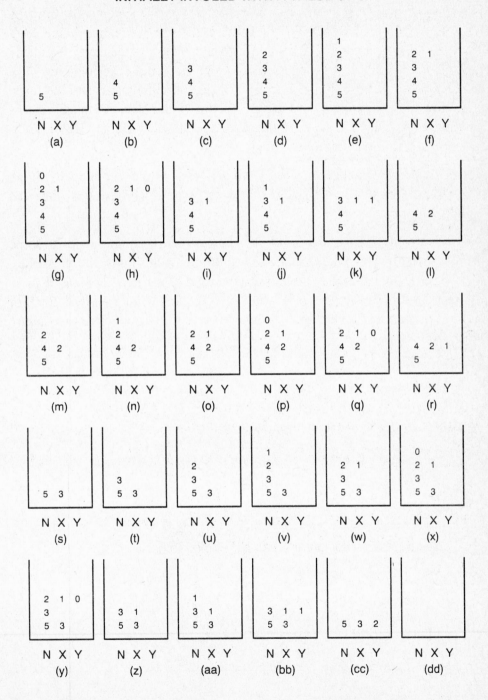

When N = 1, Fibonacci returns a value of 1 for X giving the first Fibonacci number. As a part of this process an activation record is deallocated and popped off the stack resulting in Figure 13.3.3.f.

At this point, Fibonacci is called by the statement **Y:= Fibonacci (N − 2)**. Since N = 2 in the top activation record, N − 2 = 0 (Figure 13.3.3.g). In the new invocation of Fibonacci with N now equal to zero, Fibonacci returns a zero to Y (Figure 13.3.3.h).

Now our activation record has a value for X and Y so Fibonacci returns a value of X + Y = 1 + 0 = 1 for the second Fibonacci number. This value is returned to X in the previous activation record (Figure 13.3.3.i).

This process continues until Fibonacci returns a 5 for N = 5 (Figure 13.3.3.cc: X + Y = 3 + 2 = 5). Note that when Fibonacci returns this value, the stack is empty.

Recursion, when used properly, is a powerful programming tool. In some cases, it can improve performance over iterative algorithms. In other cases, a recursive algorithm may be more natural and easier to understand than its iterative counterpart even if the former is not quite as efficient as the latter. For another example of recursion, the reader is referred to the quicksort procedure in Section 6.

13.4 Sample Program

```
program PrimeDivisors(Numfile, Primefile);

{   This program reads a file of integers and generates their prime divisors }

var
    NumFile, PrimeFile: text;

    procedure OpenFiles(var NumFile, PrimeFile: text);

    begin { OpenFiles }
        reset(NumFile);
        rewrite(PrimeFile);
    end;

    procedure CloseFiles(var NumFile, PrimeFile: text);

    begin { CloseFiles }
        close(NumFile);
        close(PrimeFile);
```

```pascal
        end;

procedure ProcessFile(var NumFile, PrimeFile: text);

var
    Number: integer;

    procedure FindNextPrimeNumber (var PrimeNumber: integer);

{   FindNextPrimeNumber receives the current prime number and          }
{   calculates and returns the next larger prime number.               }

    var
        prime:      boolean;
        divisor:    integer;

    begin { FindNextPrimeNumber }
        if PrimeNumber= 2 then
            PrimeNumber:= 3
        else
                begin { else }
                    Prime:= false;
            while not Prime do
                begin { while }
                    Prime:= true;
                    PrimeNumber:= PrimeNumber + 2;
                    divisor:= 3;
                    repeat
                        If PrimeNumber mod divisor = 0 then
                            Prime:= false;
                        divisor:= divisor + 2;
                    until (not Prime) or
                        (divisor > sqrt(PrimeNumber));
                end; { while }
        end; { else }
    end; { FindNextPrimeNumber }

procedure WritePrime(var PrimeFile: text; Prime Number: integer;
                                        var First: boolean);
    begin ( WritePrime }
        If First then
            begin { if }
                write(PrimeFile, PrimeNumber);
                First:= false;
            end { if }
```

```
      else
            write(PrimeFile,' * ', PrimeNumber);
   end; { WritePrime }


procedure FindPrimeDivisors(var NumFile, PrimeFile: text;
                                                  Number: integer);
```

```
{  FindPrimeDivisors calculates all of the prime divisors of        }
{  Number including prime divisors which occur more than once.       }
{  This procedure will need to be studied closely in order to be     }
{  fully understood. Some enhancements have been made to             }
{  make it more efficient — albeit, somewhat more difficult to       }
{  understand. The procedure begins by storing the value of          }
{  Number in TempNumber and then setting PrimeNumber to 2.           }
{  The code in the repeat loop determines whether PrimeNumber is a   }
{  divisor of TempNumber. If so, the PrimeNumber is written to the   }
{  output file and TempNumber is set equal to TempNumber div         }
{  PrimeNumber. This process continues until PrimeNumber >           }
{  sqrt(Number) or TempNumber = 1. Note: This algorithm works if the }
{  boolean expression in the until statement is comprised of only    }
{  TempNumber = 1, although it is not nearly as efficient for large values }
{  of Number. There is one difficulty, however. If the value of TempNum- }
{  ber is greater than the square root of Number, then TempNumber is a }
{  prime divisor of Number and needs to be written to the output file. }
{  Thus the if statement if TempNumber > sqrt(Number) then ... after }
{  the repeat loop.                                                  }
```

```
var
      First: boolean;
      TempNumber, PrimeNumber: integer;


begin { FindPrimeDivisors }
      TempNumber:= Number;
      write(PrimeFile, TempNumber:5, ' = ');
      PrimeNumber:= 2;
      First:= true;
      repeat
         if TempNumber mod PrimeNumber = 0 then
               begin { if }
                     TempNumber:= TempNumber div PrimeNumber;
                     WritePrime(PrimeFile, PrimeNumber, First);
               end { if }
         else
               FindNextPrimeNumber (PrimeNumber);
      until (PrimeNumber > sqrt(Number)) or (TempNumber = 1 );
```

```
    If TempNumber > sqrt(Number)
        then WritePrime(PrimeFile, TempNumber, First);
    writeln(PrimeFile);
end; { FindPrimeDivisors }

begin { ProcessFile }
    while (not eoln(NumFile)) do
        begin { while }
            read(NumFile, Number);
            if Number <= 1 then
                writeln(PrimeFile, Number:5,
                ' is an ILLEGAL number.')
            else

{    The code in the repeat loop determines whether PrimeNumber is a    }
{    divisor of TempNumber. If so, the PrimeNumber is written to the    }
{    output file and TempNumber is set equal to TempNumber div          }
{    PrimeNumber. This process continues until PrimeNumber >            }
{    sqrt(Number) or TempNumber = 1. Note: This algorithm works if the  }
{    boolean expression in the until statement is comprised of only     }
{    TempNumber = 1, although it is not nearly as efficient for large values }
{    of Number. There is one difficulty, however. If the value of TempNum- }
{    ber is greater than the square root of Number, then TempNumber is a }
{    prime divisor of Number and needs to be written to the output file. }
{    Thus the if statement if TempNumber > sqrt(Number) then...after     }
{    the repeat loop.                                                    }

var
    First: boolean;
    TempNumber, PrimeNumber: integer;

begin { FindPrimeDivisors }
    TempNumber:= Number;
    write(PrimeFile,TempNumber:5, ' = ');
    PrimeNumber:= 2;
    First:= true;
    repeat
        if TempNumber mod PrimeNumber = 0 then
            begin { if }
                TempNumber:= TempNumber div PrimeNumber;
                WritePrime(PrimeFile, PrimeNumber, First);
            end { if }
        else
            FindNextPrimeNumber (PrimeNumber);
    until (PrimeNumber > sqrt(Number)) or (TempNumber = 1);
```

```
    if TempNumber > sqrt(Number) then
        WritePrime(PrimeFile, TempNumber, First);
    writeln(PrimeFile);
end; { FindPrimeDivisors }

begin { ProcessFile }
    while (not eoln(NumFile)) do
        begin { while }
            read(NumFile, Number);
            if Number <= 1 then
                writeln(PrimeFile, Number:5,
                ' is an ILLEGAL number.')
            else
```

14. STRING PROCESSING

A string is a finite sequence of characters. Many implementations of Pascal provide a predefined string data type and predefined functions and procedures to operate on them. Standard Pascal provides the character type and string constants. However, it does not provide a predefined string type. Therefore, arrays are used to process strings of characters. Consider the following declarations:

```
type
    NameArray = array[1. .15] of char;

var
    Name, Name2: NameArray;
```

A string can be assigned to Name in the following manner:

Name:= 'Heather Lynne ';

The contents of Name may be assigned to Name1 in the following manner:

```
for I:=1 to 15 do
    Name2[ I ]:= Name[ I ];
```

This method is somewhat laborious. The contents of an array may be assigned to another array of the same type using the form:

array-variable-identifier-1:= array-variable-identifier-2;

Therefore, Name can be assigned to Name2 in the following manner:

Name2:= Name;

Most computer encoding schemes use one byte (8 bits) to store a character. In many computers, the size of a memory word is more than one byte, most often four bytes. Most Pascal compilers will store a character string in memory, one character per word. If a memory word is four bytes long, this means that three bytes per word of memory are wasted. Memory utilization is improved if **packed arrays** are used to store strings. Name and Name2 may be declared as packed arrays using the declarations:

type
    NameArray = **packed array**[1 . .15] of char;

var
    Name, Name2: NameArray;

As before, the contents of Name may be assigned to Name2 using the assignment statement:

Name2:= Name;

Now, however, memory is saved. If a memory word is four bytes long, then four characters will be stored per memory word.

Arrays, including packed arrays, may be compared using relational operators provided that they are the same length. For example,

'buick' < 'chevy'

is true since 'b' comes before 'c' in the collating sequence.[3] However, 'buick' cannot be compared to 'ford' because they are not the same length. The boolean expression

'ford' >'chevy'

is valid because both strings have five characters. Furthermore, the expression is true since 'f' comes after 'c' in the collating sequence.

Some Pascal compilers will allow the name of an array of character type to appear in an input list of a read or readln statement or in the output list of a write or writeln statement. Thus, the following statements

```
read(Name);
write(Name);
readln(Name);
writeln(Name);
```

would be valid. However, some compilers do not allow the name of an array of character type to appear in an input list or output list. Under such circumstances, the characters in a character string must be read or written one character at a time:

```
for I:= 1 to 15 do
read(Name[ I ]);
```

_____

(3) A collating sequence is the computer's character set. All the letters, numerals, and punctuation that the computer can input or output are in a particular order known as its collating sequence.

CHAPTER 4

FUNDAMENTAL DATA STRUCTURES

1. INTRODUCTION

1.1 DATA AND PROGRAMS

All computer programs involve information or **data.** A program is of little use if there is no information produced at the end of its execution. Some programs merely *generate* data, such as a program to generate prime numbers. These types of programs usually do not require any input data, but merely create the information desired by the programmer. Other programs *process* input data and create more data as a result, such as bookkeeping and billing programs that examine files of charges and then generate bills to be mailed to customers. Whether a program needs input data or not, it nonetheless needs to *store* some data, which is then used to generate other data desired by the programmer.

The study of *data structures* is a study of the possible ways of organizing and storing information; that is, a study of the various ways to *structure data,* and a study of the way that some data is related to other data. Depending on the way data is arranged ("structured"), computer operations involving that data may become less or more efficient, or less or more complex operations such as information retrieval and modification.

A study of data structures usually involves examining the operations, programs or algorithms associated with the various structures, although a detailed analysis of these algorithms is normally part of a separate field of study, usually called the *Theory of Algorithms.* In general, good algorithms lead to good programs. But the efficiency of programs can be improved by an intelligent and prudent choice of the data structures used to store the needed information.

1.2 ABSTRACT DATA TYPES

Certain data structures (e.g., scalar data and arrays) are built into every computer language. However, not every language has the full range of the more complex structures (e.g., pointer variables frequently used in linked lists). To overcome some of the difficulty encountered when converting from one language to another and also to allow for improvement in the internal implementation of more complex structures in various versions of a program, certain data structures are now commonly termed **Abstract Data Types.**

An **Abstract Data Type** (abbreviated as ADT) is any unit of data (usually complex) not built into a specific programming language. For example, the structure *stack* (see Chapter 3) can be called an ADT since most languages do not contain "stack" as an elementary data type or structure. In a data-base management program, the *database* might be considered an ADT.

Once an ADT has been identified, operations can be associated with the ADT (such as insertion, deletion, searching, testing whether empty, etc.), and specifications can be drawn up detailing what the ADT contains, and what each operation does.

In many computer languages, a given ADT (such as a stack) may be implemented in several different ways, using different possible fundamental data types and structures. In some languages (such as Modula-2 and Ada), it may even be impossible for someone to know how such an ADT is actually implemented, particularly if the program segment containing the definition of the ADT and its operations was written by another programmer.

ADTs provide a beneficial distinction between *external representation* of data structures along with their related operations, and the actual *internal implementation.* This distinction becomes particularly useful in larger programs. If the modifications of ADTs are done only by using carefully written operations, then fewer errors usually occur. If a more efficient method to implement an ADT is developed, in a carefully written program the sections defining the ADT and its operations can be replaced by the newer code without affecting the other segments of the program. A programming team can determine which ADTs will be used, how the related operations are to work, and what the external specifications should be, thus leaving the actual internal implementation to someone else. As long as users follow the external specifications, they should not need to know anything about the internal implementation. The ADT can form a protective fence around the internal implementation both to guard the data structure and also to allow it to be improved without disturbing the rest of the program.

Some of the more complex data structures are frequently described as ADTs. Sometimes several implementations are discussed in detail (as in the case of stacks). Other times, implementations are not discussed at all or only one brief example is given (as in the case of trees). However, programming with ADTs has become a more and more important part of the contemporary study of Data Structures, even though they are not always explicitly mentioned.

2. LINKED LISTS

Study the Linked Lists for the 'AB' exam.

2.1 BASIC DEFINITIONS

2.1.1 LISTS AND NODES

A **linked list** is an ADT (abstract data type) consisting of a collection of items called **nodes.** Each node is a record containing at least two fields, an *information* field (usually abbreviated to *info*) and a *next address* field (sometimes called a *link* field). The simplest type of linked list has only one address field and is called a *singly linked list*. However, there may be multiple information fields in each node. The *address field* contains the address of the next node on the list, i.e., the memory location that begins the next node.

The *address* of a node is frequently called a **pointer** to a node.

The **first node** in a list (to which no other node points) is called the **head** of the list. The **last node** in a list (which does not point to any other node) is called the **tail.**

The "dummy" address that points nowhere is called the **nil pointer** or **null pointer** or simply **nil** (or **null**). It is used as an address in the *next* field of a tail node to indicate the end of a list and is often depicted with a slash bar (/) through the *next* field of a node.

A list with no nodes is called the **empty list** or the **nil list.**

2.1.2 POINTERS

As mentioned above, a pointer is merely an *address* to a node, i.e., to a memory location. The pointer variable that points to the head node is commonly also used to designate the entire list.

Pascal uses an uparrow (caret) after a pointer variable to indicate the "node to which a pointer points." For example, if *p* is a pointer variable, then *p*^ is the "node to which the pointer variable *p* points."

The distinction between a pointer (pointer variable) and the item pointed to can be confusing, and this confusion can be a source of programming errors. It is necessary to be clear about the distinction. Thus, the following example, taken from a non-computer environment, may help clarify the difference.

Suppose a town has a hospital named Mercy whose address is 1400 West Park. Suppose several blocks away (at Sixth and White Streets) there is a sign that points to Mercy Hospital and suppose someone named the sign "Sam." Sam is not Mercy Hospital. Sam is merely a street sign, but Sam points to Mercy Hospital. To use Pascal notation, Sam is a street sign at Sixth and White, the value of Sam is 1400 West Park, and Sam^ is Mercy Hospital. The address of Mercy Hospital (1400 West Park) is different than the address of Sam (Sixth and White). The two are interrelated yet distinctively different. In a similar way, *p* is not a node, but merely points to (gives the address of) a node. *p* and *p*^ are located in two different places in computer memory, but are interrelated.

2.1.3 DIAGRAMMING LISTS AND EXAMPLES

The ADT of a linked list is normally depicted by using divided *boxes* to indicate *nodes* and *arrows* to indicate *pointers* to nodes as in the following diagram:

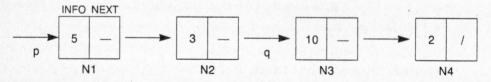

This list has four nodes that can be labeled *N1, N2, N3,* and *N4.* (In most programs, such labels of individual nodes in a linked list are never used.) The *head node* is *N1* and the *tail node* is *N4.* Node *N4* has a nil pointer depicted in its *next* section. *p* is the name of the pointer to node *N1,* but since *N1* is the head node, *p* is also considered the pointer to the entire list.

The pointer between node *N2* and node *N3* is also labeled *q* for purposes of example. Using Pascal notation, node *N1* is usually designated as *p*^ and node *N3* as *q^*. Thus, *p^.info* is 5 and *p^.next* is a pointer variable pointing to the node *N2*. So, *p^.next^.info* is 3. Similarly, *q^.next.info* is 2 and *q^.next^.next* is NIL.

A second related diagram may help clarify the difference between pointers and nodes pointed to. Nodes are combinations of two or more memory locations, one used to store information, one used to store the address of the next node. These two memory locations can be assumed to be adjacent. As was emphasized earlier, in memory a computer stores only numbers — it cannot store the arrows used in diagrams. The following diagram emphasizes this by using numbers in place of arrows.

	Memory Location	Contents	Node Name	
(p-pointer)	2501	2813		Mem. loc. 2814 is a
(q-pointer)	2502	4559		pointer to the next
		...		node that consists of
	2813	5	N1	the 2 mem. loc.'s
	2814	2815		2815 & 2816.
	2815	3	N2	
	2816	4559		
		...		
	3218	2	N4	
	3219	0<nil>		
		...		
	4559	10	N3	— **info** field
	4560	3218		— **next** field

The numbers contained in the *next* fields of the nodes depicted in this second diagram did not appear in the original diagram since the arrows took their places. The numbers have replaced the arrows since arrows cannot exist in computer memory. Even though the two diagrams are significantly different, they nevertheless contain the *same* information. Note also that the second diagram emphasizes the difference between a pointer variable and what it points to. *p* is at memory location 2501, but *p* points to memory location 2813 which is where node *N1* is located.

2.1.4 LISTS AND ARRAYS

Lists have several advantages over arrays in certain situations. A major advantage is the *dynamic allocation* of nodes in a list as opposed to the unchanging *static* allocation of arrays. In other words, a program can request more space for lists when needed at *run time*, rather than pre-determining all the space at *compile time* as with arrays.

Another advantage involves inserting items into and removing items from the data structure. It is difficult to insert a new item into a sorted array in the correct location. Many items need to be shifted and there may be no room for more information. Similarly, deleting an item from an array means that many other items must be moved to fill in the gap. Such operations are relatively trivial with linked lists since only one or two pointers need to be shifted and none of the other items in the list needs to be shifted. For example, suppose an item needs to be added to a list in a specific place, say right after node $p^\wedge$. First a new node, say $q^\wedge$, is created, then $q^\wedge.next$ is set to point to $p^\wedge.next$, and the $p^\wedge.next$ is reset to q. (See the diagram in section 2.4.2.) None of the other elements in the list needs to be shifted.

There can be disadvantages associated with lists as well. A list is a **sequential access structure** (rather than a random access structure as with an array). To access any item in a list, one must start at the head of the list and move through the list, one node at a time, until the desired node is reached. Another disadvantage concerns computer memory. For each node, not only is room to store the information needed, but also an extra memory location to store the address of the next node. This illustrates the trade-off that occurs many times in computer science: to gain some advantages, one endures a loss of some available memory.

Up to this point, linked lists have been discussed as ADTs without referring to implementation. The various operations on lists could also be described in detail solely by using box and arrow diagrams. Actual implementation techniques will be discussed next. As mentioned in Chapter 1, implementation of ADTs should be done in such a way that the implementation can be changed or improved without significant change to the program that uses the ADT.

2.1.5 IMPLEMENTING LISTS

There are two major ways of implementing a linked list:

1) *explicitly* using an *array* of available list nodes (called the linear implementation of linked lists);

2) *implicitly* using the special features of a given language, such as pointer

variables and records (called the *pointer* implementation of linked lists). Languages that have pointer variables as a built-in data type hide most of the messy bookkeeping necessary to keep the pointers straight.

2.2 LINEAR IMPLEMENTATION

2.2.1 UNDERLYING DATA STRUCTURE

The ADT of a linked list can be implemented by using an array of records, such that each array element is a node. This implementation may be necessary if the language being used does not have pointer variables.

Initially an array of nodes is explicitly declared and made large enough so that the program would never run out of nodes for linked lists. For example (using Pascal),

```
CONST numbernodes = 500;

TYPE nodetype = RECORD
            info: INTEGER;
            next: INTEGER;
        END;

VAR nodesupply : ARRAY[1. .numbernodes] OF nodetype;
```

2.2.2   PRESUPPOSITIONS

Certain presuppositions regarding our data structure and how it will be used need to be determined.

The array *nodesupply* will be used as the supply of all available nodes and nodes will be "obtained from it" as well as "returned to it" when no longer needed. In reality, the nodes themselves always remain in the array, and "active" nodes (that are part of one or more active linked lists) may be intermingled with "inactive" nodes (that are available for use). The inactive nodes and the various lists of active nodes are kept separate by the way they are linked together through the *next* fields.

The "pointer" that will be stored in the *next* field of each node will be the *index* of the array *nodesupply* where the next node is located.

To simplify the code, the array of nodes, *nodesupply*, the total number of nodes, *numbernodes*, and the pointer to the next available node, *avail*, are assumed to be global variables.

2.2.3 INITIALIZATION

The array *nodesupply* needs to be initialized so that the next available node can always be found. This is done by setting the pointers so that *nodesupply[i]* links to *nodesupply[i + 1]* resulting in a linked list of available nodes that will be referred to as the "available list." Without this initialization and linkage, there would be no easy way to distinguish which nodes are available and which are part of active lists. The initialization is done via the following procedure.

```
PROCEDURE Initialize;
VAR i: INTEGER;
BEGIN
        (* Link first numbernodes – 1 nodes to successors *)
        FOR i:= 1 TO numbernodes – 1 DO
            nodesupply[ i ].next := i + 1;
        (* Link last node to nil-pointer = 0 *)
        nodesupply[numbernodes].next := 0;
        avail := 1
END;     (* Initialize *)
```

This code makes *nodesupply[i]* point to *nodesupply[i + 1]* and the last node point to 0, which is the signal for a *nil* pointer. It ends by setting *avail* equal to 1, indicating that the first element in the *nodesupply* array is the first available node for use by a list.

2.2.4 OBTAINING AND RELEASING NODES

When a node is needed, it is taken from the head of the available list. When a node from an active list is disposed of, it is tacked onto the head of this available list. Thus, it may be that at some point of a running program, the head of the available list may be *nodesupply[23]* which links to *nodesupply[12]* which links to *nodesupply[50]* which links to *nodesupply[51]*, etc. This fact helps explain the code of the next section.

2.2.5 OBTAINING A NODE FROM THE AVAILABLE LIST

The following procedure takes a node from the available list for use by a list. The available list is properly altered.

```
PROCEDURE Getnode(VAR p: INTEGER);
BEGIN
        IF avail = 0 THEN
            Writeln('list overflow') (* error *)
        ELSE
          BEGIN
            p := avail;
            avail := nodesupply[avail].next
        END
END;   (* Getnode *)
```

The initialization procedure set *nodesupply[i].next* equal to *i + 1*. But note that *avail* is *not* merely incremented by 1, since, as mentioned above, after getting nodes for lists and freeing nodes, it may be that the original "natural" link order is totally rearranged. Instead, it has been set to what the *next* field says the next available node is.

2.2.6   RETURNING (FREEING) A NODE TO THE AVAILABLE LIST

A program may need so many nodes that all the nodes created in the *nodesupply* array may be used up. However, not all nodes may be actively part of any list at any one moment of the program. By somehow returning inactive nodes to the available list, an "overflow" (i.e., running out of available nodes) can be avoided. This is the purpose of the following procedure. In addition, if one does not de-allocate (i.e., free up) the node space at an appropriate point of a program, one may lose a pointer to the node and *not* be able to use it or dispose of it later.

When a node is freed up and returned to the available list, it is placed at the *head*. The *next* section of this freed node is set to point to the old head of the available list, and the pointer to the first available node *(avail)* is adjusted to point to this last node freed.

```
PROCEDURE ReturnNode (p: INTEGER);
BEGIN
        nodesupply[p].next := avail;
        avail := p
END;   (* ReturnNode *)
```

2.2.7   EXAMPLES

Example A — Creating a List.

To create an ADT of a linked list (regardless of how it is implemented) the following steps are needed:

(1) create a new node;
(2) give a value to the **info** section of the node;
(3) link up the **next** section to another node.

The following code recursively generates a list of length *n* by getting a node and then generating a list of length *n – 1* which it points to. The information section of each node is filled with the number of its reverse order in the list, i.e., the head node contains *n,* etc. Code such as this is purely for demonstration purposes and would never be used in a major program.

```
FUNCTION Genlist(n: INTEGER): INTEGER;
        (* Recursive code *)
VAR    p: INTEGER;
BEGIN
        Getnode(p);
        If n>1 THEN
            nodesupply[p].next := Genlist(n – 1)
        ELSE
            nodesupply[p].next := 0;
        nodesupply[p].info := n;
        Genlist := p
END;   (* Genlist *)
```

Example B — Printing a List

```
PROCEDURE Printlist(list: INTEGER);
        (* Iterative code *)
BEGIN
        WHILE list <> 0 DO
            BEGIN
                Writeln(nodesupply[list].info);
                list := nodesupply[list].next
            END (* WHILE *)
END;   (* Printlist *)
```

2.3   POINTER IMPLEMENTATION

2.3.1   DEFINING POINTER TYPES AND DECLARING POINTER VARIABLES

To implement the ADT of a linked list using pointer variables in those languages that possess them (e.g., C, Pascal, Modula-2, Ada), normally, *two* new types are defined: one a pointer variable type, and the other a node type. For example, in Pascal one could write:

```
Type ptr   =   ^node;
     node   =   RECORD
                     info: INTEGER;
                     next:ptr
                END;
```

(Note that in Pascal, in the TYPE definition, the uparrow (or caret) comes *before* the type identifier of what it points to. This is the only case in Pascal where an identifier (e.g., "node") can be used without being first declared.)

After the definition of the new types, variables of the type **ptr** are merely declared. For example,

```
VAR p,q,list: ptr;
```

Note that the pointer variables *p, q,* and *list* exist, but they are places to keep addresses only. As yet, *no nodes have been created!*

2.3.2   OBTAINING NODES — THE PASCAL *NEW* PROCEDURE

In Pascal, nodes are created using the standard Pascal procedure **New** that takes a **pointer** variable as an argument. For example, the following code segment takes a declared pointer variable *p,* and then allocates space for a node of the type that *p* points to. After this "new" space has been allocated, the fields of the node are given values.

```
New(p);
p^.info := 5
p^.next := NIL;
```

New allows a programmer to *dynamically* create as *many* nodes as needed, *when* they are needed. *New* does for pointer variables what *Getnode* in Section 2.2.5 did for the linear implementation.

2.3.3   RELEASING NODES — THE PASCAL *DISPOSE* PROCEDURE

Pascal allows a programmer to dispose of unneeded nodes by using the library procedure **Dispose,** which also takes a pointer variable as an argument. The node pointed to then becomes part of the available space for use. Thus *dispose* functions like the procedure ReturnNode in Section 2.2.6 above.

In a Pascal program, one simply writes

Dispose(p);

After this procedure call, *p* no longer points to any valid node, and if one tries to use *p^* (without first obtaining a node by using *New(p)*), one normally gets an error.

EXAMPLES

Example A — Creating a List

Much of the code that follows is very similar to the code presented in Section 2.2.7 that used the linear (array) implementation of lists. The logic underlying each of the functions is unchanged — only the actual implementation of the ADT of a linked list has changed, and thus, the only changes in the code of the various procedures and functions are those that are necessary for the new implementation.

```
FUNCTION Genlist(n: INTEGER): ptr;
        (* Recursive code *)
VAR     p: ptr;
BEGIN
        New(p);
        If n > 1 THEN
            p^.next := Genlist(n – 1)
        ELSE
            p^.next := NIL;
        p^.info := n;
        Genlist := p
END;    (* Genlist *)
```

Example B — Printing a List

```
PROCEDURE Printlist(list:ptr);
        (* Iterative code *)
BEGIN
        WHILE list <> NIL DO
            BEGIN
                Writeln(list^.info);
                list := list^.next
            END (* WHILE *)
END;    (* Printlist *)
```

2.4   COMMON OPERATIONS

2.4.1   TYPES OF OPERATIONS

Operations for the ADT of a linked list can be determined without knowing anything about a particular implementation. For example, some or all of the following might be desired:

```
PROCEDURE Create(Var list:ptr);
        (to create a new list with one node)
FUNCTION IsListEmpty(list:ptr):BOOLEAN;
        (to test to see if the list is empty)
PROCEDURE InsAfter(p:ptr; x:item);
        (to insert x after the node that p points to)
PROCEDURE InsEnd(list:ptr; x:item);
        (to insert x at the end of the list that list points to)
PROCEDURE DelAfter(p:ptr);
        (to delete the node after the node that p points to)
FUNCTION Search(list:ptr; x:item):ptr;
        (to search a list for an item and return a pointer to the correct node)
```

Not all of the operations listed above will be shown below. Enough samples are given to enable other routines to be written.

For now, it is presupposed that the "position pointer" p used as a parameter actually points to the node one suspects it points to. There are other alternatives possible, and one will be mentioned below in Section 2.5.1. Choosing different presuppositions or variations on the basic linked list structure (see Section 2.5 below) may lead to a different set of basic operations or an easier implementation of those chosen.

2.4.2   INSERTION

First, a consideration of what any insertion routine must do for a list as an ADT is presented before any code for specific implementations of lists is seen. A new node needs to be inserted after the node to which p points, and then information x is placed into the *info* section of that node. To do this, first a new node is obtained, then its *next* pointer is assigned to the node to which $p^.next$ points, and then $p^.next$ is reassigned to point to the new node. This process can be envisioned by using a diagram of the ADT of a linked list as follows.

Notice that existing information in the list is *not* rearranged. This property of linked lists makes them a preferred data structure when many insertions (and/or deletions) take place.

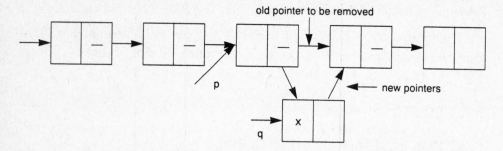

The following two sections of code present the procedure *InsAfter* (for "Insert After") based on the two different implementations discussed above.

A. ARRAY IMPLEMENTATION

```
PROCEDURE InsAfter (p:INTEGER;x:INTEGER);
VAR    q:INTEGER;
BEGIN
       IF p = 0 THEN (* check to see if p is nil *)
           Writeln('Void insertion') (* error *)
       ELSE
       BEGIN
           Getnode(q);
           nodesupply[q].info := x;
           nodesupply[q].next := nodesupply[p].next;
           nodesupply[p].next := q
       END (* IF..ELSE *)
END;   (* InsAfter *)
```

B. POINTER IMPLEMENTATION

```
PROCEDURE InsAfter (p:ptr; x:item);
VAR    q:ptr;
BEGIN
       IF p = NIL THEN (* check to see if p is nil *)
           Writeln('Void insertion') (* error *)
       ELSE
           BEGIN
               New(q);
               q^.info := x;
               q^.next := p^.next;
               p^.next := q
           END (* IF..ELSE *)
END;   (* InsAfter *)
```

Sometimes a special procedure is desirable for tacking on new nodes to the *end* of existing lists. The following procedure *InsEnd* (for "Insert at End") performs that task, given the pointer to the *list* (rather than to a *node* as in the previous code). The procedure first creates the new tail node, and then uses the pointer q to locate the old tail node and then connects it to the new node.

```
PROCEDURE InsEnd (VAR list:ptr; x:item);
VAR     p,q:ptr;
BEGIN
        (* create and fill new node *)
        New(p);
        p^.info := x;
        p^.next := NIL;
        IF list = NIL THEN
            list := p
        ELSE (* search for end of the list *)
            BEGIN
                q := list;
                WHILE q^.next <> NIL DO
                    q:=q^.next;
                    (* reset former nil-pointer to point to the new node *)
                    q^.next := p
            END ( IF..ELSE *)
END;   (* InsEnd *)
```

2.4.3   DELETION

First a consideration of what any deletion routine must do for a list as an ADT is presented before code for specific implementations of lists is seen. A procedure "DelAfter" that deletes the node *after* the node pointed to by p and returns the value of its *info* section in the variable x is to be created. It must check whether the proposed deletion is valid by checking to see if the list has more than one node. It deletes a node by redirecting the pointer of the previous node to point to the following node. This process can again be envisioned by using a diagram of the ADT of a linked list as follows.

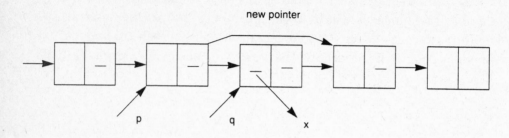

new pointer

p   q   x

The following two sections of code present the procedure *DelAfter* based on the two different implementations discussed above.

A. ARRAY IMPLEMENTATION

```
PROCEDURE DelAfter (p:INTEGER; VAR x:INTEGER);
VAR    q:INTEGER;
BEGIN
    IF p = 0 THEN (* nil pointer *)
        Writeln('Void deletion')
    ELSE
        IF nodesupply[p].next = 0 THEN
            (* no next node *)
                Writeln('Void deletion')
        ELSE
            BEGIN
                q:nodesupply[p].next;
                x:nodesupply[q].info;
                nodesupply[p].next=nodesupply[q].next;
                ReturnNode(q)
        END (* else *)
END;   (* DelAfter *)
```

B. POINTER IMPLEMENTATION

```
PROCEDURE DelAfter (p:ptr; VAR x:item);
VAR    q:ptr;
BEGIN
        IF p = NIL THEN (* nil pointer *)
            Writeln('Void deletion')
        ELSE
            IF p^.next = NIL THEN
                (* no next node *)
                    Writeln('Void deletion')
```

```
        ELSE
            BEGIN
                q := p^.next;
                x := q^.info;
                p^.next:=q^.next;
                Dispose(q)
            END (* IF..ELSE IF..ELSE *)
END;   (* DelAfter *)
```

2.4.4   SEARCHING

This next function is basically a "linear search" scheme for linked lists (rather than arrays). The list *list* is searched for x and the function *Search* returns the pointer to the *first* node containing x.

```
FUNCTION Search(list:ptr; x:item):ptr;
VAR    p:ptr;
       found:boolean;
BEGIN
       p := list;
       found := FALSE;
       WHILE (p <> NIL) AND (NOT found) DO
           IF p^.info = x THEN
               found := TRUE
           ELSE
               p := p^.next;
       Search := p
END;   (* Search *)
```

This *Search* function may not be useful in certain situations, as when the node containing x needs to be deleted. In this case, the pointer to the *previous* node is needed rather than to the node containing x. *Search* can be easily modified to return two pointers, and the interior code expanded to retain the previous value of p.

The efficiency of this search is the same as for the linear search for arrays, i.e., it is $O(n)$ for a list of n nodes. Since lists are sequential access structures (as mentioned above in Section 2.1.4), it is impossible to develop a routine for lists comparable to binary search for arrays with the same efficiency.

2.5 VARIATIONS

2.5.1 HEADER NODES

It is occasionally desirable to keep some bookkeeping information about a list, e.g., the number of nodes in the list, the use of the list, etc. Depending on the conventions decided upon when coding a procedure or function, it may even be desirable to have a "dummy" node in which no information is stored.

To store the bookkeeping information, one can use another node, called the *header node,* which itself points to the first (active and regular) node of the list. In this arrangement, even the "empty" list has one node, its header node.

The use of a header node means that most of the list routines need minor modifications. However, with a header node, certain applications may be simplified.

For example, if a "dummy" header node is used, the notion of a position pointer to a node (i.e., the pointer used as a parameter in routines) could be re-defined. The *coded* pointer could be implemented as the *actual* pointer to the *previous* node. Using this implementation, for a delete routine, only the "pointer" to the node to be deleted is needed (since it is actually the pointer to the previous node) (see discussion above in Section 2.4.1 and 2.4.4).

This brief example again shows some of the trade-offs involved in working with data structures and related algorithms. We sometimes choose to make a data structure slightly more complicated (e.g., by including a header node) and to modify our meaning of a "pointer to a node." One result is that the code for our routines will need to be developed with more care (to avoid any errors due to the new meaning of "pointer"). However, the end result is a set of routines that will be easier to use in programs that need them.

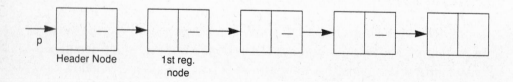

p   Header Node   1st reg. node

2.5.2 CIRCULAR LISTS

It is often convenient to have the *next* field of the end node of a list *not* be *NIL,* but rather point back to the head of the list. This convention makes the list *circular.*

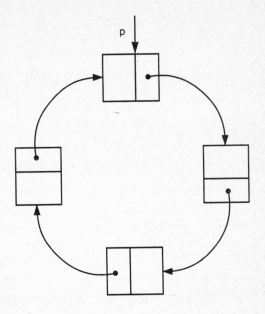

In some situations, a circular list can be a better data structure than a non-circular list. For example, it is always possible to reach any node from any other node since by going forward, eventually one reaches the head of the list. Examples of the use of circular lists will be seen in subsequent chapters when various implementations of ADTs are discussed.

2.5.3 DOUBLY LINKED LISTS

A major problem with linked lists is the **in**-ability to back up. This problem can be eliminated by using both a *forward* (right link) and also a *backward* (left link) pointer, which results in a new ADT of a "Doubly-Linked List." It is also impossible with regular linked lists to delete a node of a linked list, given just the actual pointer to the node (unless the technique mentioned in Section 2.5.1 is used). This problem can also be eliminated by using a "doubly-linked list." The drawback of this ADT is that one must use an additional memory location for each node. The standard trade-off in computer science once again appears — ease of use and some efficiency is gained at the expense of memory.

The node type for a "doubly-linked list" can be defined as follows:

```
TYPE node = RECORD
                leftlink: ptr;
                info: INTEGER;
                rightlink: ptr;
            END;
```

When using a "doubly linked list," the *leftlink* of the head node is set to

NIL as well as the *rightlink* of the tail node. It is also possible to have a header node with a doubly linked list and to make it circular.

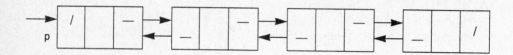

3.   STACKS

Study this section for the 'AB' exam.

3.1   STACK STRUCTURE AND OPERATIONS

A **stack** is an ADT (abstract data structure) used for information storage in which data is inserted or removed from one "end," called the "top of the stack." A common (physical) example of the data structure *stack* is a stack of dishes in a cafeteria counter dish storage receptacle.

There are *three* common primitive stack operations.

1) **Push(x,s)** – *inserts* item *x* onto stack *s* (making *x* the new element at the top of the stack). (This operation is usually coded as a *procedure.)*

2) **Pop(s)** – *removes* the item at the top of the stack from stack *s*. This operation is usually coded as a *function* and so the item removed from the stack is returned as the function value.)

3) **Peek(s)** – *copies* the value of the top of the stack but does *not* remove it from the stack *s*. (This operation is also usually coded as a *function* and so the item copied is returned as the function value.) This function is sometimes called *Visit(s)* or *Stacktop(s)*.

To guarantee against errors, a fourth operation is commonly implemented:

4) **Empty(s)** – *checks* to see if there are any elements in stack *s*. (This operation is also usually coded as a *function* returning the boolean value of *true* if *s* is empty and False if there are elements in *s*.

NOTES ON STACK OPERATIONS:

a) Normally *Pop* or *Peek* cannot be performed on an empty stack, so the stack should be checked somehow before using either function. This can be done internally in *Pop* and *Peek* or it can be done before calling these functions if *Empty is* available.

b) Trying to *Pop* an empty stack induces an "underflow" error.

c) Trying to *Push* onto a "full" stack (if it does have any implementation-dependent limit) is called an "overflow" error.

d) Since *Push* and *Pop* both abbreviate to *P*, often *Stack* is used for *Push* (abbreviated *S*) and *Unstack* is used for *Pop* (abbreviated *U*).

3.2 USING STACKS

A stack can be most useful when it is necessary to remember the "last" unit of information stored. It is sometimes referred to as a LIFO structure (*Last In, First Out*), a title that emphasizes the order in which the structure "remembers" items in it. The following examples will illustrate this. In all examples involving stacks, the assumption is that once an element has been popped off the stack, it cannot be pushed a second time back onto the stack.

(1) Given the input stream

ABCDE

and given the following sequence of stack operations (where *S* stands for Push [**S**tack], and *U* for Pop [**U**nstack])

SSUSSUSUUU

what is the output stream?

The operation of the stack will be given in detail for this first example:

INPUT STREAM	STACK OPERATION	:	STACK ← bottom	OUTPUT STREAM
A B C D E	S	⇒	A	
B C D E	S	⇒	A B	
C D E	U	⇒	A	B
C D E	S	⇒	A C	B
D E	S	⇒	A C D	B

E	U	$\Rightarrow$	A C	B D
E	S	$\Rightarrow$	A C E	B D
–	U	$\Rightarrow$	A C	B D E
	U	$\Rightarrow$	A	B E E C
	U	$\Rightarrow$	–	B D E C A

Thus the output stream is B D E C A.

(2) Given the input stream

A B C D E

and given the following OUTPUT streams, what is the command sequence that generated it?

a) B A C E D $\underline{\text{S S U U S U S S U U}}$

b) E D C A B $\underline{\text{impossible output stream}}$

Example 2b shows that even stacks have limitations. Although significant rearrangement of elements can take place, there are certain output combinations that are not possible, no matter how one arranges the order of pushes and pops. The problem arises in example 2b with item A. For E to be the first item out of the stack, it must have been the last one in, which implies that A is at the bottom of the stack. Thus, A must be the last element out.

Depending on the order of pushes and pops, one can change or even reverse the input order of data. Assume the input stream for both of the following examples is again:

A B C D E.

(3) Assume the command stream is:

S U S U S U S U S U.

The corresponding output would be

A B C D E.

(4) Assume the command stream is:

S S S S S U U U U U.

The corresponding output would be

E D C B A.

Because of these order properties, stacks can be useful in developing an algorithm to store information and then recall it in a certain *order!*

3.3   SAMPLE IMPLEMENTATION

3.3.1   ARRAY IMPLEMENTATION

Up to this point a stack has been presented merely as an ADT, without any consideration about how it is implemented in a given language or the many different ways it might be implemented. This section now addresses these implementation questions.

One way to implement a stack is to use the underlying data structure of an array. However, the same problems arise using arrays to implement a stack as occur when arrays are used to implement a linked list. The size of a stack is constantly changing, which makes it difficult to implement a stack exactly using an array, since arrays are *static* structures with predetermined sizes.

Nevertheless, as was done with linked lists, an array can be declared of a size large enough to hold all the elements that would even be in a stack at one time. For each stack, a top-of-stack pointer is also needed that will serve as the (array) index to the top-of-stack element.

The following code implements a stack as a record, with one field being the array of elements, and the other being the top-of-stack pointer.

```
CONST    maxstack  =   100;
TYPE     stackitem =   INTEGER;
         stack     =   RECORD
                          item: ARRAY[1..maxstack]
                             OF stackitem;
                          top: INTEGER
                       END;

VAR      s         :   stack:
```

3.3.2   CODING THE OPERATIONS

There are several ways of implementing stacks as arrays depending on whether one chooses to have the top-of-stack pointer point to the *last used* space or to the *next available* space, and whether the first used space has the subscript of *one* or the subscript of *maxstack*. The code below assumes (1) that the top-of-stack pointer points to the *last used* space and (2) that the first used space has the subscript of *one*.

The following code can easily be misused by combining operations together, thereby making the revised code much more difficult to read and reducing the analogy between the abstract data type (and its operations) and the implemented data structure. Newer languages such as Modula-2 and Ada allow data encapsulation so that the code is safe from such interference, but that does not prevent a programmer from writing the original code poorly.

Before using any stack *s*, it must be initialized by setting *s.top* equal to zero.

EMPTY
```
    FUNCTION Empty(s:stack): BOOLEAN;
    BEGIN
            IF s.top = 0 THEN
                Empty := TRUE
            ELSE
                Empty := FALSE
    END; (* Empty *)
```

PUSH
```
    PROCEDURE PUSH(VAR s:stack; x:stackitem);
    BEGIN
        IF s.top = maxstack THEN
            Writeln('stack overflow error')
        ELSE
            BEGIN
                s.top := s.top + 1;
                s.item[s.top] := x
            END (* else *)
    END; (* Push *)
```

POP
```
    FUNCTION POP(VAR s:stack): stackitem;
    BEGIN
        IF Empty(s) THEN
            Writeln('stack underflow error')
        ELSE
            BEGIN
                Pop := s.item[s.top];
```

```
            s.top := s.top - 1;
        END (* else *)
    END; (* Pop *)
```

PEEK

```
    FUNCTION Peek(s:stack): stackitem;
    BEGIN
        IF Empty(s) THEN
            Writeln('stack underflow error')
        ELSE
            Peek := s.item[s.top]
    END; (* Peek *)
```

Notice that the only difference between Pop and Stacktop is that the top-of-stack pointer is changed in Pop.

3.3.3 POINTER IMPLEMENTATION

Stacks can be very simply implemented as linked lists. The top of the stack is merely the head node of the list. If the list is nil, the stack is empty. Elements are inserted and deleted from the head of the list. Using linked lists, a stack overflow will not normally occur since there is no array limit to worry about. However, when popping elements from the stack, care should be taken to dispose of unneeded nodes properly.

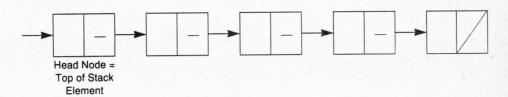

Head Node =
Top of Stack
Element

3.3.4 CODING SOME OPERATIONS

To show the similarity in the operations, even with using a different underlying data structure, the following examples are given.

DECLARATIONS OF DATA STRUCTURE

```
TYPE  stackitem  =  INTEGER;
      stack      =  ^node;
      node       =  RECORD
                        info: stackitem;
                        next: stack
```

```
                    END:

VAR   s          :    stack;
```

PUSH
```
    PROCEDURE Push(x:stackitem; VAR s:stack);
    VAR p:stack;
    BEGIN
        New(p);
        p^.info := x;
        p^.next := s;
        s := p
    END;   (* Push *)
```

POP
```
    FUNCTION Pop(VAR s:stack): stackitem;
    VAR p:stack;
    BEGIN
        IF Empty(s) THEN
            Writeln('stack underflow error')
        ELSE
            BEGIN
                Pop := s^.info;
                p :=s;
                s := s^.next;
                Dispose(p)
            END (* else *)
    END;   (* Pop *)
```

3.4   APPLICATIONS

Stacks are used in many ways, particularly when it is necessary to store information temporarily and then retrieve it in a reverse order. Two primary examples of this type of applications are (1) the evaluation of arithmetic expressions and (2) the analysis and removal of recursion. The connection between stacks, arithmetic expressions and recursion will be merely sketched here.

Some hand calculators require that operators be entered last, after the operands. These are called "stack" or "RPN" (for Reverse Polish Notation) calculators. In other words, to add 3 and 5, first the 3 is entered, then the 5 and finally the + sign is pressed. In other words, 3 + 5 is equivalent to 3,5 + in RPN. A more complicated conversion is 3 + 4 x 5 which converts to 3, 4, 5, x, +. Notice that in this second example, the order of the operators (+ and x) are reversed. However, in a similar expression using parentheses, $(3 + 4) \times 5$, the RPN expression keeps the operators in the original order, 3, 4, +, 5, x. A program to convert between the standard arithmetic notation and RPN involves the use of a stack to store the operators.

When a subprogram recursively calls itself, the computer does not duplicate the code. Rather, the values of all variables along with a return address are stored on stacks. During any use of the subprogram at any level of call, only the values that appear at the top of the stack on the various variable stacks are used. In this way, the subprogram "remembers" all the previous values of the variables it needs at any level. When it is desirable to eliminate recursion, a stack needs to be explicitly coded to keep track of the various values.

4. QUEUES

Study this section for the 'AB' exam.

4.1 QUEUE STRUCTURE AND OPERATIONS

A **queue** is a waiting line. This is a standard dictionary definition and the word is commonly used in British countries to designate any waiting line, not merely a computer science concept.

In computer science, a queue is an ADT (abstract data type) in which new data is inserted at one "end," called the *rear,* and stored data is removed from the other "end," called the *front.* Thus, in action it is identical to a waiting line that people experience while waiting for food in a cafeteria or for transportation at a terminal.

Since intermediate information in a queue *cannot* be reached, in action a queue is somewhat similar to a stack. However, whereas a queue is a FIFO (*first* in, first out) a stack is a LIFO (last in, first out) structure. Thus, unlike a stack, a queue does *not* (and cannot) change the order in which the elements are removed, relative to the order of their insertion.

There are *two* common primitive queue operations.

1) **Enqueue(x,q)** (often written Enq(x,q)) — *inserts* item *x* onto a queue *q* at its *rear.* (This operation is usually coded as a *procedure.*)

2) **Dequeue(q)** (often written Deq(q)) — *removes* the item at the front of queue (q). (This operation is usually coded as a *function* and so the item removed from the queue is returned as the function value.)

To guarantee against errors, a third operation is commonly implemented.

3) **Empty(q)** — *checks* to see if there are any elements in queue *q*. (This operation is also usually coded as a *function* returning the boolean value of *true* if *q* is empty and *false* if there are elements in *q*.)

Sometimes a fourth operation is found that is similar to the *Peek* operation on stacks. This function copies the value of the element at the front of the queue but does not remove it from the queue.

4.2   IMPLEMENTING QUEUES USING ARRAYS

4.2.1   THE UNDERLYING DATA STRUCTURE

Implementing the ADT of queues using the underlying data structure of an array involves the same problems as occurred with implementing stacks as arrays. Queues are dynamically changing in size, while arrays are static. But, similar to what was done with stacks, an array can be declared that is large enough to hold all items expected to be in the queue at any one time.

A queue needs *two* pointers: one indicating the index of the *front* and the other the index of the *rear*.

The following code implements a queue similar to the way a stack was implemented, i.e., via a record consisting of the storage array and two pointers.

```
CONST    maxqueue = 100;

TYPE     queueitem =    INTEGER;
         queue =        RECORD
                        item: ARRAY[1..maxqueue] OF queueitem;
                        front,rear: INTEGER;
                        END;

VAR q : queue;
```

4.2.2   PRESUPPOSITIONS

As with linked lists, certain presuppositions regarding the data structure and how it will be used need to be determined before coding the operations. In general, issues regarding the coding of queue operations require more thought and preliminary planning than did those regarding stack operations. As a result, a study of these issues provides an excellent example of some of the numerous (and frequently unexpected) problems that arise when dealing with more complicated data structures in applications programs.

There are three main issues for discussion:

Issue 1 — How should items be stored in the queue?

Issue 2 — What happens when the last space (i.e., the space with the greatest subscript value) in the underlying array has been filled?

Issue 3 — How is the test for an empty queue performed?

4.2.3 ISSUE 1: STORAGE OF ITEMS IN A QUEUE

There are two major options for storing items in a queue when the underlying data structure is an array.

(a) They can be always butted up to the front, so that the next items to be removed always is in array location 1. However, this option requires that all items in the queue be moved after each deletion, which can be highly time-consuming if there are numerous items and, thus, inefficient. However, this option would lead to a certain simplicity in coding the *Dequeue* function and in keeping track of the items in the queue.

(b) They can be left wherever they happen to be when inserted. This option complicates the computation of the *front* and *rear* pointers, but eliminates the time-consuming process of moving queue elements around. This option also makes it likely that after the queue has been used, an item will be inserted into the queue so that it is located in the last space of the underlying array, which leads to a discussion of the second issue.

4.2.4 ISSUE 2: FILLING THE UNDERLYING ARRAY

Even when a large array is used for the underlying data structure, after some use it is likely that a new element will be stored in the last space (i.e., the space with the largest subscript) in the array, but only a few elements will be "active" in the queue. To avoid wasting space and to be able to reuse the beginning of the array again, normally the array is thought of as "circular," in that after using the last space, the first space is then reused (or "recycled"). However, this convention complicates the calculation of the pointers *rear* and *front.*

The choice of a circular array assumes the choice of the second option in resolving the first issue: namely that an item is not moved in the array after its insertion in the queue. However, these conventions may lead to the situation where *rear < front.* Thus, the code of the queue operations must take this into account. A circular array will be assumed in the discussion that follows, and it will also be assumed that when a Dequeue is performed, the *front* pointer is incremented by one and when an Enqueue is performed the *rear* pointer is incremented by one.

4.2.5   ISSUE 3: TESTING FOR AN EMPTY QUEUE

This issue actually leads to two new, but related, issues: (4) Can the array ever be completely filled with queue elements? and (5) Where should the front pointer actually point to? These new issues may seem ludicrous, but their importance will be seen in the discussion that follows. For now, assume that *front* and *rear* are the actual array indices of the first and last items stored in the queue, and that the array can be filled to capacity. There are several possible conditions for a queue to be empty that should be examined.

1) The condition *front = rear* would be an appropriate test for whether there is *one* element in the queue, but *not* whether the queue is empty.

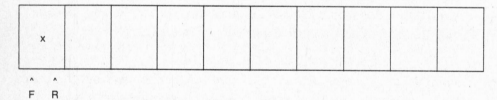

2) The condition *front > rear* would work if the array was not considered to be circular. With a circular array, there could be many elements in the array with the first element stored near the end of the array and the last element stored near the beginning, leading to *front > rear.*

Case 1: Natural Order — *front < rear* when non-empty.

	X	X	X	X	X	X		

    ^   ^

    F   R

Case 2: Wrap-around Order — ***front*** > ***rear*** when non-empty.

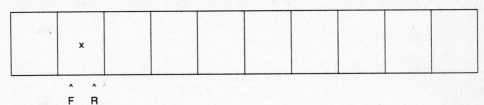

3) The condition *front* = *(rear* MOD maxqueue) + 1 would work if not for the fact that the array is circular and could be filled to the limit. Because of the circularity of the array, this same condition is true when the array is *full* (if every space is permitted to be used)!

Case 1: Almost empty queue.

BEFORE DELETION

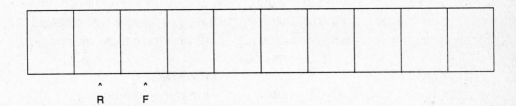

AFTER DELETION (*front* is increased by 1 and *front* = *rear* + 1)

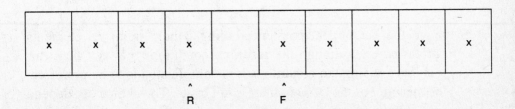

Case 2: Almost full queue.

BEFORE INSERTION

AFTER INSERTION (*rear* is increased by 1 and *front* = *rear* + 1)

x	x	x	x	x	x	x	x	x	x

$$\quad\quad\quad\quad\quad\quad\quad\quad\quad\quad\quad\quad ^\wedge \quad\quad ^\wedge$$
$$\quad\quad\quad\quad\quad\quad\quad\quad\quad\quad\quad\quad R \quad\quad F$$

The dilemma raised by the third issue is usually resolved by making choices based on the two related issues mentioned: (4) Can the array ever be completely filled with queue elements? and (5) where should the *front* pointer actually point to?

In answer to (4), most implementations are coded so that one space is left "wasted" in the array. Thus, in an array of length *maxqueue* only *maxqueue* – 1 elements can be stored. This eliminates the double meaning of the third possible condition.

Thus, the following conditions have these meanings:

CONDITION	MEANING
1. front = rear	One item in queue
2. (rear MOD maxqueue) + 1 = front	Empty queue
3. (rear MOD maxqueue) + 2 = front	Full queue

In answer to (5), because the conditions just listed seem non-intuitive, some implementations prefer to use the convention that *front* actually points to the "wasted" space in the array that is immediately *before* the first element. If this convention is chosen, the following conditions have these meanings.

CONDITION	MEANING
1. (front MOD maxqueue) + 1 = rear	One item in queue
2. rear = front	Empty queue
3. (rear MOD maxqueue) + 1 = front	Full queue

The last condition can be implemented so that when trying to *Enqueue* an item, *rear* is incremented first and then tested to see if it equals *front*. If it does, then overflow has occurred.

Some feel that keeping the pointers pointing to their "intuitive" elements is to be preferred even though the resulting conditions may not be clear. Others feel that keeping the conditions less complicated is to be preferred, even if the meaning of the *front* pointer is not exact. The choice can depend on the environment in which a queue is used. In either case, the questions raised by this (relatively simple) implementation provide excellent examples of the many issues that often need to be considered before coding operations related to data structures.

4.2.6 CODE FOR THE OPERATIONS

Based on the discussion above, *the following conventions have been chosen for the code that follows:*

1) Once inserted, an item is *not* moved in a queue.

2) The array is thought of as circular, i.e., after *q.item[maxqueue]* comes *q.item[1]*. Therefore, *front* (and *rear*) can also be increased to the next legal number by using the formula *front := front MOD maxqueue + 1*.

3) *q.front* is the index of the array element *immediately preceding* the first element in the queue. Therefore, if *q.front* equals *q.rear*, the queue is empty or overflow has occurred.

4) To enable a test for emptiness (and overflow), one element of the array is sacrificed as a queue element and used instead as a "dummy" element.

Before using any queue *q*, it must be initialized by setting *q.front* and *q.rear* both equal to zero.

EMPTY

```
FUNCTION Empty (q:queue: BOOLEAN);
BEGIN
        Empty := (q.front = q.rear)
END;   (* Empty *)
```

A longer way to code this function is to use the structure of the function Empty found in Section 3.3.2 and the condition (q.front = q.rear). However, the code above provides an alternate example, and shows the compactness that results by using a logical expression in an assignment statement.

ENQUEUE

```
PROCEDURE Enqueue (x:queueitem; VAR q:queue);
BEGIN
    BEGIN
        q.rear := q.rear MOD maxqueue + 1;
        IF q.rear = q.front THEN
            Writeln ('queue overflow error')
```

```
        ELSE
             q.item[q.rear] := x
END;    (* Enqueue *)
```

DEQUEUE

```
PROCEDURE Dequeue (VAR q:queue): queueitem;
BEGIN
        IF Empty(q) THEN
             Writeln ('queue underflow error')
        ELSE
           BEGIN
                 q.front := q.front MOD maxqueue + 1;
                 Dequeue := q.item[q.front]
                 END (* ELSE WITH q * )
END;    (* Function Remove *)
```

4.3   IMPLEMENTING QUEUES USING LINKED LISTS

Queues can also be implemented as linear linked lists. Often the choice is made that the head of the list is the front of the queue and the tail is the rear. Implementation is simplified if a second pointer to the rear of the list is also used, since insertions will constantly be made there, and it is more efficient to have a pointer always available to that part of the list. The head of the list is the "front" of the queue and is the point where elements are dequeued.

Certain implementation problems are also eliminated if the list has a header node, since otherwise coding is complicated when the queue is empty and when an item is inserted into an empty queue. However, this demands a function *Createqueue* that creates a new queue with merely a header node. The following diagram depicts a queue as a linked list with a header node.

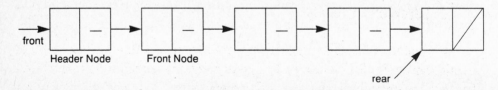

front

Header Node   Front Node

rear

The following definitions show how a queue can be implemented in Pascal using the underlying data structure of a linked list.

```
TYPE  queueitem    =   INTEGER;
      ptr          =   ^node;
      node         =   RECORD
```

```
                          info: queueitem;
                          next: ptr
                       END;
        queue       =  RECORD
                          front, rear: ptr
                       END;
```

VAR   q: queue;

Given the data structure definition, code for the various operations can now be written. Only one sample subprogram code is given, a linked list (pointer) version of the function *Dequeue*. Since linked lists are used, care must be taken with disposing of the formerly used node (as was done in the function Pop in Section 3.3.4), so the node space (no longer needed by the queue) can be reused by the program.

```
FUNCTION Dequeue (VAR q:queue):queueitem;
VAR p:ptr;
BEGIN
    IF q.front = q.rear THEN
        Writeln ('queue underflow error')
    ELSE
        BEGIN
            p := q.front^.next;
            (* p now points to the real front node *)
            q.front^.next := p^.next;
            Dequeue := p^.info;
            Dispose(p)
        END (* IF..ELSE *)
END;   (* Dequeue *)
```

4.4   IMPLEMENTING QUEUES USING CIRCULAR LINKED LISTS

If a queue is implemented using a circular list, certain implementation details can be simplified further. Only one pointer is needed which can be used for both the enqueuing and dequeuing operations. This queue pointer points to the *rear of the queue*, but this rear (tail) node points to the head of the queue, since the list is circular. Thus, if *q* is a pointer to this queue structure, to enqueue an item the *InsAfter* procedure of Section 2.4.2 can be used and applied to *q*. To dequeue an item the *DelAfter* procedure of Section 2.4.3 can be used and applied to *q^.next*.

4.5 DEQUES

A **deque** (pronounced 'deck' as in a 'deck' of cards) is a *Double Ended Queue*. It is an ADT (abstract data type) in which insertions and deletions can be performed at either of two ends, usually called the *right* and the *left*.

Because of its configuration, a deque can function both as a stack (if insertions and deletions are done only at one end), or as a regular queue (by restricting insertions to one end and deletions to the other). If it functions as a queue, it can also act as a queue in either direction!

Deque operations are usually labeled as Right-Insert, Right-Delete, Left-Insert, Left-Delete, and Empty. They are modeled after the operations defined in stacks and queues. Implementation can be done via an array (as with a queue) or with a "doubly-linked list." The coding of the various operations is similar to the codes given for the various implementations of other ADTs.

4.6 EVALUATION

The following is a brief comparison and evaluation of some of the many data structures seen thus far.

ARRAYS: Random access to any information cell.

If information is ordered, insertion (retaining the order) means shifting a lot of information.

STACKS: Sequential access.

One must pop the topmost cells of information off the stack to get to the desired cell. In many implementations, it is hard to "save" the popped information for reuse.

Cannot insert in the middle.

QUEUE: Sequential access.

One must dequeue to get to the desired cell of information. However, one can immediately enqueue the unneeded information to avoid loss.

Cannot insert in the middle immediately, without dequeuing and enqueueing in the correct order.

5.   ARRAYS AND RECORDS

5.1   AGGREGATE STRUCTURES

Scalar variables do not fill all needs. There are many situations that demand that many scalar variables be associated together. A structure of several memory locations that together form one data structure is often termed an **aggregate structure.** The structure usually is given only one variable name, even though composed of many memory locations. Two of the simplest aggregate structures are *arrays* and *records*.

5.2   ONE-DIMENSION ARRAYS

In general, an **array** is homogeneous data structure with multiple dimensions. In this context, **homogeneous** means that all the elements of the array are of the same data type. Each dimension can be arbitrary in size, but once the sizes of the various dimensions of an array have been determined, in most languages they are fixed for the duration of the program. The memory locations in an array are *sequential* and *consecutive*, like items (e.g., songs) on a magnetic tape cassette. Every array has one name by which it is identified, but the individual elements in an array are accessed by means of one or more subscripts (like the components of a mathematical *vector* or *matrix*). For example, vector a of dimension 4 has components a_i where i ranges from 1 to 4.

A one-dimension array is the simplest non-scalar data structure, and its structure and use is similar to that of a mathematical *vector*.

In computer languages, array subscripts are indicated by being enclosed in a pair of parentheses or a pair of square brackets, depending on the rules of the language. For example, the ith element in the array A would be indicated as $A[i]$ in Pascal and $A(I)$ in FORTRAN.

Information in an array is accessed directly and randomly. Thus, an array is sometimes termed a *random access* structure. Some of the items in the structure do not have to be accessed first in order to get to others.

5.3   STORAGE OF ARRAYS

Besides the data stored in the elements of an array, each array also has associated information stored. For each array, a *base location* is stored and, frequently, other information (depending on the language and compiler) such as the number of subscripts (i.e., dimensions), and the maximum/minimum values of each subscript. The *base location* indicates the memory location of the *base*, i.e., the first element of the array.

The locations of the elements of an array are never all stored. The memory location of any element is computed when needed using the base location and the element's subscript(s), as seen in this example.

mem. loc.

Suppose A(1) was stored at
memory location 253.

base (A) = location of 1st element
of array A = 253

mem. loc.		
253		A(1)
254		A(2)
255		A(3)
256		. . .
. . .		. . .
. . .		. . .

Under the assumption that array elements are stored consecutively, A(2) is located in the first (=2 − 1) place after A(1). Similarly, A(5) is the fourth (=5 − 1) element after A(1).

$$
\begin{aligned}
\text{location (A(5))} \quad &= \quad \text{base (A)} \quad + 5 - 1 \\
&= \quad 253 \quad\quad + 5 - 1 = 257
\end{aligned}
$$

In general,

$$
\text{location (A(N))} \quad = \quad \text{base (A)} \quad + N - 1.
$$

For some languages and in some implementations, the relevant information for arrays is stored in memory before the data contained in the array, and only the base location is stored in a symbol table. This collection of array information is commonly called the **dope vector** (or **dummy vector**). When used, the base location found in the symbol table sometimes gives the address of the first element of the dope vector rather than the first element in the array. The dope vector in these cases contains the location of the first element of the data.

5.4 TWO- AND HIGHER-DIMENSION ARRAYS

For many problems, one-dimension arrays do not suffice and so two- or higher-dimension arrays must be used. Two-dimension arrays are frequently thought of as representing a table (with rows and columns), and three-dimension arrays as a box with multiple storage compartments (with levels, rows, and columns). The individual storage cells are accessed as in the one-dimension case, via subscripts. With two-dimension arrays, the same convention is followed as with mathematical matrices, in that the first subscript indicates the row, and the second the column. There is no universal agreement on the interpretation of the different subscripts for three- or higher-dimensions.

Any array of any dimension is a data structure with one name for many memory locations. The number of total cells in the array can be calculated by examining the maximum number of each dimension. For example, a two-dimension array A with first element $A(1,1)$ and last element $A(3,5)$ has 3 x 5 = 15 total cells for storage. Similarly, a three-dimension array B with first element $B(1,1,1)$ and last element $B(3,2,4)$ has 3 x 2 x 4 = 24 total cells for storage.

As mentioned above, computer memory is numbered sequentially (i.e., linearly), like the inch counter on a tape recorder. Given this fact, the question of how to store a two- or higher-dimension array in a linear computer memory must be discussed.

Storage of a multidimension array is done by decomposing the array into subsections, each of which is in some sense linear, and then storing all the subsections in some sort of order. For two-dimension arrays (i.e., matrices or tables), there are two choices for the decomposition:

— by rows (called "row-major order")
— by columns (called "column-major order").

In other words, one can imagine taking a (two-dimension) table or matrix printed on a piece of paper and cutting it into strips by rows or by columns. These paper strips can then be fastened together in some order (the first row or column followed by the second, followed by the third and so on) to form one long linear list of data from something that was originally a two-dimension structure.

Knowledge of the storage order is necessary in order to determine which memory location contains which array cell, and different computer languages use different schemes. For example, FORTRAN stores its two-dimension arrays by columns, and Pascal stores them by rows.

To determine where a particular element of a two-dimension array is in memory, both the base location and at least one dimension (either row or column depending on the storage scheme of the language) must be known.

To derive a formula associated with a language that uses the column-major order, like FORTRAN, how many elements are in each column (i.e., the number of *rows*) must be known. This information is available to the compiler since it can be derived from the *first* subscript in the array declaration statement.

Suppose a real array A with three rows and five columns is given. In other words, A has been declared as $A(3,5)$ in FORTRAN. Suppose base(A) is 130, in other words, suppose $A(1,1)$ is stored in memory location 130. Where is $A(2,3)$ stored?

Before answering this question, a couple of other questions should be considered first.

Assuming a language that uses column-major order, and given that $A(1,1)$ is stored in 130, what element of the array is stored in memory location 131 (i.e., what is stored right after $A(1,1)$)? The answer to this question is $A(2,1)$. This element is the second element in the first *column* of the two-dimension array, and thus is stored next to $A(1,1)$.

Where is $A(1,2)$ stored? This is the first element of the second column and it should be stored right after the last element of the first column, i.e., right after $A(3,1)$. $A(3,1)$ is stored in base(A) + **3** (the number of elements per column) − 1 (correction factor because base(A) contains the first element) = $130 + 3 - 1 = 132$. Therefore, the answer is that $A(1,2)$ is in the next location after $A(3,1)$, $130 + 3 - 1 + 1 = \textbf{133}$.

For this array, the following standard two-dimension visualization can be used:

1,1	1,2	1,3	1,4	1,5
130	133	136	139	142
2,1	2,2	2,3	2,4	2,5
131	134	137	140	143
3,1	3,2	3,3	3,4	3,5
132	135	138	141	144

An arbitrary element $A(I, J)$ is stored in base$(A) + \textbf{3} *(J-1) + I - 1$ (where 3 is the length of the column).

Therefore, $A(2,3)$ is in

$$130 + 3(3-1) \quad + 2 - 1$$
$$= 130 + 3(2) \quad + 2 - 1$$

$$= 130 + 6 \qquad\qquad + 2 - 1$$
$$= 138 \qquad\qquad + 2 - 1 = 137$$

Another rule is often used to determine a storage location. It is based on the fact that with column-major storage, if the elements of the array are listed in the order in which they are stored in memory, then the *first* subscript varies the fastest. This rule holds also for three- and higher-dimension arrays as well. In the example given above, the elements are stored in the following order (subscripts only): 1,1; 2,1; 3,1; 1,2; 2,2; 3,2; 1,3; 2,3; 3,3; 1,4; 2,4; 3,4; 1,5; 2,5; 3,5. Notice that the first subscript is always changing.

In a language that uses row-major storage (like Pascal) the basic theory for deriving a formula to determine the storage location of an element in the array is the same as above, except that in this case, the number of elements in each *row* needs to be known.

Similarly, there is an easy to remember rule to determine storage locations for arrays stored in row-major order. If the elements of the array are listed in the order in which they are stored in memory, the *last* subscript varies the fastest.

5.5 DECLARING ARRAYS

In general, arrays must be declared before use. They are declared along with their dimensions and the sizes of each dimension. In some languages that allow the definition of new types (e.g., Pascal), rules of style suggest that arrays of a given dimension and size be defined as a new type and given a unique name, and then variables of that new array type can be declared in the variable section. Some languages permit the use of characters as subscripts and some languages permit the initial subscript to be something other than 1 (as in BASIC) or 0 (as in C).

5.6 RECORDS

A two-dimension array is sometimes used to store associated units of information. For example, one row may all refer to information associated with a single person, and each column may refer to a specific category of information for each person, e.g., the first column may always indicate bank balance, the second the account number, etc.

If an array is arranged in this way, each row is called a *record*, i.e., a number of discrete units of information all associated together. Each subsection of a record is called a *field*.

The problem with using an array to store records of information is that an array is a homogeneous structure, i.e., all the units of information in an array must be of the same *type* (e.g., all integers, all reals, all characters, etc.). Therefore, one cannot store a name (an array of *characters*) with an *integer* account number, with a balance (a *real* number).

In some languages (such as C or Pascal), a new *record* type of variable can be defined, and individual variables and arrays can then be declared to be of this new (user-defined) type. (In C, these are called *structures*.) Each of the fields in a record can be of its own type without any restrictions. Thus a record is a heterogeneous aggregate of data structure. It is of fixed-sized, however, once a specific record type has been defined.

For example, in Pascal a new *record* type can be defined for use in storing information for an address label and this new type can be given the name "addressline." After defining the type "addressline," scalar variables and arrays can be declared to be of this type.

```
TYPE addressline     =   RECORD
            name   :   ARRAY[1..30] OF CHAR;
            street :   ARRAY[1..30] OF CHAR;
            city   :   ARRAY[1..30] OF CHAR;
            state  :   ARRAY[1..2] OF CHAR;
            zip    :   INTEGER
        END;

VAR      students  :   ARRAY[1...100] OF addressline;
         line      :   addressline;
```

In most languages, both the record variable name and also the specific field are indicated together to specify a particular cell. Pascal uses a period to unite these two identifiers. For example, *line.zip* indicates the *zip* field of the record variable *line*. Also, *students[24].name[1]* indicates the first character of the *name* field of the 24th element in the array *students* (each element of which is a record variable). *students[5]* would indicate the fifth variable in the *students* array, each of which is a complete record variable. Thus, *students[5]* would indicate all five fields together.

As with arrays, all the data associated with a record variable are stored in adjacent memory locations. Thus, in the example given above, the *name* field is stored next to the *street* field and so on. In each field, the normal rules for storage apply. Thus, in the array *students* given above, the *name* field of *students[1]* is separated from the *name* field of *students[2]*, but is adjacent to the *street* field of *student[1]*.

It should also be noted that the declaration used above can hide the true size of a variable that contains records. *students* is an array of 100 elements, but since each element is a record variable of type *addressline*, it contains several parts, most of which are arrays. Each individual variable of type *addressline* consists of 93 independent memory locations (assuming one memory location for each character and integer variable). Thus the array *students* uses 9,300 memory locations.

6. TREES

Study this section for the 'AB' exam.

6.1 BASIC DEFINITIONS

A **tree** can be considered to be a version of the ADT of a linked list in which each node can point to more than one other node, but no node has two or more nodes pointing to it. Thus, a tree can be viewed as a generalized list, and a singly linked list can be seen as a special case of a tree.

A **binary tree** is a tree in which each node points to at most two other nodes.

The head node of a tree is called its *root*.

The tail nodes of a tree are called its *leaves*.

Nodes on trees are given relationship names based on the long-standing use of trees to keep genealogy records. Thus, the nodes pointed to by some node are called the children, sons, daughters, or offspring of that node, and the node that points to other nodes is called the parent, father, mother, or ancestor of those nodes.

Other family relationships are also used as if the tree were a family genealogy tree, i.e., the "family" relationships between nodes of a tree are labeled as grandparent, grandchild, uncle, (co-)siblings, (first) cousins, second cousins twice removed, etc. At any node, every offspring starts a new *branch* from its parent node.

The root of a tree is said to be at level *0*. Its immediate descendants are at level *1*, etc.

The *degree* of a node is the number of its offspring.

A collection of trees is termed a *forest* or an *orchard*.

A *complete* binary tree of level n is a tree such that at level n, each node is a leaf and at level $n-1$ (or less), each node has both left and right offspring.

The *depth* (sometimes called the *height*) of a tree is the maximum level of all its leaves. The *ply* of a tree is the number of nodes in its longest branch, and equals depth + 1.

Trees are commonly depicted with the root at the top of a diagram and branches going downwards (the opposite of the way trees grow in nature). The following examples are meant to illustrate some of the definitions just presented.

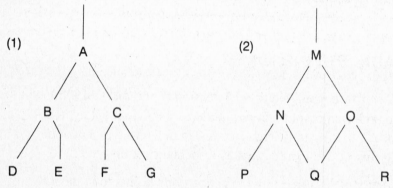

(1) and (3) are trees.
(2) is NOT a tree since Q has two nodes pointing to it.
(1) is complete, but (3) is **not** complete.

A is the root of tree (1).
B is the parent of D.
A is the grandparent of F.
E and F are (first) cousins.
X is the nephew/niece of W and W is the aunt/uncle of X.
D, E are (co-)siblings
V is of degree 2.
Y is of degree 1.
(3) is of depth 3.
V is in level 1.
The leaves of tree (1) are D, E, F, and G.

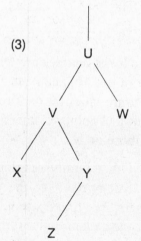

6.2 TRAVERSING BINARY TREES

There is a unique inherent order in a singly linked list, namely the order that starts at the head node and ends at the tail node. There are no real options in traversing (i.e., going to each one of) the nodes of such a list, since each node points to only one other node. Thus, it is a trivial task to list the elements of a singly linked list in linear order.

A tree is graphically represented in two dimensions by necessity. What is needed is a logical method of listing the (contents of the) nodes of a tree in one dimension (i.e., linearly). Since trees are two-dimension structures in some sense similar to two-dimension arrays, there are options in the way that information in such a structure can be listed in linear order (see Section 5.4). Thus, different linear orderings do exist for the same binary (two-dimension) tree, even though only one tree is being traversed.

There are three standard orders for traversing the nodes of a tree and these correspond to the three standard ways of writing arithmetic expressions (See C.9.2). In each order, a parent and its two children (left child before the right) are listed. The names of the orders are based on whether the parent is listed before (pre-), between (in-), or after (post-) its children. On a larger tree, the same order scheme is recursively used on each node that has children.

(1) PREORDER: *parent,* left child, right child.

(2) INORDER: left child, *parent,* right child.

(3) POSTORDER: left child, right child, *parent.*

It is emphasized once again that this is not a way to obtain three different trees out of one tree. This is a way to take one (two-dimension) tree and obtain three different linear (one-dimension) listings of the nodes contained in that tree. An example of one tree and its three different traversals follows:

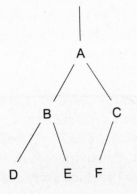

(1) PREORDER: *A* B D E C F

(2) INORDER: D B E *A* F C

(3) POSTORDER: D E B F C *A*

Notice that the root *A* (emphasized in the three listings) occurs in its "correct" place (before, between, after) relative to the other nodes. Also notice that if a node is missing (as with the right child of C), its proper place is noted but nothing appears in the listing. (i.e., the inorder traversal of the subtree $C - F$ is $F - C$ rather than $C - F$ since the right child is missing rather than the left.)

A tree is frequently used to describe an arithmetic expression (where the leaves are variables or numbers and interior nodes are always the operators). The following is such an example.

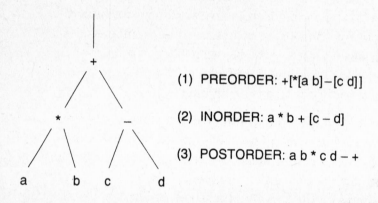

(1) PREORDER: +[*[a b]−[c d]]

(2) INORDER: a * b + [c − d]

(3) POSTORDER: a b * c d − +

The square brackets have been included for readability, and to help recognize that the three tree traversal orders correspond to the three methods of describing a mathematical binary function: prefix (functional), infix (arithmetic), and postfix (Reverse Polish Notation, "RPN") notations. However, the ultimate meaning of the expression is the same no matter what the form in which it is written.

There is one other traversal order, called *level order traversal*, which is used in special situations (see Heap sort and Section E.5.1.3). In this traversal scheme, all elements of one level are listed left to right, starting with the root in level 0, and proceeding level by level until the last one. A level order traversal of the first tree in the example above would give: A B C D E F and of the second tree would give: + * − a b c d. Unlike the three other traversals, a level order traversal cannot be implemented recursively, but is usually simply implemented using a queue.

Traversal algorithms are important since they are related to searching algorithms — if information is desired in some data structure (whether an array or a tree), there needs to be some systematic way to check each node of the structure to retrieve and possibly modify the information stored there. A traversal algorithm provides a systematic procedure by which every node in an ADT can be guaranteed to be checked.

6.3 OPERATIONS ON TREES

6.3.1 POINTER IMPLEMENTATION AND EXAMPLE

The ADT of a tree is usually implemented using pointer variables although a linear implementation with arrays is also possible. The pointer variable code for trees is similar to the code for linked lists in Section 2.3.1, except that there are two "next" fields.

```
TYPE  tree   =  ^node;
      node   =  RECORD
                  left: tree
                  info: INTEGER;
                  right: tree
                END;
```

The following sample code that uses this definition of a tree node consists of three segments: a tree generator, a tree printer (in inorder), and a driver main program. The generator segment recursively generates a tree of depth n by creating a node and then generating two trees of depth $n - 1$ which it points to. The information section of each node is filled with a number corresponding to the order of its creation, i.e., the root node contains a 1. Code such as this is primarily for demonstration purposes similar to the code found in Section 2.2.7 and would rarely be used in a major program.

GENERATING A COMPLETE TREE OF DEPTH N

```
FUNCTION Gentree(n:INTEGER):tree;
(*  Recursive function to generate a complete tree of depth n.
    The nodes are labeled from 1 to 2^n – 1 in the order created. *)
VAR t: tree;
BEGIN
    New(t);
    numnode := numnode + 1; (* note that numnode is a global variable *)
    t^.info := numnode;
    IF n <= 0   THEN t^.left := NIL
                ELSE t^.left := Gentree(n – 1);
    IF n<= 0    THEN t^.right:=NIL
                ELSE t^.right := Gentree(n – 1);
    Gentree := t
```

END; (* Gentree *)

PRINTING A TREE — INORDER

```
PROCEDURE Inprint(t:tree);
(*   Recursive procedure to print a tree in Inorder traversal — left, parent,
     right *)
BEGIN
    IF t <> NIL THEN
        BEGIN
            Inprint (t^.left);
            Write(t^. info);
            Inprint(t^.right)
        END
END;
```

MAIN PROGRAM

```
BEGIN
    numnode := 0;
    Inprint (Gentree(4))
END.
```

The code for Inprint can be easily modified by rearranging the center three lines if a routine to print a preorder or postorder traversal is desired.

6.3.2   ORDERED TREES

Trees can be used for ordering purposes. First of all, the traversal order to be used and the resulting output order must be chosen. The common *traversal* used is *inorder*, and the desired resulting order of the linear listing of the nodes is commonly $l < p < r$ which results in numerical or alphabetical order.

A tree whose node contents are such that the inorder traversal results in an ordered linear listing is called a *lexicographically ordered tree* or a lexically ordered tree (or a binary search tree). A lexicon is another name for a dictionary. Thus, this is equivalent to saying the tree is in "dictionary" or "alphabetical" order. Example:

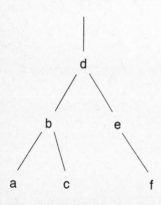

The inorder traversal of this tree gives the linear list of: a b c d e f, i.e., alphabetical order. Thus, this is a lexicographically ordered tree.

A binary tree that is lexicographically ordered can be an efficient alternative to an array for ordered data storage, especially if many insertions and deletions take place with the stored data. What are needed are efficient ways to insert and retrieve (or find) information in such a tree. The following section describes an algorithm for inserting an item into an ordered tree. A retrieval algorithm can be obtained by modifying this insertion algorithm slightly. A second comparison line is added before the present one and this new comparison would test for equality (and return a pointer to the "found" node). Instead of inserting a new node when reaching a nil-pointer, a retrieval algorithm returns a "not found." This retrieval algorithm is essentially a tree version of binary search (see Section 2.3), each time eliminating half of the tree from further consideration.

6.3.3 INSERTING INTO AN ORDERED TREE

Any algorithm for inserting new items into a lexicographically ordered tree must retain the ordering in the enlarged tree. The following is one version of such an algorithm.

ALGORITHM TO INSERT AN ITEM INTO AN ORDERED TREE
— Choose root to be the initial COMPARE-NODE
— REPEAT
    (* Compare item-to-be-inserted
       with contents of COMPARE-NODE *)
    — IF item-to-be-inserted > COMPARE-NODE contents
        THEN IF right child of COMPARE-NODE exists
            THEN choose the right child
               as the new COMPARE-NODE
            ELSE insert item as new right child
               and STOP!
        ELSE IF left child of COMPARE-NODE EXISTS
            THEN choose the left child
               as the new COMPARE-NODE
            ELSE insert item as new left child
               and STOP!
— UNTIL item has been inserted.

6.3.4 EXAMPLE: REPEATED INSERTIONS INTO AN ORDERED TREE

The following example starts with an empty tree, and repeatedly inserts items into the tree so that at each point, the tree is always lexicographically ordered. In other words, at every point, if an inorder traversal of the tree is performed, the output list of items will be in alphabetical order.

INPUT LIST: N S I A L P J M

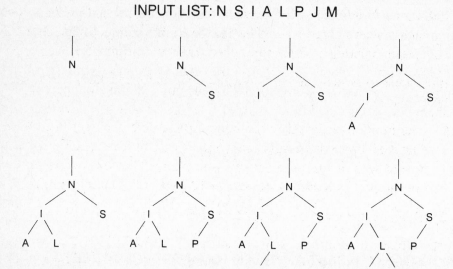

6.3.5 DELETING FROM AN ORDERED TREE

Any algorithm for deleting a node from a lexicographically ordered tree must retain the ordering in the reduced tree. However, this task is more difficult than in the case of the insertion algorithm. Given the following tree:

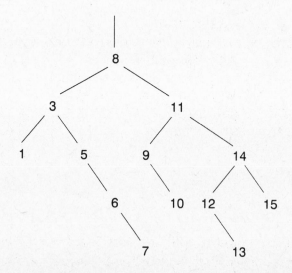

the way nodes 15, 5, or 11 are deleted differ drastically. The procedure used depends on whether the node has no children (i.e., is a leaf), has only one child, or has two children.

A) If the node-to-be-deleted has no children (i.e., is a leaf), merely delete it. (See deleting 15.)

B) If the node-to-be-deleted has only one child, the descendants of that node are each moved up one level, so that the child takes the place of the deleted node. (See deleting 5 — the right descendant of 3 is now 6.)

C) If the node-to-be-deleted has both children, a major adaptation to the tree takes place:

1) The inorder successor to the node-to-be-deleted is identified. Note that the inorder successor cannot have a left child, else that (left) child would be the actual inorder successor. If node 11 is to be deleted in the tree above, its inorder successor is 12 (which has no left child).

2) Replace the node-to-be-deleted with its inorder successor.

3) Replace the inorder successor with its right child (if it exists) (and move all successive descendants up one level). Since the inorder successor has no left child (see 1 above), there are no left descendants to have to worry about.

After deleting 11 in the previous example, the tree looks like:

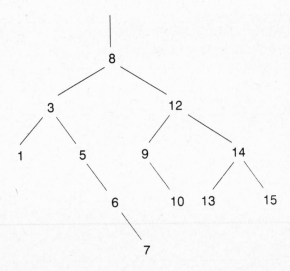

The deletion algorithm will also work if the inorder predecessor takes the place of the deleted node, with necessary changes to the rest of step (C). The final tree will be ordered, but will be a different tree than that which appears here.

6.4   BALANCING AND ROTATING

A *balanced binary tree* is one in which for every node, the heights of the two subtrees do not differ by more than 1. A balanced binary tree is also called an *AVL-tree*, named for Georgii M. Adelson-Velskii and Yevgenii M. Landis, (who developed a height-balancing algorithm in 1962).

Balancing is the process of converting an arbitrary tree into a balanced tree.

The *balance factor* of a node is the height of the left rooted branch minus the height of the right rooted branch. By "left (or right) rooted branch" is meant the left subtree from the node including the node. (Thus, for example, if a node has no left child, the left rooted branch consists of that node alone and has height 0.)

THEOREM

In a balanced binary tree, each node has a balance factor of either – 1, 0, or 1.

PROBLEM

Insertions and deletions in a (lexicographically ordered) binary tree may make it highly imbalanced, so that searching for an item (in two different ordered trees, both containing the same set of items) may vary drastically in the number of steps. For example, the two following trees are both ordered and

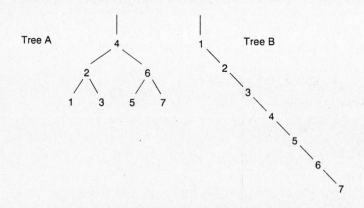

both contain the same information, but have drastically different shapes.

Tree A and tree B both have the same inorder traversal, but tree B is, in a sense, a degenerate tree and is equivalent to a singly linked list.

To find 3, 5, or 7 in tree A would only take 3 comparisons (at maximum) using the search algorithm mentioned earlier in Section 6.3.2. However, in tree B, it takes 3 comparisons to find 3, 5 to find 5, and 7 to find 7.

For some applications, it can be important to be able to search quickly, so it is important to make a tree as balanced as possible.

Balancing is accomplished by performing an action called *rotation* about certain nodes.

A *simple rotation* about a node is a rearrangement of a subtree rooted at that node such that the inorder traversal remains the same and one of the children of the node has now become the root (of that subtree).

A *right [left] rotation* is one in which the root has become the right [left] child of the new root (which was formerly the left [right] child of the old root).

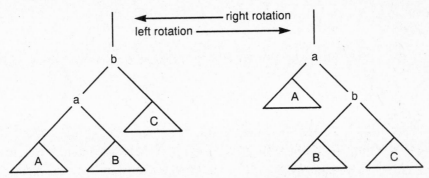

Note: Subtree B switches parents!

In the process, one of the subtrees switches parents as depicted in the diagram above.

The process of a left rotation can be coded simply as follows:

```
PROCEDURE Leftrotate (VAR a:tree);
VAR b,temp:tree;
BEGIN
    b:=a^.right;
    temp := b^.left;
    b^.left := a;
    a^.right := temp;
    a:= b
END;
```

What follows is a general description of a *balancing algorithm* for ordered trees. It does not take into account special situations.

1) After an insertion/deletion, check balance factors of the various nodes from the point of insertion/deletion to the root.

2) If the balance factor = 2 for a node, rotate right.

3) If the balance factor = – 2 for a node, rotate left.

NOTES

(a) After rotation, the balances of the nodes should be rechecked. Additional rotations may be necessary.

(b) If two nodes happen to be unbalanced in opposite directions, a double rotation in opposite directions is necessary.

The following is an example of a single rotation.

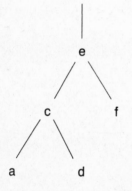

Add node b (right child of a) to this tree.

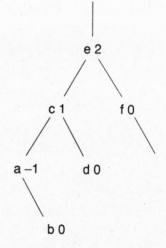

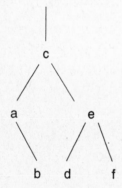

Balanced tree after rotation.

Since e now has a balance factor of 2, a right rotation is performed making e the right child from the new root c.

6.5 THREADING TREES

Tree traversal is a common operation and is naturally described recursively. However, if a traversal routine is not or cannot be implemented recursively, it is possible to explicitly include a stack in the routine. An explicit stack is usually more efficient. However, pushes and pops still can take more time than desired.

One common approach to increase efficiency in a traversal routine is to *thread* a tree, i.e., to insert additional links (pointers) to aid in the traversal. Commonly, these threads are added from leaves (and even other nodes that do not have both children) to the inorder successor (and/or the inorder predecessor).

Nil-pointers at nodes can be modified to indicate they are now threads or "back"-pointers. To do this, it must be determined:

1) whether a node has a nil-pointer as a pointer in either right or left child field, and

2) what the inorder successor (and predecessor) to that node is.

In addition, the definition of a tree is modified to allow more than one pointer to any node.

Tree-threading can be limited to just right (inorder) successors, if desired, obtaining a partially (inorder) threaded tree.

NOTES

(a) Threads always point to an ancestor, never to a descendant.

(b) Threads take the place of a nil-pointer (left or right child). Therefore, the total number of children and threads at any node (in a binary tree) must always equal two.

(c) A thread from the right-most node of a tree (which never has an inorder successor) points to a special header node that in turn points to the root of the tree.

(d) When depicting threads visually, in order not to be misleading, a thread is always drawn on the same side as the pointer to a child that it replaces. For example, a thread that points to the inorder successor of a node and replaces a pointer to a right child is drawn on the right side of the node.

The following are examples of a partially (inorder successor) threaded and a completely threaded tree.

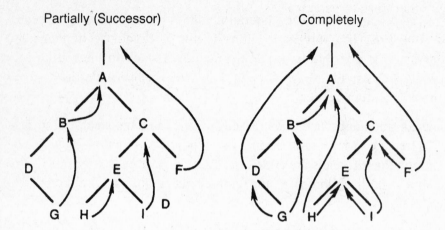

Partially (Successor)   Completely

Code for threaded trees must distinguish between threads and links to offspring. Various methods have been developed to do this. In linear implementations, the link pointer values are often negated if they are threads. Thus, by checking if a link value is negative, it can be determined whether the pointer is a thread or a link to an offspring, i.e., whether the pointer is pointing to a child or to an ancestor.

In linked implementations, (at least) one other field (which can merely be a boolean flag called *rthread*) is added to each node record, indicating whether the right link is a thread or not. Rthread is true if the right link is a thread to an ancestor, and false if it is not a thread (i.e., if it points to a child). The code for tree traversal is so written that each time a right branch is chosen, rthread is tested first to determine what action is taken next.

6.6 GENERAL TREES

The theory and use of binary trees is fairly well-developed. But things complicate rapidly if the tree is not binary. It is difficult even to decide how a tree should be stored if the maximum degree of its nodes is not known.

A standard practice to handle general trees is to transform the arbitrary tree into a binary tree (or even to transform a forest of general trees into a binary tree). The common transformation is done via what is called "Knuth(ian) natural correspondence" (named after Donald Knuth at Stanford University). The procedure is straightforward and is described as follows:

l) All co-siblings are linked together (and, given a forest, the roots of each of the trees are linked together);

2) the left-most offspring remains linked to its parent, but

3) all other links to parents are removed;

4) the transformed structure is rotated 45° clockwise to exhibit a new binary tree.

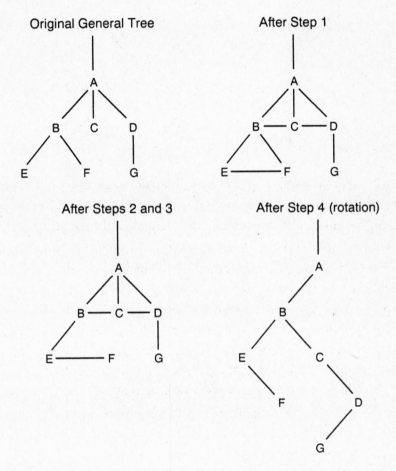

The previous is a simple example of such a transformation.

In the new tree created, some of the relationships of the original general tree can be determined. For example, a left child in the new tree corresponds to the first child in the original tree (cf. left child of A is B). A node and its right descendants in the new tree correspond to co-siblings in the original tree (see E and its left child F).

CHAPTER 5

ALGORITHMS

1. INTRODUCTION

How do we differentiate a good program from a bad one? The answer to this depends on several factors.

One way is to analyze the algorithm used by the program. An algorithm is a general method for solving some kind of problem. A program is the application of the specific algorithm. Efficiency is the measure of the algorithm's impact on a computer. An algorithm is efficient if it accomplishes its goals with a minimum of computer resources. These resources are space (memory) and time.

Of the two factors, time is a more important consideration. This is not the # of minutes a program takes to execute. Here, time refers to the # of steps it takes to carry out an algorithm. Thus, when analyzing an algorithm, we examine the number of steps it takes to carry out a function: an algorithm that takes N steps to carry out is twice as fast as an algorithm that takes 2 * N steps.

1.1 BIG O

Big O, meaning "order of", is the notation used to express the running time of an algorithm in terms of N, the size of the data inputs. Saying that an algorithm is $O(N^2)$ means that it takes N^2 steps to complete. Some typical Big O values are:

$O(1)$: Constant time. The running time of the algorithm won't be affected by the data.

$O(\log N)$: Logarithmic time. Running time increases very slowly with N, since log N only doubles when N is squared.

O(N): Linear time. Running time is dependent on N.

O(N^2): Quadratic time. Running time increases with the square of N.

O(2^N): Exponential time: If N is 10, then the running time is 1,000, but doubling N increases it to 1,000,000. Algorithms of exponential time are considered to be impractical.

2.   SEARCHING

2.1   SEARCHING ALGORITHMS

It is often necessary to locate certain information stored in a data structure. To do this, consideration must be given to various possible ways of traversing the data structure in question. If a way can be found to traverse a data structure so that *every* cell can be accessed, then this method can also be used to search that structure for stored information. In this chapter, algorithms to search arrays will be examined. Traversals and searching algorithms for other data structures will also be considered in later chapters.

Frequently an array of records is searched according to one field to locate a specific record and be able to access and even modify other fields. Typical examples would include searching through a list of names to find (and retrieve) a telephone number, or searching a list of account numbers to modify a bank balance (or other related information).

The items actually searched are called *keys*. Usually a *key* is left unchanged, but another piece of information associated with the *key* is copied. Often this other piece of information is the index of the array element in which the desired item is stored. The index is then used to find what is really wanted, e.g., another field in the record of data. Frequently one field of a record is used as a key (e.g., the name field or the account number field), and other fields associated with the key (e.g., the telephone number or bank balance) are operated on (i.e., retrieved or modified).

There are two major search techniques associated with arrays: *Linear (Sequential) search* and *Binary search*.

Linear search can *always* be used. The underlying principle is to examine each element of an array in order, starting at the first one, until the desired *key* is found. This method is particularly suited for an *unsorted* array, and can be considered similar to the procedure often used for searching a shuffled deck of cards for a given card.

Binary search can be used *only* with a *sorted* array. It is a stylized version of what someone does when searching a telephone book for a number. In general, one starts in the *middle,* and keeps eliminating part of the book until the desired name is found. (Note again for the sake of emphasis, that when the name is found in the book, it is not copied since it is already known, but rather, the *associated information* of the *phone number* is copied and used.)

2.2 LINEAR SEARCH

Linear search (sometimes called *sequential search*) is a straightforward algorithm that starts with examining the first key in the array and continues until it finds the desired item or it reaches the end of the array (without finding it). When the algorithm finds the item, it returns the array index of the item in the parameter *place.* If the desired item is *not* found, the final value of *place* is zero. If two or more records in the array have the same key, only the first one is located. This algorithm can be used with either sorted or unsorted arrays. The following is a version of the algorithm in Pascal.

```
PROCEDURE LinSearch (stuff:ArrayType; n:INTEGER; key:ArrayItemType;
VAR place: INTEGER);
(*   STUFF is the array of records being searched,
     N is the number of items being searched
     (which may be less than the total size if the array is not full)
KEY is the key item being searched for,
     PLACE indicates where KEY is in the array, or if it is zero, indicates that
     KEY was NOT FOUND *)

VAR       i   :   INTEGER;
          found  :   BOOLEAN;
BEGIN
    (* initialization *)
    found := FALSE;
    i :=1; (* the first item in the array is assumed to have subscript 1 *)
    place := 0;
    (* search loop *)
    WHILE (i <= n) AND (NOT found) DO
        IF key = stuff[ i ] THEN (* we have found it! *)
            BEGIN place := i; (* location of KEY in stuff *)
    found := TRUE (* flag to get out of loop *)
            END
        ELSE
```

```
        i := i + 1;
END; (* procedure *)
```

The following segment gives an example of how to use this code in a program.

```
(* assume that AccountNumbers contains Num account numbers *)
Read(key);
linsearch(AccountNumbers,Num,key,location);
write('Account',key', is stored in location',location);
```

A brief analysis of the efficiency of linear search is appropriate. In the worst case, the sought-after item is not in the array, but every element in the array will have been examined in the attempt to find it. If there are n items, then the number of comparisons is n. Therefore, for the number of comparisons, linear search is $O(n)$ in the worst case.

2.3 BINARY SEARCH

To understand how *binary search* works, its operation is demonstrated by the following example.

The location of account number 350 in the following array of account numbers is sought.

subscript	1	2	3	4	5	6	7	8
CONTENTS	110	112	156	210	257	296	350	892
	^1			^1				^1
	F			M				L

(The digits "1" above the letters F, M and L indicate the *first* values of these variables that point to elements in the array.) Initially, the entire array is examined. Thus *First* initially points to the item 1 and *Last* points to item 8. The "*Middle*" item is computed by the formula:

$$M = (F + L) \text{ div } 2.$$

The **div** operator gives an integer result, e.g., 5 div 2 is 2 and not 2.50.)

With F being 1 and L being 8, M is 4, as shown above.

Next, what is sought (i.e., 350) is compared to what is in the 4th element of the array (i.e., 210). Since what is sought (350) is greater than the "middle" item, the middle element and the first half of the list are ignored. This "ignoring" of the first half is accomplished by resetting F to be one past the middle item, i.e., $F = M + 1$. F is now 5, and the procedure is started again (and the fact that there ever was a first half of the array is ignored). Thus the following situation now exists:

subscript	1	2	3	4	5	6	7	8
CONTENTS	110	112	156	210	257	296	350	892
					^2	^2		^2
					F	M		L

$F + L = 5 + 8 = 13$
$\Rightarrow M = 13$ div $2 = 6$

Since $M = 6$ is not the correct array location, F is recomputed: $F = M + 1 = 6 + 1 = 7$, resulting in:

subscript	1	2	3	4	5	6	7	8
CONTENTS	110	112	156	210	257	296	350	892
							^3	^3
							F	L
							^3	
							M	

$F + L = 7 + 8 = 15$
$\Rightarrow M = 15$ div $2 = 7$
ARRAY[middle] = ARRAY[7] = 350 which is what was sought!

The code of the algorithm which follows merely translates this procedure.

```
PROCEDURE BinSearch (Stuff:ArrayType; n:INTEGER;
                            key:ArrayItemType; VAR place: INTEGER;

(* parameters have the same purpose as in linear search *)

VAR first, last, middle: INTEGER;

BEGIN
     (* initialization *)
     first :=1;
     last := n;
     place := 0;
     (* major loop *)
     WHILE first <= last DO
         BEGIN
             middle := (first + last) DIV 2;
```

```
            IF key = stuff[middle] THEN
            (* we have found it! *)
                BEGIN
                    first := last + 1;
                    (* trick to get out of loop *)
                    place := middle
                    (* save location of KEY *)
                END
            ELSE (* we have not found it but which half do we ignore ? *)
                IF key > stuff[middle] THEN
                (* omit first half *)
                    first := middle + 1
                ELSE (* omit last half *)
                    last := middle − 1
        END (* while *)
END; (* procedure *)
```

A brief analysis of the efficiency of binary search is also appropriate. The worst case is related to how many times the array size can be subdivided in half and still be an integer. The calculations are easier if the size of the array, n, is assumed to be a power of 2, e.g., $n = 2^i$ for some i. A careful analysis shows that in this case, the maximum number of times that the array can be divided by 2 is i.

But $\log_2 n = \log_2(2^i) = i$.

Therefore, at worst, there are $i = \log_2 n$ subdivisions and, for each subdivision there are at most *two* comparisons in the loop of the code given above. In other words, in the worst case, the number of comparisons is $O(\log_2 n)$.

To compare linear search with binary search, if $n = 1024$, the *linear* search worst case = *1024 comparisons*, and the *binary* search worst case = 2 x $\log_2 1024 = 2$ x $\log_2 2^{10} = 20$ *comparisons*.

2.4   HASHING

2.4.1   PRELIMINARIES

There are situations that arise in which information needs to be retrieved from a data structure quickly, but even the use of binary search with arrays is too slow. Binary search would also be difficult to use if the array were constantly being updated by insertions and deletions, since using binary search would demand that an array be adjusted so it remains sorted after each insertion or deletion, a process that could slow down the procedure even more. (Linear search would be even slower, although there would be no need to sort after insertions.) An alternative is to dispense with any ordering and instead use a *hash function*.

A **hash function**, *h*, is a function that maps a *key* (i.e., one field in a record) into an *address* (i.e., array subscript) that is then used to store the associated record (in that array). If the symbol *S* designates some key (e.g., a number or character), then *h(S)* is its hash address or hash number. *Hashing* refers to the use of hash functions for data storage and retrieval.

For a specific set of keys, an ideal hash function is bijective (i.e., $1 - 1$, unique). In other words, the ideal function is one that makes two different keys correspond to two different addresses, yet is easy to compute. However, such a function is rarely, if ever, obtained.

When two symbols. S_1 and S_2 are used as keys and when $h(S_1)$ equals $h(S_2)$ for the hash function *h*, then a **hash collision** or **hash clash** is said to have occurred. Good hash functions are those that lead to new such collisions, but since collisions regularly occur, procedures exist to resolve the resulting difficulties.

The *general procedure for using a hash function* to store and retrieve information is as follows:

(1) Given the key symbol **S,** compute its hash value, *h(S);*

(2) Access the record in the data storage structure (normally an array) corresponding to *h(S);*

(3) If a collision occurs, resolve any ambiguities.

2.4.2 HASH FUNCTIONS

There are different possibilities for hash functions, and no one function is ideal for all purposes. The major types of functions are now briefly mentioned.

2.4.2.1 DIVISION

This is the earliest type of hash functions. It is very widely used and is one of the easiest functions to calculate. It presupposes a range in which the output of the function lies, e.g., the permitted values for the array subscript. If the elements are to be stored in an array of size *m*, the hash function would be

$h(x) = x \bmod m$ (if the range were 0 to $m - 1$)

or

$h(x) = (x \bmod m) + 1$ (if the range were 1 to m).

The modulus m is usually chosen to be a prime number slightly larger than the number of elements to be stored. As an example, with $m = 11$, $h(35) = (35 \bmod 11) + 1 = 2 + 1 = 3$. It has been suggested that a prime of the form $4k + 3$ for some integer k is particularly effective as a modulus.

The major problem with this type of hash function is that it is very easy to get clashes. For example, if m is 101,

$h(125) = 125 \bmod 101 + 1 = 24 + 1 = 25.$
$h(226) = 226 \bmod 101 + 1 = 24 + 1 = 25.$

2.4.2.2 MIDSQUARE

This method attempts to introduce a certain randomness into the computation of the hash number, and can be viewed as a specific version of a more general approach of computing a hash number by means of a (repeatable) *random number generator*. In other words, given two different keys, the hash function should produce two different numbers with little or no relationship to the keys or to each other, except that the same function will produce the same hash numbers given the same input anytime it is used.

The name "mid-square" is derived from the steps taken by the hash function to produce a result: taking the *mid*dle of the *square* of the input number. In other words, given x, one first squares it, and then removes the center few digits to use as the hash number. This method is sometimes used as a random number generator. It can be formulated as:

$h(x) = (x^2 \text{ div } n) \bmod n$

where $n = 10^i$ or 2^i for some i. For example, if x equals 123456

then $x^2 = 15241383936.$

If $n = 10^4,$

then $h(x) = 138.$

2.4.2.3 FOLDING

This method is sometimes called *bit* or *digit compression*. The general strategy is: (1) *subdivide* the key x into groups of n-digits (bits) (the leading or last group can have fewer than n-digits or bits); (2) *combine* the different groups together by an operation such as *sum, exclusive-or,* or *or*; (3) *extract* the last n digits (bits) of the resulting number as the hash number (i.e., mod the number by 10^n if it has more than n digits). For example, with n being 3,

$$
\begin{aligned}
h(97434658) &= (974+346+58) \bmod 1000 \\
&= 1378 \bmod 1000 = \mathbf{378} \\
h(32169857) &= (321+698+57) \bmod 1000 \\
&= 1067 \bmod 1000 = \mathbf{67}
\end{aligned}
$$

2.4.2.4 DIGIT ANALYSIS

This is sometimes called *digit* or *character* or *bit extraction*. The general strategy is: (1) *select* certain digits (bits) of the key x; (2) *transform or rearrange* them as the hash number. The following procedure may be taken as a simple example of this approach:

          (1) Take the digits in positions 3 – 6,
and   (2) Reverse them.

          Thus, $h(75{:}4612{:}3) = 2164$

This approach is less desirable than others since, in general, it is better to use a method that makes use of *all* the input information, i.e., all bits or digits. However, in some situations, some of the input information is biased and can skew the computation of a hash number. For example, the majority of social security numbers begin with either the digit 5 or the digit 3. It would be better to ignore the first digit and use the other digits, perhaps transforming them by one of the other types of hash functions.

2.4.2.5 MULTIPLICATION

This method derives its name from the two multiplications involved in obtaining the hash number. The combination of multiplication and other arithmetic operations suggests that the resulting hash numbers will be more evenly distributed throughout the storage array. It can be formulated as:

$$h(x) = \mathrm{trunc}(m * \mathrm{fraction}(x * z))$$

where m is the size of the storage array, z is a number between 0 and 1, *trunc* is the truncation function (that eliminates the fractional part of a number) and *fraction* eliminates the integral part of a number. The resulting number will be an integer between 0 and m and could possibly be 0. Some studies indicate that the best choice of z is $(-/5-1)/2$ or $1-(-/5-1)/2$.

EXAMPLE

Suppose the following records are to be stored via a hashing scheme:

ID # (key)	Name	Other Information
2651	Smith	...
3412	Jones	...
1183	Brown	...
9356	Kelly	...

(1) Using **Digit Analysis**, by taking digits 2 and 4 and adding them, the following hash numbers are obtained:

ID # (key)	Hash Numbers
2651	6 + 1 = 7
3412	4 + 2 = 6
1183	1 + 3 = 4
9356	3 + 6 = 9

Therefore, the storage array would look like:

1	2	3	4	5	6	7	8	9	10
			1183 Brown		3511 Jones	2651 Smith		9356 Kelly	

(2) Using a **Division** method, with $m = 10$ (including the shift by 1), the following are obtained:

ID # (key)	Hash Numbers
2651	2
3412	3
1183	4
9356	7

3. ELEMENTARY SORTING

3.1 SORTING ALGORITHMS

One common operation performed on arrays is **sorting** the array elements, i.e., putting them in some kind of order.

There are a number of different approaches to sorting. The usual problems associated with any algorithm affect these various approaches. The less complicated (and easier to understand) methods are also less efficient, while the more efficient methods are usually more complicated (and difficult to understand).

This chapter will examine two straightforward sorting algorithms that can be used with one-dimension arrays. They are also inefficient. However, more efficient methods appear later (in Chapter 4) after the discussion of more complex data structures.

There are two major elementary approaches to sorting:

a) **Exchange Sorts:** These methods *exchange adjacent* items in an array. The best known exchange sort is **bubble sort.**

b) **Selection Sorts:** These methods search for the next desired item, *select* it, and put it in its proper place in the array.

3.2 BUBBLE SORT

The most common example of an exchange sort is the algorithm known as *bubble sort*. This name is derived from comparing the operation of the algorithm to air bubbles going up slowly in a glass of carbonated water. The bubbles move up bumping other bubbles that get bigger and go up faster. Thus, the lightest bubbles get to the top faster than the others.

The basic principle underlying this algorithm is simple:

— examine adjacent items in an array pair by pair;

— if they are out of order, exchange them.

The algorithm consists of repeatingly performing *passes* on the array, each time applying the basic principle until the array is sorted.

Analyzing the action of the algorithm shows that it divides the array into a sorted section and an unsorted section. Each pass adds at least one more item to the sorted section. Thus, at maximum, $n - 1$ passes are needed to sort any array of length n (n passes are *not* needed since after $n - 1$ items are arranged in order, the last item must also be in its proper place). The action of the algorithm indicates that the algorithm should stop when

a) the number of passes equals $n - 1$ where n is the number of items in the array, or

b) no exchanges have been made in a pass (since that indicates that no items were out of order, i.e., that the array is all sorted).

When implemented, many algorithms actually do a "bubble-down" sorting, in which the "heaviest" (largest) item moves to the end the fastest.

The following is an example of the algorithm's operation:

Original array	25	57	48	37	12	92	86	33
check pair 1	(25	57)	48	37	12	92	86	33
no exchange needed								
check pair 2	25	(57	48)	37	12	92	86	33
exchange	25	(48	57)	37	12	92	86	33
check pair 3	25	48	(57	37)	12	92	86	33
exchange	25	48	(37	57)	12	92	66	33
check pair 4	25	48	37	(57	12)	92	86	33
exchange	25	48	37	(12	57)	92	86	33
check pair 5	25	48	37	12	(57	92)	86	33
no exchange needed								
check pair 6	25	48	37	12	57	(92	86)	33
exchange	25	48	37	12	57	(86	92)	33
check pair 7	25	48	37	12	57	86	(92	33)
exchange	25	48	37	12	57	86	(33	92)
after pass 1	25	48	37	12	57	86	33	**92**

Note that the greatest item is in its proper place at the last place in the array.

The same procedure of checking and exchanging (if necessary) is followed for each pass. The details are omitted. The results after the next two passes are:

after pass 2	25	37	12	48	57	33	**86**	**92**

Note that now the two largest items are in their proper places and order in the last two places in the array.

after pass 3		25	12	37	48	33	57	86	**92**

There are several ways to implement bubble sort. Note that after *j* passes, the last *j* elements are sorted and need never be looked at again. Thus most versions only check the first $n - j$ elements on pass $j + 1$. Also, the various versions differ as to which condition is used to determine when the algorithm should stop. The most inefficient method is to write the code so that all $n - 1$ passes are always performed (i.e., stopping condition (a)). A better way is to use a boolean variable (usually called a *flag)* to determine whether an exchange has taken place and stop if no exchanges have taken place in a particular pass (i.e., stopping condition (b)). Such a code is sometimes called a *flagged* bubble sort, and an example of it follows in Pascal.

```
PROCEDURE Bubblesort(VAR stuff:ArrayType; n:INTEGER);
(*   This procedure sorts a 1-dimension array using the flagged bubble sort
     algorithm.
     The input array *stuff* is returned at the end of the procedure sorted
     with the minimum element in the first location and the maximum
     element in location n.
     The array is of type ArrayType and the number of elements in the array
     to be sorted is n. Each item in the array is a scalar variable of type
     ArrayItemType. *)

VAR exchanged : BOOLEAN; (* the flag that indicates that an exchange has
                                                          taken place *)
    pass,j  :   INTEGER; (* loop counters *)
    temp    :   ArrayItemType; (* temporary variable for exchanging
                                             elements in the array *)

BEGIN (* procedure bubblesort *)
    (* initialization *)
    exchanged := TRUE;
    pass := 0;
    (* checking and exchanging loop *)
    WHILE (pass < n – 1 ) AND exchanged DO
        BEGIN (* WHILE LOOP *)
            exchanged := FALSE;
            pass := pass + 1;
            FOR j :=1 TO n-pass DO
            (* check if adjacent items are out of order *)
                If stuff[ j ] > stuff[ j+1 ] THEN
                    BEGIN (* exchange elements *)
                        temp := stuff[ j ];
                        stuff [ j ] = stuff[ j +1 ];
```

```
                    stuff[ j+1 ] := temp;
                    exchanged := TRUE
                END (* IF and FOR *)
            END (* WHILE *)
END; (* procedure bubblesort *)
```

The following code shows how the *bubblesort* procedure would be used.

```
PROGRAM Test (input,output);

TYPE   ArrayItemType = INTEGER;
       ArrayType = ARRAY[1...20] of ArrayItemType;

VAR    testarray: ArrayType;
       i:   INTEGER;

BEGIN
    (* first initialize first 10 items in array *)
    FOR i:=1 TO 10 DO
        testarray[ i ] := 25 – i;
    (* bubblesort is now called, with a size parameter of 10, since only 10
    items were given values and need be sorted *)
    bubblesort(testarray, 10);
    (* the sorted array is now printed out *)
    FOR i:=1 TO 10 DO
        Writeln(testarray[ i ])
END.
```

In order to evaluate algorithms used with data structures, it is helpful to get some idea of how long they take to complete their task. A detailed analysis can be found elsewhere, but an overview is given here. Note that in pass j, the number of *comparisons* is $n - j$, and in the worst case, the number of passes is $n - 1$. Adding the number of comparisons together for each pass gives us $n(n-1)/2$ *comparisons* in the *worst case*. Since the dominant term in this expression is a multiple of n^2, this algorithm is said to be "of order n^2" for the number of comparisons and this is written as $O(n^2)$. In the worst case, one **exchange** is performed for *each* comparison. Therefore, the number of exchanges equals $n(n-1)/2 = O(n^2)$ for the *worst case*.

This formula is useful since it gives some indication of the speed of the algorithm relative to the size of the input. In particular, since $(2n)^2$ equals $4n^2$, if the size of the input is doubled, this indicates that it would take about four times longer to sort an array using bubble sort!

3.3   STRAIGHT SELECTION SORT

The most common example of a selection sort is the algorithm known as *straight selection* (or *jump down sort*).

The basic principle underlying this algorithm is this:

— examine all the items in the **unsorted subsection** of the array and **select** the smallest [largest];
— place the selected item in the first [last] place of the subsection being examined, reduce the size of the subsection.

As with the bubble sort, the algorithm consists of repeatedly performing *passes* on the array, each time applying the basic principle until the array is sorted. As with bubble sort, this algorithm also stops after *n – 1* passes.

The following is an example of the algorithm's operation:

(array subscript)	1	2	3	4	5	6	7	8
original array	25	57	48	37	12	92	86	33

subsection size = 8—largest item is x[6] <=> 92
x[6] is exchanged with x[8]

after pass 1	25	57	48	37	12	33	86	92

subsection size = 7—largest item is x[7] <=> 86
x[7] is exchanged with x[7], i.e., nothing happens.

after pass 2	25	57	48	37	12	33	86	92

subsection size = 6—largest item is x[2] <=> 57
x[2] is exchanged with x[6]

after pass 3	25	33	48	37	12	57	86	92

There are variations on the code for straight selection sort, but fewer than with bubble sort. There can be no "flagged" version of this sort, but there are fewer exchanges. The following is a version of it in Pascal.

```
PROCEDURE StraightSelection(VAR stuff:ArrayType; n:INTEGER);
(*   This procedure sorts a 1-dimension array using the straight selection
     sort algorithm.
     The input array *stuff* is returned at the end of the procedure sorted
     with the minimum element in the first location and the maximum
     element in location n.
     The array is of type ArrayType and the number of elements in the array
```

to be sorted is *n*. Each item in the array is a scalar variable of type
ArrayItemType. *)

```
VAR    i,j,index   :   INTEGER;
(*  i, j, and index are counters to be used as subscripts. *)
       large  :  ArrayItemType
(*  large is the value of the largest element in *stuff* *)
BEGIN (* Procedure StraightSelection *)
   FOR i := n DOWNTO 2 DO
     BEGIN
              (* first initialize the "largest" item in *stuff* and save its subscript
                 in index *)
              large := stuff[1];
              index :=1;
              (* check through the other elements to find something "larger" *)
              FOR j :=2 TO i DO
                  IF stuff[ j ] > large THEN
              (* save the new large element and remember its place *)
                     BEGIN
                         large := stuff[ j ];
                         index := j
                     END; (* IF and FOR j *)
              (* completes the rest of the exchange *)
              stuff[index] := stuff[ i ];
              stuff[ i ] := large
   END (* FOR i *)
END;   (* straightselection *)
```

In order to evaluate this algorithm, note that in pass *j*, the number of
comparisons is *n − j* and the number of passes is *always n − 1*. Adding the
number of comparisons together for each pass again gives $n(n − 1)/2$ comparisons, written as $O(n^2)$. However, in this algorithm, there is only *one* exchange per pass. Thus, the total number of exchanges is *n − 1* or $O(n)$.

Although this algorithm has significantly fewer exchanges than bubble
sort, it still is slow because of the number of comparisons performed.

3.4   STABLE SORTS

Suppose an array of records with several fields is given, and suppose one
field is called the *key* field. Let *i* and *j* be the indices of two records in this array
and suppose *key[i] = key [j]*. In other words, suppose two records had the same
zip code that is stored in the *key* field. Let us also suppose that, in the array,
the *i*[th] record *precedes* the *j*[th] record. In other words, suppose the *i*[th] record

corresponds to Mr. Brown's information and the ith record corresponds to Mrs. Smith's and the records are in alphabetical order.

A sort is called *stable* if, after sorting based on the *key* field, the record formerly associated with *i* still precedes the record formerly associated with *j*. In other words, a stable sort will not "undo" existing orders based on other keys, when sorting based on a different key and then examining items with equal key values.

The stability or non-stability of a sorting scheme can be an important consideration when several sorts are successively done on the same file. For example, suppose one wishes to alphabetize a list and then sort by zip code, hoping that the resulting list will have everyone in the same zip code in alphabetical order. To ensure this, the second sort used *must* be stable.

Of the two elementary sorting schemes, bubble sort is *stable,* but straight selection sort is *not*. Thus, even though bubble sort makes more exchanges than straight selection sort, for certain applications it may actually be a preferred sorting scheme.

4. HASHING

4.1 RESOLVING CLASHES

Ideally, $h(x)$ is chosen to be as unique as possible, but collisions and clashes do occur, i.e., two different keys are hashed to the same number. The situation in which numerous keys are hashed to the same numbers is sometimes called *clustering*, and a good hash function avoids clustering. Yet, since it rarely can be eliminated completely, strategies are needed to resolve ambiguities that occur.

There exist several categories of techniques that attempt to resolve ambiguities. The techniques that will be examined are: *linear probing, quadratic probing, rehashing, bucket,* and *chaining.* Each technique has its own advantages and disadvantages. It should be remembered that all of them are "patch-up" techniques that try to correct problems due to collisions resulting from the hash function being used. The better the hash function, the less need there is for a highly efficient collision resolution technique.

In most collision resolution techniques, when retrieving information a search (and subsequent comparison) needs to be performed until the desired key is found. The hope is that even combining such a search with the initial hash number calculation, the total time and energy is less than occurs using a binary or linear search. Moreover, with a proper choice of a hash function, collisions can be kept to a minimum.

4.1.1 LINEAR PROBING

Linear Probing is also called *open addressing* and even, by some authors, *rehashing* (a title also used for the approach found in Section 4.1.3). The basic technique is this: suppose the information associated with key is being inserted into the storage array, but location h(key) is already in use. The algorithm then searches for the next available space and stores the information there. In other words, since h(key) is occupied, the information is stored in h(key) + 1 if that is free, or if not, then h(key) + 2, or else h(key) + 3, etc. (This procedure of looking for the next available space is called linear probing or even a rehash rule. Here "linear" is used in the same way as it is used in "linear" search, i.e., the next one in a line.)

This procedure can be described more succinctly as follows: if the location h(key) is occupied in the storage array, the first alternative space tried is h(key) + 1. However, if that is occupied also, the second alternative space tried is h(key) + 2. In general, the kth alternative space tried is h(key) + k (with wraparound of the array taken into account as usual using the mod operator).

To locate an item already stored in the array, the hash number is first computed, and the contents of that location are checked. If the item in question is not found there, then a (short) linear search is performed (starting at the computed address) until the item is found.

As an example, let h(key) equal key mod 100 + 1,

then h(321) = 321 mod 100 + 1 = 21 + 1 = 22
and h(121) =121 mod 100 + 1 = 21 + 1 = 22.

The record with key 321 would be stored in location 22 in the storage array, and then linear probing done on the address for key 121, which would be stored in location 23 (if that is available).

Although straightforward, this procedure also tends to result in clustering.

4.1.2 QUADRATIC PROBING

The technique known as *quadratic probing* is similar to linear probing while trying to avoid the clustering problem. If the location h(key) is occupied, the first alternative space tried is the same as with linear probing, i.e., $h(\text{key}) + 1$. However, if that is occupied also, the second alternative space tried is $h(\text{key}) + 2^2$. In general, the kth alternative space tried is $h(\text{key}) + k^2$ (with wraparound of the array taken into account as usual). The gaps forced by the squared term spread out items that have the same hash number. However, it makes retrieving information already stored slightly more difficult because of the computation of the squared term.

4.1.3 REHASHING

Both linear and quadratic probing can be seen as specific examples of a more general approach usually called *rehashing* or *double hashing*. (Although sometimes "rehashing" is the name given to an algorithm that constructs a new hash table after the first one has become inefficient due to numerous deletions of elements.) This technique has several variants.

One version is a probing version, in that if $h(\text{key})$ is occupied, the kth alternative space tried is $h(\text{key}) + z_k$ (with wraparound of the array taken into account as usual). Here z_k is not simply k (as in the linear probing case) or k^2 (as in the quadratic probing case), but a more general function, such as $k * p$ where p is relatively prime to the size of the array (which ideally is a prime number as well).

Another version uses a sequence of hashing functions, h_1, h_2, h_3, etc. In other words, if $h_1(\text{key})$ is occupied, the $h_2(\text{key})$ is tried and so on, using a new hash function on the original key rather than merely modifying the first hash number obtained.

4.1.4 BUCKET

A different approach to the collision problem is taken by the *bucket* approach in which collisions are expected and integrated into the procedure. The storage array is subdivided into a number of contiguous regions called "buckets," and all records that hash to the same value are stored in the same bucket. Ideally, even though a secondary linear search is often necessary, since records with the same hash value are stored in a contiguous region, this approach can be faster than the previous three methods.

This method can be particularly useful when the number of items stored is large and an external disk file is used. The hash number can actually correspond to an address on the disk. Since disk reads are frequently done by blocks of information rather than by a single byte, the entire bucket can be read quickly from disk into fast memory for a secondary search.

4.1.5 CHAINING

Chaining is conceptually similar to the *bucket method,* and some writers refer to both methods by one title. Chaining is also called a *linked* method. It is sometimes subdivided into *separate chaining* (if a dynamic allocation of nodes in the chain is used) and *coalesced chaining* (if all the storage space has been previously declared in a linear storage scheme as in the linear implementation of lists in Section D.2.2).

The basic technique is this: suppose information is being inserted into an array and location h(key) is occupied. A linked list (i.e., a "chain") is created rooted at h(key), and all records having the same hash value are stored in it. In many implementations, nothing is actually stored in the head node, since it is merely a pointer to the storage nodes that form the chain. In the following example, the hash function is h(key) = key mod 10.

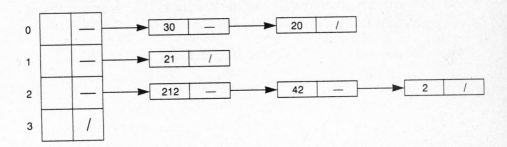

Chaining has many of the same advantages and disadvantages as does the bucket method. Both require a sequential search after the proper chain or bucket has been found. However, both avoid possibly lengthy searches (or involved calculations) that may occur with the probing methods.

5. ADVANCED SORTING

5.1 HEAP SORT

5.1.1 BASIC DEFINITIONS

Heap sort is the first sorting algorithm to be examined that does not make use of an array as its fundamental data type for its derivation and analysis. It is based on the ADT of a binary tree. Before examining the algorithm itself, some new terminology is presented.

A *strictly binary tree* is a binary tree in which every node has degree 0 or 2.

An *almost complete binary tree* is a strictly binary tree of depth $k+1$ such that:

1) every leaf is either at level k or level $k + 1$;

2) at level k, all leaves are to the right of nodes with children, (i.e., the internal nodes).

A *heap structure* is either an almost complete binary tree of depth $k + 1$ or a modified almost complete binary tree of depth $k + 1$ such that the rightmost internal node at level k has just a left child (and, thus the tree is not strictly binary).

A *heap* is a heap structure such that the key at any node is greater than the keys at each of its (possible) descendants.

The following example illustrates these definitions.

Strictly binary, but   not almost complete binary.

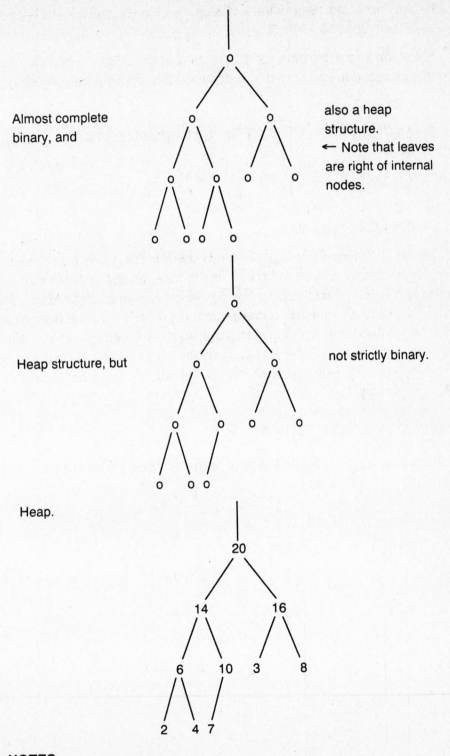

Almost complete binary, and also a heap structure.
← Note that leaves are right of internal nodes.

Heap structure, but not strictly binary.

Heap.

NOTES

A) In a heap, the root contains the largest key.

B) Any path from the root to a leaf is ordered. For example, in the last tree above, $20 \geq 14 \geq 10 \geq 7$.

The *Heap Sort Algorithm* consists of three major steps, the first of which is done once, and the other two repeated until the sorting is completed.

1) CREATE a heap.

2) EXCHANGE the last item of the sublist (last active leaf) with the first (root).

3) ADJUST the heap.

5.1.2   CREATING THE HEAP

There are various ways to perform this step. One way is to take elements from an input source, and add them, one by one, as new leaves to a heap structure (all the while keeping the figure a heap structure). After each insertion, the tree is adjusted to make sure it is properly ordered. Because of the nature of the structure and the fact that it was a heap before each insertion, only the path from the new leaf to the root needs to be checked and, if necessary, elements in that path readjusted. This algorithm is illustrated by the following example.

Input list to be sorted: 2 7 5 4 1 9 8 3

(The starred nodes indicate the only path that needs to be checked and re-adjusted if necessary.)

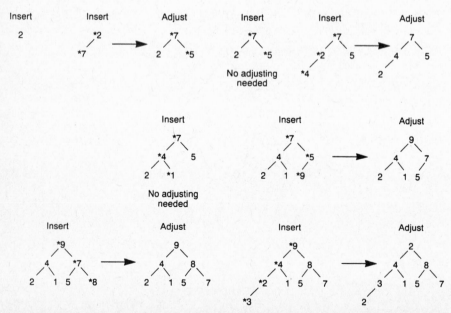

A common alternate algorithm is to put all elements into a heap structure first and then turn the structure into a heap. This process is done by looking at each parent node, starting with the rightmost parent in the next to last level, and moving right to left in each level and upwards level by level until the root is reached. Each parent is compared with its children and is exchanged with the larger of its children, if necessary. If a child itself has descendants, this process is repeated until a leaf is reached. Only one path from a parent node to a leaf offspring needs to be checked.

5.1.3 EXCHANGING ELEMENTS AND ADJUSTING

By definition, in a heap the root contains the largest item. This item can be stored by being moved to the last leaf (which is then ignored), and replacing the root with the previous contents of the last leaf. Then the heap structure needs to be adjusted back to be a heap. However, (once again) this means only having to examine one path from the root to a leaf. Starting with the root, the item in a node is exchanged with the larger of the two children, and this process is repeated either until both children are smaller than the parent node, or until a leaf has been reached.

The complete algorithm consists of a loop that repeats the exchange of the root with the "last" leaf of the "active" section of the tree and the re-adjustment of the heap structure into a heap. Each time through this exchange-adjustment step, the "active" section of the tree is shortened by one leaf. At the end, if the entire tree is traversed, in what is sometimes called a "level" order traversal (i.e., one level at a time, from left to right, starting at level 0, i.e., the root) (see Section D.6.2) the elements will be in order. This algorithm is illustrated by the following example that starts with the completed tree at the end of the previous example.

(The starred nodes indicate the only path that needs to be checked and re-adjusted if necessary).

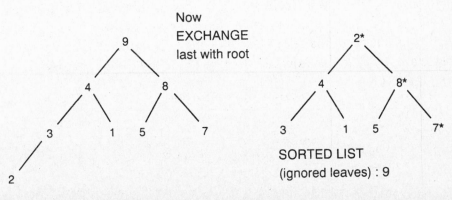

Now
EXCHANGE
last with root

SORTED LIST
(ignored leaves) : 9

Now READJUST tree

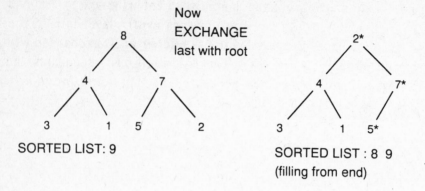

Now
EXCHANGE
last with root

SORTED LIST: 9

SORTED LIST : 8 9
(filling from end)

Now READJUST tree

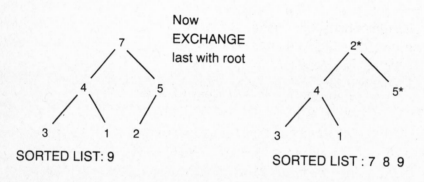

Now
EXCHANGE
last with root

SORTED LIST: 9

SORTED LIST : 7 8 9

The rest of the steps are similar and are omitted.

5.1.4 IMPLEMENTATION

A tree that is a heap structure can be stored linearly in an array fairly simply, level by level, starting with the root at level 0. Not every tree can be stored so easily, but in a tree that is a heap structure, each level (except possibly the last) has all possible nodes, and in the last level any missing nodes are to the right of all the rest. The following heap structure has the nodes labeled according to the array locations in which they would be stored.

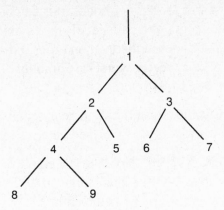

Given this tree, the relation between the locations of a node and its children can be established by doubling the parent's location (and adding 1) to get the child's location. For example,

the children of node 1 are nodes 2 and 3
the children of node 3 are nodes 6 and 7
the children of node 4 are nodes 8 and 9

Using this scheme for determining the locations of child nodes and parent nodes, heap sort is usually implemented linearly, using an array, even though the theory of trees was needed to design the algorithm.

5.1.5   BRIEF ANALYSIS

The theory of trees is also helpful in analyzing heapsort. A heap-structure is a binary tree, and a binary tree of depth m has $2^{m+1} - 1$ nodes maximum. For example,

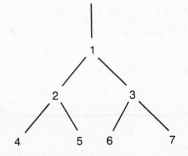

has depth 2 — THEREFORE the maximum number of nodes is $2^{2+1} - 1 = 8 - 1 = 7$

After the heap is set up, only elements in one path from a root to a leaf need to be examined, and this is done only once for each node. Since the length of a path, at most, is *m* for a tree of $2^{m+1} - 1$ nodes, this can be written as $\log_2 n$ for a tree of *n* nodes. The length of a path equals the (maximum) number of comparisons needed to put nodes in that path in order. Since this process of ordering is repeated for each node, the worst case amount of work needed for the heap sort algorithm is (less than) *n* times $\log_2 n$ or $O(n \log n)$.

Because this is significantly faster than the elementary algorithms presented in Chapter 2, heap sort is usually termed an advanced method.

To compare heap sort with an elementary method, a list of 32 items requires around 160 comparisons for heap sort, but 1024 comparisons for bubble sort (since bubble sort is an $O(n^2)$ algorithm).

5.2   QUICK SORT

Many versions of quick sort exist. Some of them are recursive while others are non-recursive in the hopes of obtaining greater efficiency. The recursive versions generally follow this pattern.

Given a list of elements in an array *L* as follows:

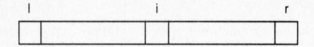

quick sort subdivides the list appropriately, and calls itself on both sections of the divided list. The subdivision of the list is done by routine *Split* which does most of the work in this algorithm. Split can be said to "semi-sort" the items in the array by rearranging them and choosing the division point so that all the elements in the left section are less than all the elements in the right section. The following sample code shows how straightforward the overall quick sort algorithm is. For simplicity, the array to be sorted, *L*, is assumed to be a global variable. The two arguments, *l* and *r,* are the pointers to the left and right items in the subsection being processed.

```
PROCEDURE Quicksort(l,r:INTEGER)
VAR i:INTEGER;
BEGIN
    IF l < r THEN
        BEGIN
            Split(l,r,i);
            Quicksort(l,i–1 );
            Quicksort(i+1,r)
        END
```

END;

The routine Split (sometimes called Partition or Rearrange) "semi-sorts" the elements in the array by the following steps:

1) It chooses some comparand element x.

2) It divides the list into two sections (not necessarily of equal lengths), such that,

   a) in the left (first) section, $L[1]$ to $L[i]$, each element is less than x and

   b) in the right (other) section, $L[i + 1]$ to $L[r]$, each element is greater than (or equal to) x.

There are numerous ways to code the routine Split, as well as numerous ways to choose the comparand element x. Some of the major choices for x are: the first element in the array, the middle element, or the first element not equal to a previous element. The following diagrams and codes demonstrate one version of Split.

Array L (to be sorted):

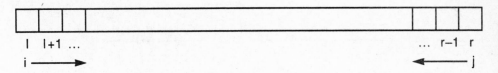

Let x be some element (see choices given above).

```
i:=l; j:=r; (* local pointers to left and right ends *)
REPEAT
    WHILE L[ j ] >= x DO j:=j–1; (* locate an item too small *)
    WHILE L[ i ] < x DO i:=i+1; (* locate an item too large *)
    IF i<=j THEN
        BEGIN (* switch misplaced items *)
            temp:=L[ j ];
            L[ j ]:=L[ i ];
            L[ i ]:=temp
        END
UNTIL j <= i;
```

Example:
First time through REPEAT loop.

x=5   3   2   8   5   9   4   1   (j does
(middle   not
element)   move)

i ──────────► i ─────────────────── j

Second time through REPEAT loop.

3   2   1   5   9   4   8

i ──► i   j ◄── j

Third time through REPEAT loop (pointer cross — no exchange).

3   2   1   4   9   5   8

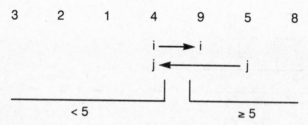

i ──► i
j ◄────── j

        < 5   ≥ 5

Quick sort is $O(n^2)$ for the worst case, but in the average case it is $O(n \log n)$. Tests published in the book "Data Structures + Algorithms = Programs" by Niklaus Wirth (the designer of the language Pascal) indicate that quick sort even beats heap sort by a factor of 2 to 3.

5.3   INDEX SORTING

Sometimes an auxiliary array is used in a sorting routine such that this auxiliary array modifies the indices of the actual array containing the information, and such that the items in the auxiliary array are exchanged, rather than (the possibly huge number of) items in the main array. Such a strategy is called **index sorting** (or key sorting, auxiliary array sorting, or sorting by address).

Instead of being a separate sorting scheme, this approach is used in conjunction with other standard methods. A favorite sorting scheme is actually used, but the code is modified so that items in the auxiliary array are exchanged rather than those in the main array. This strategy is especially appropriate when dealing with large records, especially when the records are stored in separate arrays (as is sometimes necessary in FORTRAN or BA-SIC).

COMMENT

Whether one writes in FORTRAN or Pascal, the amount of work done to exchange large records is the same. However, the coding may be (deceptively) simpler in Pascal. For example, given

```
TYPE  line = RECORD
          id: INTEGER
          name: ARRAY [1 . . 30] OF CHAR;
          address: ARRAY [1 . . 30] OF CHAR;
          state: ARRAY [1 . . 2] OF CHAR;
          zip; INTEGER
          END;

VAR list   :   ARRAY [1 . .100] OF line;
    temp   :   line;
```

then
```
          line[ i ] := temp;
```

is actually equivalent to *64* separate assignment statements. Whether it is written out as 64 statements (FORTRAN or BASIC) or written out as one (Pascal, Modula-2, Ada), the amount of work done and the time involved is the same.

When index sorting is used, an auxiliary array is set up that contains the indices (i.e., subscripts) of the elements of the array containing the items to be sorted. Then the code of the sorting routine is modified so that (1) the elements in the information array are always accessed by means of an index array element and (2) only elements in the index array are exchanged. This process is illustrated in the following:

STRATEGY

(1) compare x[index[i] with x[index[j]]
(2) exchange index[i] with index[j] if necessary.

(**Note:** The original array x remains unchanged!)

Using the bubble sort scheme:

subscript	1	2	3	4	5
x array	15	0	1	20	4
index array	1	2	3	4	5

The following comparisons are done:

x[index[1]] = x[1] = 15 ?<? x[index[2]] = x[2] = 0 NO!
    Exchange index[1] and index[2]
x[index[2]] = x[1] = 15 ?<? x[index[3]] = x[3] = 1 NO!
    Exchange index[2] and index[3]
x[index[3]] = x[1] = 15 ?<? x[index[4]] = x[4] = 20 ok
x[index[4]] = x[4] = 20 ?<? x[index[5]] = x[5] = 4 NO!
    Exchange index[4] and index[5]

After one pass, the original array stays the same, but the index array has been modified.

Using the bubble sort scheme:

subscript	1	2	3	4	5
x array	15	0	1	20	4
index array	2	3	1	5	4

The following comparisons are done in the next pass:

x[index[1]] = x[2] = 0 ?<? x[index[2]] = x[3] = 1 ok
x[index[2]] = x[3] = 1 ?<? x[index[3]] = x[1] = 15 ok
x[index[3]] = x[1] = 15 ?<? x[index[4]] = x[5] = 4 NO!
    Exchange index[3] and index[4]
x[index[4]] = x[1] = 15 ?<? x[index[5]] = x[4] = 20 ok

The index array now is:

subscript	1	2	3	4	5
x array	15	0	1	20	4
indexarray	2	3	1	5	4

The elements in the x array have now been ordered (even though only two passes were done). Notice that the index array gives this order, i.e., the second element (in the *x* array) is the smallest, then comes the third then the fifth then the first, and finally, the fourth (which is the largest element).

Any regular version of a sorting algorithm can be modified to be an index version. An index array must be included in the code, and the array must be initialized properly (normally such that index[*i*] = *i*). In addition, any comparison lines need to be altered so that the items are compared through the index array (as in the example above), and the switching section modified so that the elements of the index array are switched rather than the items in the main array.

6.   NUMERICAL INTEGRATION

Study this section for the 'AB' exam.

Some of the first applications of computers were complex numerical calculations. These involved issues such as solving equations, evaluating functions, numerical integration (finding the area of a region of a plane that is not necessarily bounded by a polygon), and working with differential equations. In several of these areas the methods of calculation were known, but they were complex and cumbersome for human work.

Equations may be solved either by the use of known formulas or by methods of approximation. The bisection method and Newton-Rapson method involve approximating solutions over smaller and smaller intervals. Where formulas exist for the solutions of an equation, such as the quadratic formula, these formulas may be used. In some cases other numerical methods may be used if the number of calculations is unreasonable. Similarly, there are formulas for approximation of values of functions which may be used instead of calculating the function directly. An example of the Monte Carlo method, being used to find an approximation of pi, follows.

Various methods exist for performing numerical integration. The area of a region of the plane which is bounded by differentiable functions may be determined exactly using methods of integral calculus. These areas may be approximated using a computer. All of the methods involve approximating the area of the region by calculating the area of many polygons. These polygons, such as rectangles or trapezoids, are constructed so they approximate the region whose area is to be determined. By increasing the number of polygons and determining the area of each we can determine a good approximation of the area of the region.

Differential equations are equations which deal with the rate of change of a function. Numerical methods, calculations, for solving these were well known before the advent of digital computers. Since these methods can be specified precisely with an algorithm, it is not difficult to use a computer for these methods.

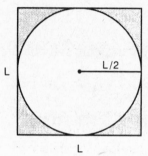

L

L/2

L

FIG. 1

Ex. Monte Carlo methods typically use random digits to solve problems which have no inherently random properties. For the approximation of pi, we need the dart board analogy. We have a square board with an inscribed circle, as in Fig. 1. Suppose we have monkeys that have been trained to toss darts at the board. Now, assuming all the darts land somewhere on the board, and assuming that a dart can land anywhere with equal likelihood, we ask: what is the probability that a dart will land inside the circle?

If you remember the equations for the areas of a circle and a square ($A = \pi(L/2)^2$ and $A = L^2$, respectively), you can discover that the probability equals the ratio of the circle's area to the square's area, or $\pi/4$, which is about 0.7854. For our example, we do not know π. However, if we could get the monkeys to throw a large number of darts at the board, we could compute the proportion of hits falling inside the circle. From this proportion, we can find an approximation for π.

The following pseudocode generates randomly the X- and Y- coordinates of each "dart" thrown at the board. Since these coordinates lie between 0 and 1, darts appear only in the positive quadrant of the square (the top right corner). However, the full figure can be built from four identical pieces, so the result remains the same. We must multiply $\pi/4$ by 4 to get the desired result.

Also note that if we increase the number of darts thrown, the degree of deviation from the expected result decreases. This axiom is called in statistics the "law of large numbers." We are testing for 4-digit accuracy in this problem. Our output consists of the number of darts, the approximate value of π, and the deviation from the expected result.

(Monte Carlo method for finding the approximation of pi)

```
program montecarlo;
var i, darts, n, count: integer
    approx, x, y: real;
begin
    n := 0;
    count := 0;
    writeln('input the number of darts to be tossed')
    readln(darts);
    while darts > 0 do begin
        for i := 1 to darts do begin
            x := random; {Assume random to be an expression}
            y := random; {that finds a random #}
    {Check to see if dart has landed inside circle}
            if ((x*x) + (y*y)) < 0 then count := count + 1;
            end; {for}
        n := n + darts
        approx := count/n * 4
        writeln(n,approx,approx - 3.1416);
        end;
end.
```

A NOTE ON ETHICAL ISSUES

Computers have become the core of modern technology — society would not be able to function as it does without computers. Yet there are ethical concerns that arise with the use of computers.

Such issues arise with respect to the copying of software programs, the compilation of private information of individuals, the unauthorized use of hardware, etc. As society becomes increasingly computerized, new problems such as these result. Is copying your friend's software program for yourself immoral, not to mention illegal? Should companies be allowed to reveal whatever statistics their computers have generated on individuals?

It is not the purpose here to provide answers to these dilemmas. Rather, students should make themselves aware of the social ramifications of computers and understand the possible solutions.

ADVANCED PLACEMENT EXAMINATION IN
COMPUTER SCIENCE A

Test 1

ADVANCED PLACEMENT EXAMINATION IN
COMPUTER SCIENCE

Answer Sheet

1. Ⓐ Ⓑ Ⓒ Ⓓ Ⓔ
2. Ⓐ Ⓑ Ⓒ Ⓓ Ⓔ
3. Ⓐ Ⓑ Ⓒ Ⓓ Ⓔ
4. Ⓐ Ⓑ Ⓒ Ⓓ Ⓔ
5. Ⓐ Ⓑ Ⓒ Ⓓ Ⓔ
6. Ⓐ Ⓑ Ⓒ Ⓓ Ⓔ
7. Ⓐ Ⓑ Ⓒ Ⓓ Ⓔ
8. Ⓐ Ⓑ Ⓒ Ⓓ Ⓔ
9. Ⓐ Ⓑ Ⓒ Ⓓ Ⓔ
10. Ⓐ Ⓑ Ⓒ Ⓓ Ⓔ
11. Ⓐ Ⓑ Ⓒ Ⓓ Ⓔ
12. Ⓐ Ⓑ Ⓒ Ⓓ Ⓔ
13. Ⓐ Ⓑ Ⓒ Ⓓ Ⓔ
14. Ⓐ Ⓑ Ⓒ Ⓓ Ⓔ
15. Ⓐ Ⓑ Ⓒ Ⓓ Ⓔ
16. Ⓐ Ⓑ Ⓒ Ⓓ Ⓔ
17. Ⓐ Ⓑ Ⓒ Ⓓ Ⓔ
18. Ⓐ Ⓑ Ⓒ Ⓓ Ⓔ
19. Ⓐ Ⓑ Ⓒ Ⓓ Ⓔ
20. Ⓐ Ⓑ Ⓒ Ⓓ Ⓔ

21. Ⓐ Ⓑ Ⓒ Ⓓ Ⓔ
22. Ⓐ Ⓑ Ⓒ Ⓓ Ⓔ
23. Ⓐ Ⓑ Ⓒ Ⓓ Ⓔ
24. Ⓐ Ⓑ Ⓒ Ⓓ Ⓔ
25. Ⓐ Ⓑ Ⓒ Ⓓ Ⓔ
26. Ⓐ Ⓑ Ⓒ Ⓓ Ⓔ
27. Ⓐ Ⓑ Ⓒ Ⓓ Ⓔ
28. Ⓐ Ⓑ Ⓒ Ⓓ Ⓔ
29. Ⓐ Ⓑ Ⓒ Ⓓ Ⓔ
30. Ⓐ Ⓑ Ⓒ Ⓓ Ⓔ
31. Ⓐ Ⓑ Ⓒ Ⓓ Ⓔ
32. Ⓐ Ⓑ Ⓒ Ⓓ Ⓔ
33. Ⓐ Ⓑ Ⓒ Ⓓ Ⓔ
34. Ⓐ Ⓑ Ⓒ Ⓓ Ⓔ
35. Ⓐ Ⓑ Ⓒ Ⓓ Ⓔ
36. Ⓐ Ⓑ Ⓒ Ⓓ Ⓔ
37. Ⓐ Ⓑ Ⓒ Ⓓ Ⓔ
38. Ⓐ Ⓑ Ⓒ Ⓓ Ⓔ
39. Ⓐ Ⓑ Ⓒ Ⓓ Ⓔ
40. Ⓐ Ⓑ Ⓒ Ⓓ Ⓔ

Use a separate sheet of paper to answer the free-response questions.

COMPUTER SCIENCE A

TEST 1

SECTION 1

TIME: 1 hour, 15 minutes
40 Questions

DIRECTIONS: Choose the best answer and darken the corresponding oval on your answer sheet.

1. Suppose the variables number and sum are declared and intitialized as follows.

   ```
   VAR
           number, sum : integer;
   BEGIN
           number := 16; sum := 9;
   ```

   Which of the following statements will produce the output 1.77 ?

   (A) writeln (number/sum :2 :2)

   (B) writeln (trunc(number/sum): 2)

   (C) writeln (trunc(number/sum) div 100 :2)

   (D) writeln (trunc(number/sum * 100)/100 :2 :2)

   (E) writeln (round(number/sum * 100)/100 :2 :2)

2. Suppose that a program contains only the following declarations

   ```
   CONST
           MIDDLE = 12;
   VAR
           trial: integer;
   ```

x: char;

zonae: real;

and the procedure Test has been declared as

procedure Test(var high: integer; low: real);

Which of the following procedure calls is correct?

(A) Test (trial, MIDDLE/trial)

(B) Test (MIDDLE, MIDDLE/trial)

(C) Test (MIDDLE, zonae)

(D) Test (zonae, trial)

(E) Test (MIDDLE, 53.6, zonae)

3. Which of the following best represents the output of the program

```
PROGRAM ttt( input, output);
TYPE
        color = ( red, orange, yellow, green, blue, indigo);
VAR
        x: color;
        y,z: integer;
BEGIN
        y : =0;
        z : =0;
        FOR x := red TO indigo DO
        BEGIN
                y:= y + 1;
                z := z + ord(x);
        END;
        writeln( y, z);
END.
```

(A) 6   10

(B) 6   15

(C) 6   21

(D) 5   10

(E) No output. The program contains an error.

4. Assume that the computer system upon which the following statement is executed uses the ASCII collating sequence. Which of the following best describes the output produced by the statement writeln(chr(ord('a') –1)) ?

(A) The character immediately following 'a' in the ASCII collating sequence.

(B) The character immediately preceding 'a' in the ASCII collating sequence.

(C) The character 'Z' (an upper-case Z).

(D) The integer corresponding to the character which precedes 'a' in the ASCII collating sequence.

(E) No output. The statement contains an error.

5. What are the values stored in the variables x and y after the following sequence of statements is executed?

```
x := 600;
        IF( x >= 0 ) THEN
                IF( x < 1000 ) THEN
                BEGIN
                        y: = 2 * x;
                        IF( x < 400 ) THEN
                        x := x div 10;
                END
                ELSE
                        y: = 3 * x
        ELSE
        y := –x;
```

(A) x = 600   y = –600

(B) x = 600   y = 1200

(C) x = 600   y = 1800

(D) x = 60   y = 1200

(E) x = 60   y = 1800

6. Consider the following program.

```
program aaa;
var n: integer;
procedure ccc(M:integer);
var u: integer;
begin
        if ( M > 0) then begin
                u := m div 2;
                ccc ( u );
                u:= m mod 2;
                write(u:1);
        end;
end;
begin
        read(n);
        while ( n < > 0 ) do
        begin
                write( n:12, ' ');
                if(n = 0)then
                        write ("0")
                else ccc(n);
                writeln;
                read(n);
        end;
end.
```

If the input is 5 34 0 what is the output?

(A)   5   101

         34   100010

(B)   5   101

         34   100010

                0 0

(C)   5   555

                 34   444333

(D)   No output. The program contains an error.

(E)   None of the above since the program contains an infinite loop.

Use the following loops for questions 7 through 11.

```
{LOOP A}
x = 0;
while (x < 99) do
begin
    readln(i);
    x := x + i;
end;
```

```
{LOOP C}
x := 0;
for i:= 1 to 99 do
begin
            readln(x);
            x:= x + x;
end;
```

```
{LOOP B}
x:= 0;
i:= 0;
while ( i <> 99 ) do
begin
    readln(i);
    x: = x + i
end;
```

```
{LOOP D}
x:= 0;
i:= 0;
while ( i <> 99 ) do
begin
        x :=x + i;
        readln(i);
end;
```

7. The statement "The statements in this loop are executed 99 times" best describes the actions indicated by

(A) LOOP A

(B) LOOP B

(C) LOOP C

(D) LOOP D

(E) LOOP A and LOOP C

8. The statement "This loop terminates after i has the value 99 and before i has been added to x" best describes the actions indicated by

(A) LOOP A

(B) LOOP B

(C) LOOP C

(D) LOOP D

(E) LOOP A and LOOP C

9. The statement "This loop terminates after i has the value 99 and after i has been added to x" best describes the actions indicated by

    (A) LOOP A

    (B) LOOP B

    (C) LOOP C

    (D) LOOP D

    (E) LOOP A and LOOP C

10. The statement "This loop terminates after the value of x is greater than or equal 99" best describes the actions indicated by

    (A) LOOP A

    (B) LOOP B

    (C) LOOP C

    (D) LOOP D

    (E) LOOP A and LOOP C

11. The statement "This loop stops after the value of i is 99." best describes the actions indicated by

    (A) LOOP A

    (B) LOOP B

    (C) LOOP C

    (D) LOOP D

    (E) LOOP B and LOOP D

12. In the following program fragment the procedure SORTUM needs to be declared and defined.

    ```
    program tester;
            type intarr = array [1..100] of integer;
    var
            numbers: intarr;

    { Declare and define SORTUM here }
    ```

```
        begin
        .
        .
        .
        SORTUM(numbers);
        .
        end.
```

Assume the purpose of SORTUM is to sort the elements in its parameter list in ascending order. So before SORTUM is called as it is below we don't assume anything about the order of the elements of **numbers,** and after it is called we assume that the elements of **numbers** are arranged in ascending order. The declaration for the procedure SORTUM should be

(A) procedure SORTUM (sortarr: integer);

(B) procedure SORTUM (sortarr: intarr);

(C) procedure SORTUM (var sortarr: intarr);

(D) procedure SORTUM (var sortarr: array [1 .. 100] of integer);

(E) procedure SORTUM (var sortarr: numbers);

13. A Software system goes through specific phases called the software life-cycle. The phases in alphabetical order are analysis, coding, design, maintenance, and testing/verification. Which of the following gives the five phases in the order they usually occur?

(A) analysis, coding, design, maintenance, testing/verification

(B) coding, analysis, design, maintenance, testing/verification

(C) coding, design, analysis, testing/verification, maintenance

(D) analysis, design, coding, testing/verification, maintenance

(E) design, testing/verification, analysis, coding, maintenance

14. Consider the following statements.

1. In order to apply a binary search algorithm to a list the list must be sorted.

2. A binary search consists of deciding which half of a list contains the value in question and then which half of that half, and so on.

3. A sequential search of a list consists of examining the first item in the list and then proceeding through the list until the desired item is found or the end of the list is reached.

4. The difference in time it takes to perform a sequential search compared to the time it takes to perform a binary search decreases as the size of the list increases.

5. If we need to search a list which changes often then it is best to use a binary search.

Which of the above statements are false?

(A) 3 and 4

(B) 4 and 5

(C) 1, 2, and 3

(D) 1, 3, and 5

(E) None, all are true.

15. If we have the declaration

```
var
        A: array [1 .. 10] of boolean;
```

then which of the following is a correct statement?

(A) A has exactly two elements or members.

(B) A can hold ten elements or members.

(C) Each element of A is an integer in the range of 1 through 10.

(D) The ASCII code for each element of A is either 0 or 1.

(E) None of the statements (A) – (D) is a correct statement.

Use the program below for questions 16 and 17. The program below takes its input from a file which contains only the lines

```
34   12   –5   16   24

30   1

–10       56
```

```
program sono(inf, output);
CONST maxnum = 5;
var
        num : array[0 .. maxnum] of integer;
        k, j : integer;
        inf : text;
begin
        reset( inf, 'MWC');
        num[0] := 123;
        for k := 1 to maxnum do
                if ( k MOD 3 = 0 ) then
                        readln(inf, num[k])
                else
                        read(inf, num[k]);
{ * * * FIRST OUTPUT LOOP * * * }
        for j := 0 to maxnum do
                write(num[j]:3);
{ * * * FIRST OUTPUT LOOP * * * }
        for k := 1 to maxnum–1 do
        begin
                num[0] := num[k+1];
                j: = k;
                while( num[j] > num[0]) do
                begin
                        num[j + 1] : = num[j];
                        j := j – 1;
                end;
                num[ j + 1 ]: = num[0];
        end;
{*** SECOND OUTPUT LOOP ***}
        for j := 0 to maxnum do
                write(num[j] :3);
{*** SECOND OUTPUT LOOP ***}
end.
```

16. The output produced by the statements surrounded by the comments {*** FIRST OUTPUT LOOP ***} is

   (A) 123 34   12   -5   30   -10

   (B) 123 34   12   -5   30   1

   (C) 123 34   12   -5   16   24

   (D) 34   12   30   1   -10 56

   (E) No output. The program aborts abnormally because it runs out of input.

17. The output produced by the statements surrounded by the comments {*** SECOND OUTPUT LOOP ***} is

   (A) 56   -5   12   24   34   56

   (B) 1   -5   1   12   30   34

   (C) -10 -10 -5   1   12   30

   (D) 56   -10 1   12   30   56

   (E) No output. The program aborts abnormally because it runs out of input.

18. Assume the input to the following program fragment is

   That's as good, or better, than WonderWord.

```
repeat
    read(ch);
    if ( (ch <= 'Z') and (ch >= 'A') ) then
    repeat
        write(ch);
        read(ch);
        if ( (ch <= 'z') and (ch >= 'a') ) then
            ch := chr( ord(ch) + ord('A') - ord('a') );
    until ( ( ch = ' ') or (ch = '.') );
    write( ch );
until ch = '.';
```

   The output is

(A) THAT'S AS GOOD, OR BETTER, THAN WONDERWORD.

(B) that's as good, or better, than wonderword.

(C) That's as good, or better, than WonderWord.

(D) THAT'S as good, or better, than WONDERWORD.

(E) THAT'S as good, or better, than WONDERWord.

19. A way to declare a two-dimensional array with 60 rows and 5 columns so that each entry has a value which represents a letter grade of either 'A', 'B', 'C', 'D', 'E', or 'F' and so that if, by mistake, someone assigns a grade different from those then a run-time or compile-time error results is

(A) bobo: array [1..60,1..5] of 'A' .. 'F'

(B) bobo: array [1..60, 'A' .. 'F'] of integer

(C) bobo: array [1..60,1..5] of char

(D) bobo: array [1..60] of 1.. 5

(E) This cannot be done in Pascal.

20. Assume the input to the following program fragment is

That's as good, or better, than WonderWord.

```
read( letter );
while ( letter < > '.') do
begin
        if ( letter < > ',' ) then
                write(letter)
        else
                writeln;
        read(letter);
end
```

The output is

(A) That's as good, or better, than WonderWord.

(B) That's as good
     or better
     than wonderword.

(C) That's as good
     or better
     than WonderWord

(D) THAT'S as good,
     or better,
     than WonderWord.

(E) THAT'S as good
     , or better
     , than WONDERWord.

21. Consider the following program.

```
program goo(input, output);
var
        unix, operating    :    integer;
        dos, system        :    char;
procedure cat( var cronos: integer; zeus: char);
begin
        readln ( cronos );
        cronos := cronos + ord(zeus) – ord('a');
        zeus := 'z';
end;
begin
        readln( dos, operating);
        unix := 6;
        system := 'c';
        writeln( unix:3, operating:3, dos:3, system:3);
        cat( unix, dos);
        writeln( unix:3, operating:3, dos:3, system:3);
end.
```

If the input is in the form

    a7

    8

    6

    9

then the output is

(A) 6   7   a   c
     8   7   a   c

(B) 6   7   a   c
    10   7   z   c

(C) 8   6   a7 c
     8   6   a7 c

(D) a   c   6   7
     a   c   10   7

(E) None of these are correct.

22. Given the following type and var declarations

```
TYPE
      data     =    array [ 1..20, 'a' ...'z' ] of char
      strung   =    packed array [ 1..40 ] of char;
      wn       =    array [ 1 ..40 ] of integer;
VAR
      first, second:    data;
      long  :    strung;
      why  :    wn;
```

which of the statements below would not cause any compile-time errors?

{1} first[0, 'a'] := second [1, 'z'];

{2} why[2*4 div 4]:= ord(long[2]);

{3} first[why[2, long [why[2]]] := 'e';

{4} first[why[2], long [why[2]]] := succ (long[1]);

(A) All of them.

(B) The ones labeled {1}, {3}, and {4}.

(C) The ones labeled {2} and {4}.

(D) The ones labeled {1} and {3}.

(E) The ones labeled {2}, {3}, and {4}.

23. For the expressions

    ```
    MAXINT mod 5
    25/5
    25 div 5
    chr( 5 + ord ('0') )
    ```

    we can say

    (A) they are all of type integer.

    (B) only the last one would cause an error.

    (C) they are all equal to five.

    (D) they are of type integer, real, integer, and char.

    (E) they are all representations of zero.

Use the following function for questions numbered 24 – 26.

```
function sumn(n:integer):integer;
var
        i, j : integer;
begin
        if n < 0 then
                sumn := -1
        else if n = 0 then
                sumn := 0
        else if n > 0 then
                sumn := n + sumn(n-1);
end;
```

24. The statement sumn := n + sumn(n–1) indicates a recursive call to the function sumn. A recursive call to the function sumn will occur if

    (A) n is greater than or equal to 1.

    (B) n is greater than 1.

    (C) n is 0 or 1.

    (D) n is negative.

    (E) n is greater than 2.

25. The number of recursive calls to sumn that will be made to compute sumn(5).

    (A) 3

    (B) 4

    (C) 5

    (D) 6

    (E) 7

26. Which of the following looping constructs does the same job as the recursive function above?

    (A) function sumn(n : integer):integer;
    ```
                var i, t : integer;
                begin
                sumn := -1;
                if ( n >= 0) then
                begin
                        for i := 1 to n do
                                t := t + i;
                        sumn := t;
                end;
                end;
    ```

    (B) function sumn(n : integer):integer;
    ```
                var i, t : integer;
                begin
                sumn := -1;
                if ( n >= 0) then
                begin
                        t := 0;
                        for i := 1 to n do
                                t := t + i;
                sumn := t;
            end;
            end;
    ```

    (C) function sumn(n : integer):integer;
    ```
                var i, t : integer;
                begin
    ```

```
                    if ( n > 0) then
                    begin
                          t := 0;
                          for i := 1 to n do
                                t := t + i;
                    sumn := t;
              end;
              end;

(D)    function sumn(n : integer):integer;
              var i, t : integer;
              begin
              sumn := -1;
              if ( n >= 0) then
              begin
                    t := 0;
                    for i := 1 to n do
                          sumn := t + i;
       end;
       end;
(E)    None of the above.
```

27. There must be a relationship between the formal parameter list in a procedure heading and the actual parameter list used in a calling program. This relationship is best described as

    (A) The formal parameters and the actual parameters must match in number, type, and name.

    (B) The formal parameters must be of the same type as the actual parameters.

    (C) The formal parameters must have the same names as the actual parameters.

    (D) There must be at least as many formal parameters as actual parameters.

    (E) The formal parameters and the actual parameters must match in type and number.

28. Which of the following is not true of local variables? By local variables we mean those declared within a subprogram.

    (A) Any for statement in a subprogram must use a local variable as its control variable.

(B)   A local variable cannot have the same name of a variable declared in a block which contains the subprogram.

(C)   A local variable is not defined outside of the subprogram in which it is declared.

(D)   A local variable may be used for input and/or output.

(E)   All of the above statements are true.

For questions 29 through 33 use the following declarations.

```
CONST
        namlength = 30;
TYPE
        sex = (male, female);
        namearay = packed array [1 .. namlength] of char;
        student = record
                name : namearray;
                gpa : real;
                gender : sex;
        end;
    var
        class : array [1..100] of student;
```

29.   The identifier that represents the name field of the fifth record in the array class is

(A)   class[5].student.name

(B)   class.student.name[5]

(C)   class[5].name

(D)   class.name[5]

(E)   class[5].student

30.   In order to determine whether the gpa of the tenth and the gpa of the twentieth records in the array class are equal one would use the expression

(A)   gpa[10] = gpa[20]

(B)   gpa[10].class = gpa[20].class

(C)   class.gpa[10] = class.gpa[20]

(D)   class[10].gpa = class[20].gpa

(E)   nothing, the two cannot be compared.

31.   The statements

```
for i : = 1 to 100 do
with class[i]
        if gender = male then
                nummales := nummales + 1
        else
                numfemales := numfemales + 1;
```

are best described by

(A)   Nummales and numfemales will hold the number of males and females represented by the records in the array class.

(B)   Nummales and numfemales will hold the number of males and females represented by the records in the array class, provided that nummales and numfemales are declared and initialized properly.

(C)   May generate a run-time error if there is one record in the array class for which the field gender is not properly initialized.

(D)   Will generate a compile-time error because the proper reference to the filed gpa is class.gpa[i].

(E)   Will generate both a run-time and a compile-time error.

32.   When an array is a parameter to a procedure it is not true that

(A)   if it is declared as a var parameter then its size may change during execution of the program.

(B)   if it is declared as a var parameter then less space has to be allocated for it than if it were declared as a value parameter.

(C)   if it is declared as a value parameter then any changes to its members are not communicated to the calling program.

(D)   if it is declared as a value parameter then space must be allocated for all elements of the array.

(E)   None of these statements is correct.

33.   Which of the following declares an array with the most elements?

(A)   x : array [1 .. 3, 1 .. 5, 1 .. 5] of boolean;

(B)   x : array [−10 .. 10] of boolean;

(C)   x : array [0 .. 5, −8 .. 0] of boolean;

(D)   x : array [1 .. 6, 1 .. 9] of boolean;

(E)   x : array [1 .. 55] of boolean;

34.   Which of the following statements is not true about arrays?

(A)   Every element of an array must be of the same type.

(B)   The total number of elements in an array depends on the type of each element.

(C)   The amount of time to access an element is independent of its position in an array.

(D)   Pascal does not allow for arrays whose size change during execution of a program.

(E)   None of these statements is correct.

35.   Which of the following statements is not true about records?

(A)   Every field in a record must be of the same type.

(B)   The amount of time to access a field of a record is independent of its position in the record.

(C)   Pascal does not allow for a way in which to directly compare records of the same type.

(D)   The type of a function may not be a record type.

(E)   None of these statements is correct.

Use the following declarations and skeleton of a procedure for questions 36 – 38

```
procedure a;
    var x: integer;
    procedure b;
        var x : integer;
        begin
```

```
                    {body of the procedure b}
                        x := 4;

                            .

                            .

                    end; { of b }
            procedure c;
                    var y : integer;
                    begin
                      { body of the procedure c }
                            y := x + 2;

                            .

                            .

                    end; { of c }
            begin
                      { body of procedure a }
                      x := 5;
                      b;
                      c;

                        .

                        .

            end; { of a }
```

Questions 36 through 40 are based on the case study provided at the back of this book.

---

36. Which of the statements below has the effect of adding all the items from Boris's inventory to the player's inventory?

    (A) Items[PLAYER] := Items[PLAYER] + Items[BORIS]

    (B) Players[PLAYER].Items ;= Items[PLAYER] + Items[BORIS]

    (C) Characters[PLAYER].Items := Characters[BORIS].Items

    (D) Characters[PLAYER].Items := Characters[BORIS].Items +

        Characters[PLAYER].Items;

    (E) None of the above.

37. What would happen if the user issued the command "GET BORIS" while in the dining room?

    (A) The program would issue an "array subscript out of bounds" error and terminate.

(B)   Boris's character record would be added to the player's inventory.

(C)   The program would issue an "unexpected input" error and terminate.

(D)   The program would issue a "range" error and terminate.

(E)   The program would get caught in an infinite loop.

38.   What would happen if the user entered a command in lowercase rather than uppercase?

(A)   The program would issue an "array subscript out of bounds" error and terminate.

(B)   The program would get caught in an infinite loop.

(C)   The program would issue a "range" error and terminate.

(D)   The program would issue an "unexpected input" error and terminate.

(E)   None of the above.

39.   After having killed Boris, what would happen if the user entered the command "GET SWORD"?

(A)   Nothing at all, since the player already has a sword.

(B)   The player would have two swords in his inventory.

(C)   The program would issue an "unexpected input" error and terminate.

(D)   The program would issue an "illegal assignment" error and terminate.

(E)   The program would get caught in an infinite loop.

40.   If we wish to modify the program so that Boris attacks the player as soon as he (the player) enters the dining room, which procedures would have to be modified?

(A)   *Fight* and *GetCommand*

(B)   *Fight* and *InitialAction*

(C)   *InitialAction* only

(D)   *InitialAction* and *GetCommand*

(E)   None of the above.

SECTION 2

TIME: 1 hour, 45 minutes
5 Questions

> **DIRECTIONS:** Give a detailed answer, written in standard Pascal, to each problem.

1. While it is not possible to rewrite the following program fragment using 3 FOR Loops, it is possible to rewrite it using 2 FOR Loops and one WHILE Loop. Please do so. Assume that all variables are type integer.

```
i := 1;
j := -1;
k := 2;
ib := b;
WHILE( ib <= m ) DO
BEGIN
        jt := t;
        WHILE ( jt <= u )DO
        BEGIN
                kx := x;
                WHILE ( kx >= y ) DO
                BEGIN
                        n := ib + jt + kx;
                        kx := kx + j;
                END;
                jt := jt + k;
        END;
        ib := ib + i;
END
```

> Question 2 is based on the case study provided at the back of this book.

2. A nice improvement to this game system would be to restrict the amount of items the player could "carry" in his/her inventory by assigning a weight value to every item and a maximum amount of weight that a

character could carry. Show what changes would be made in the program to accommodate this change.

3. The type declarations below declares a type named addrs with the following fields (the size/type of each field is represented in the parentheses following the field name).

>   street (30 characters) city (30 characters)
>   state (2 characters) zip (15 characters)
>
> type
>
>   pa30 = packed array [1..30] of char;
>   addrs = record
>   street : pa30;
>   city   : pa30;
>   state : packed array [1..2] of char;
>   zip   : packed array [1..5] of char;
>   end;

a. Define a record type named **student** with 4 fields as follows

>   name of type pa30
>   age of type integer
>   address of type addrs
>   gpa of type real

b. Define an array type named **people** so that any object of that type would be an array of 1000 elements of type student.

c. Write a procedure name **sortstu** which has two parameters. The first, call it A, is the name of an object of type people and the second, call it B, is to be an integer. The procedure is to arrange in ascending order the first B elements of A according to the value in the field gpa. The parameter A is to be passed by reference and B is to be passed by value.

4. The surface area of a person, in square meters, can be roughly calculated as 7.184^{-3} * weight$^{0.452}$ * height$^{0.725}$ where weight is given in kilograms and height is given in centimeters. Assume one inch is equal to 2.54 centimeters and one kilogram is equal to 2.2 pounds.

a. Write a function named httocm which has two parameters and returns a person's height in centimeters as type real. Both parameters are type integer, the first represents the whole number of feet in a person's height and the second represents the remaining inches. If a person's height were 5 feet 8 inches then the first parameter would be 5 and the second 8.

b.   Write a function wttokg which has one parameter of type integer, a person's weight in pounds, and returns the person's weight in kilograms as type real.

c.   Write a function sarea which has three parameters of type integer, a the number of feet in a person's height, the remaining inches in a person's height, and a person's weight in pounds. The function should return the person's surface area as type real. Also this function should call the functions specified in parts a and b.

5.   Give all declarations necessary so that the following program has no compile-time errors. (This means to include a proper program statement, a const block if necessary, a var block if necessary, and any procedures or functions necessary. In the latter case you need only *declare* the procedure or function, you need not define it.)

```
begin
        reset( inf, 'xxin');
        rewrite( outf, 'xxout');
        while not eof(inf) do
        begin
                sum := 0.0;
                gpa := 0.0;
                idnum := round(gpa);
                read(inf, idnum);
                writeln( 'Processing : ', idnum:1);
                read(inf, grade, credits );
                sumc := 0;
                while( grade <> '$' ) do
                begin
                        sumc := sumc + credits;
                        if ( grade = Fail ) then
                                num := 0
                        else
                                num := ord('E') – ord(grade);
                        sum := sum + credits*num;
                        read(inf, grade, credits);
```

```
            end;
            gpa := rat(sum, sumc);
            writeln(outf, idnum, gpa );
        end;
    end.
```

COMPUTER SCIENCE A
TEST 1

ANSWER KEY

1.	(D)		21.	(A)
2.	(A)		22.	(C)
3.	(B)		23.	(D)
4.	(B)		24.	(A)
5.	(B)		25.	(C)
6.	(A)		26.	(B)
7.	(C)		27.	(E)
8.	(D)		28.	(B)
9.	(B)		29.	(C)
10.	(A)		30.	(D)
11.	(E)		31.	(B)
12.	(C)		32.	(A)
13.	(D)		33.	(A)
14.	(B)		34.	(B)
15.	(B)		35.	(A)
16.	(B)		36.	(D)
17.	(B)		37.	(D)
18.	(D)		38.	(C)
19.	(A)		39.	(B)
20.	(C)		40.	(C)

DETAILED EXPLANATIONS
OF ANSWERS

COMPUTER SCIENCE A
TEST 1
SECTION 1

1. **(D)**
    First we need to evaluate the expression before the first: within the parentheses of the writeln statement. The result of number/sum is type real and has the value 1.77777777..., and if we multiply that by 100 we get 177.777777... . Applying the function trunc to this we get 177 and dividing by 100 yields 1.770000... . The remainder of the specification with the writeln statement is :2 :2. This would produce 1.77 as output.

    Choice (E) is not correct because if we follow the explanation above, but substitute round for trunc we see we would get 1.78 as output. That value would also be produced by the statement labeled (A). Both choices (B) and (C) produce whole number output (no decimal point) so they are not appropriate. The output produced by (B) is 2 and the output for (C) is 0.

2. **(A)**
    The procedure Test has two parameters. The first is type integer and is passed by reference. That means that *only a variable* of type integer may be used as the argument. A constant cannot be used as the first argument. The second argument must be type real and can be either a constant or a variable or any other expression of type real. The call to Test given in (A) satisfies these requirements since trial is a variable and the expression MIDDLE/trial yields an object of type real.

    The call to Test in (B) and in (C) has a constant as its first argument and so is not valid. In choice (D) the first argument is type real and the second is type integer which is the reverse of how they should appear. Choice (E) has 3 arguments so it is not correct.

3. **(B)**
    The type color is declared and defined in the TYPE block. Any variable of type color can take the values symbolically represented by red, orange, yellow, green, blue, or indigo. If we apply the function ord to a variable of type color we get a numeric value associated with the symbolic value. The first possible value of the type color is associated with the numeric value 0, then next with the value 1, and so on. The FOR loop in the program initializes x at the value red and takes x through the value indigo. So the statements in the loop are each executed 6 times. Each time y := y + 1 is executed 1 is added to the previous value of y so y has the value 6 when the writeln statement is executed. Each time z := z + ord(x) is executed, the result of applying ord to x is added to the previous value of z. This is the same as computing 0 + 1 + 2 + 3 + 4 + 5. Thus z has the value 15 when the writeln statement is executed.
    Choice (A) has the correct value for y but 0 + 1 + 2 + 3 + 4 for z. Choice (C) also has the correct value for y but the value for z is 1 + 2 + 3 + 4 + 5 + 6. The values given in choice (D) would be correct if the first statement of the FOR loop were   FOR x := red TO blue DO

4. **(B)**
    The function ord maps a character to the decimal equivalent of the ASCII code for that character. So ord('a') –1 would be one less than the decimal equivalent of the ASCII code for 'a'. The function chr maps an integer in the range 0 to 255 to a character in the ASCII collating sequence. Here chr(ord('a')–1) yields the character immediately preceding the character a in the ASCII collating sequence.
    Choice (A) would correspond to writeln(chr(ord('a') + 1)). Choice (C) is not correct because uppercase Z is not the character immediately preceding 'a' in the ASCII collating sequence. However, the uppercase letters do precede the lowercase letters in the ASCII collating sequence. Choice (D) is not correct because the function chr yields a character. Finally, choice (E) is not correct because there are no errors in the statement.

5. **(B)**
    The variable x is initialized to 600. Since it is greater than or equal to 0 and less than 1000, y is assigned the value of 2*x or 1200. Since x is not less than 400, the value of x is unchanged.
    Choice (A) is not correct since the only way y could have a sign different than x would be if x were negative. Choice (C) has y with three times the value of x. This could only occur if x were not negative and less than 400. Both choices (D) and (E) have x with a value of 60. Since x is initialized at 600 it could only receive a value of 60 (600 div 10) if it were less than 400.

6.   **(A)**
Tracing through the program we see that first a value for n is read from the input, then that value is written out in a field 12 characters in width and followed by a space. If n is zero then a zero is written. Otherwise the procedure ccc is called with argument n. Then we executed a writeln and fetch another value for n. This is repeated as long as n is *not* zero. Thus the line   0 0 cannot be part of the output. This means that (B) cannot be the answer. The procedure ccc uses recursion to display the binary representation of the value of its parameter, M. If M has a value greater than 0 then we call ccc again with an argument whose value is M div 2. This continues until M div 2 is 0. In other words the recursion is used to determine the largest power of two that divides M. At that point we compute M mod 2 which is the remainder of the division of M by that largest power of 2. Then recursion deals with M div 2 as a value, etc. The call ccc(5) yields 101, and the call ccc(34) yields 100010.

7.   **(C)**
LOOP C is a for loop, so that it is possible to specify the number of times its statements are executed. In this case they are executed 99 times. The number of times the statements in the other loops are executed depend on the values of the input.

8.   **(D)**
Only LOOP B and LOOP D are guaranteed to terminate when i has the value 99. In LOOP D we add i to x before the value of i is read.

9.   **(B)**
Only LOOP B and LOOP D are guaranteed to terminate when i has the value 99. In LOOP B we add i to x after the value of i is read.

10.   **(A)**
The expression controlling LOOP A is x < 99. That loop terminates when x > = 99. None of the other loops have x as part of their controlling expression.

11.   **(E)**
The controlling expression in both LOOP B and LOOP D is i < > 99. Each terminates after i receives the value of 99 through the readln statement.

12.   **(C)**
Since we want the elements of numbers to be sorted it must be the case that the parameter to SORTUM is passed by reference. So the declaration must at least be of the form procedure SORTUM (var ....). Also the type of

SORTUM's parameter must be the same as numbers. So the declaration should be of the form procedure SORTUM (var sortarr: intarr); Choice (D) is similar, but Pascal doesn't allow for a type declaration, which is what array [1..100] of integer is, as part a parameter list in a procedure declaration.

13. **(D)**
The software life-cycle spans all aspects of solving a problem with software. The first step is analysis of the problem to be sure it is completely understood. The next phase is design during which a solution may be designed and considered. The third phase is coding during which the design is implemented using a programming language. Then the program must be tested and verified that the conditions of the problems and its proposed solution are met. Finally the system must be maintained through periodic updates or minor corrections.

14. **(B)**
If we have N items in a list then the time it takes to perform a linear search is proportional to the size of the list. In other words, k*N where k is some constant. For a binary search the search time is proportional to the $\log_2 N$. As N increases the difference between these increases. Since a list must be sorted to perform a binary search, it is best to adopt this method when the list is stable; when the changes are infrequent.

15. **(B)**
Regardless of the type of the elements of A it is an array of ten elements, A[1] through A[10]. Each element of A is Boolean type so each of the ten elements has only two values. The reference to the ASCII code in choice (D) makes no sense here.

16. **(B)**
The array num has 6 elements num[0], num[1], ..., num[5]. We see that num[0] is initialized to 123. The next five elements of num are read from the input file. This is contained in the loop with the heading for k := 1 to maxnum do. When k mod 3 = 0, in this case when k = 3, a readln is executed to fetch the input value. Otherwise a read is used. So num[1], num[2], and num[3] come from the first line and num[4] and num[5] come from the second line. If we always executed a readln after k = 3 then choice (A) would be correct. Choice (C) would be correct if we had always executed a read. If we had not noticed that num[0] was initialized to 123 we might have made choice (D). Choice (E) would be correct if we had always executed a readln to fetch the values in num.

17.   **(B)**
      The statements preceding { *** SECOND OUTPUT LOOP ** *} are an implementation of an insertion sort. That sort is controlled by a loop as k goes from 1 to 4. Each time we reach the bottom of this loop, the elements num[1] ... num[k+1] are in ascending order and num[0] the value that was in num[k+l] at the beginning of the loop. The value of num[k+1] is copied to num[0]. We then start at position k using j to represent our current position. While the element in position j is greater than the element now in position zero, we copy the element in position j one place to the right, and then decrease j. When we exit this loop we copy the value in position 0 to the position indicated by j + 1. When we reach {*** SECOND OUTPUT LOOP ***} the array has been sorted and the value of the last element placed in its proper position is 1. So 1 should be the value of num[0] and num[2]. The other choices correspond to different values for the input.

18.   **(D)**
      This loop reads characters from the input and stops when a period is read. If a character is an upper-case letter then it is written and each character following it, up to a space or a period, is converted to upper-case if it is a lower-case letter. The first character is a 'T' so all following characters are converted to upper-case. This continues until the space is read. This gives us THAT'S. After that the letters are merely read and then written until another upper-case letter is encountered. So nothing is changed until we reach 'W'. It's all upper-case from then on, since no spaces are present before the period. Choice (A) represents converting all letters to upper-case. Choice (B) represents converting all letters to lower-case. Choice (C) represents no change in the input. Choice (E) would be correct if after we were converting letters to upper-case we somehow switched to lower-case after an upper-case letter was read.

19.   **(A)**
      The problem states that the array must have 60 rows and 5 columns and that the values in the array must be in the range 'A' .. 'F'. Thus the values must be characters so either (A) or (C) would be appropriate at this point. In order to have an error occur if the value were different than a value in the range 'A' .. 'F' we must choose (A). Choice (B) declares an array whose values are integers. Choice (D) declares an array with 60 entries, it is not two-dimensional.

20.   **(C)**
      The input and output are controlled by a loop which has an exit condition letter = '.'. So the period at the end of the input is not printed. When we are in the loop we execute a write (letter) provided that letter is not a comma. If it is a comma then we execute a writeln so that the comma is not

in the output and each comma forces the output to a new line. Choice (A) represents no change from input to output. Choice (B) would be correct if the period were put into the output. Choice (D) would be correct if we executed writeln(letter) instead of writeln. Choice (E) represents executing writeln; write(letter) when a comma is encountered.

21.　**(A)**
　　　The variable dos is type char and operating is type integer. So the statement readln(dos,operating) cause dos to have the value 'a' and operating to have the value 7. Unix is initialized to 6 and system initialized to 'c'. Thus possible choices are (A), (B), and (E). When we call the procedure cat, the first argument, unix, is passed by reference and the second, dos, by value. This eliminates (B) as an answer. In the procedure cat we fetch another value from input, 8, and add 2, ord('c') – ord('a') to it. So (A) is the correct answer. Choice (C) represents a misinterpretation of the action of read when an argument is a character. Choice (D) has the correct values, but in the wrong order.

22.　**(C)**
　　　The one labeled {3} would cause a compile-time error because why is one dimensional and not two dimensional: (why[2,->])

23.　**(D)**
　　　MAXINT mod 5 is type integer and depending on the value of MAXINT might have the value 0, 1, 2, 3, or 4. 25/5 is type real and has the value 5.0. 25 div 5 is type integer and has the value 5. chr(5 + ord('0')) is type char and has the value the character 5.

24.　**(A)**
　　　If n is < 0 or negative then sumn is set to –1, that invocation of the function terminates, and the value associated with sumn is returned to the caller. If n is 0 then sumn is set to 0, that invocation of the function terminates, and the value associated with sumn is returned to the caller. If n is positive or greater than zero then sumn is set to n plus the result of a call to the function sumn. This is the recursive call.

25.　**(C)**
　　　Recursive calls to sumn will be made each time the statement sumn := n + sumn(n–1) is executed. For this problem this occurs when n has the values 5, 4, 3, 2, and 1. So 5 recursive calls are made.

26.   **(B)**

The portion of sumn that indicates recursion can be represented, in this case, by a for loop. The value associated with sumn is the sum $1 + 2 + 3 + .. + n$. Only the loop in choice (B) or choice (C) initializes t properly and computes the sum. We must also provide for sumn to return a value of -1 if its parameter is negative. Of the two, this is done only in choice (B).

27.   **(E)**

There must be a one-to-one correspondence, by position, between the actual and formal parameters to a procedure. Corresponding parameters must be of the same type. Since this is a one-to-one correspondence on a finite set, the two lists must also have the same number of elements. They do not have to have the same names. That would be impossible if we wanted to use the same procedure with different actual parameters at different points within a program.

28.   **(B)**

If, for example, we had the following declarations

```
var x,y: integer;
procedure bobo ...
```

then it is definitely possible to declare variables inside of bobo with the names x or y. If this were done then these local variables would be the ones that are referenced by the names x or y. All the other statements are true.

29.   **(C)**

The problem asks for a field from the fifth element of the array class. So the answer must include class[5]. That element is a record of type student. To access the field called name we must add .name to that reference. So class[5].name is correct. Choices (A), (B) and (E) are not correct because student is the name of a type, not the name of a variable. In choice (D) we are putting the subscript on the name field.

30.   **(D)**

To access the tenth and twentieth records in the array class we must use the syntax class[10] and class[20]. Since we wish to compare the gpa fields we see that choice (D) is correct. It is true that we cannot, in Pascal, compare class[10] and class[20] directly, but in this case we are comparing a particular field in each record.

31.   **(B)**
    One way to compute the number of males and females represented in the array class is

```
nummales := 0;
numfemales := 0;
for i := 1 to 100 do
        if (class[i].gender = male) then
                nummales := nummales + 1
        else numfemales := numfemales + 1;
```

In the problem statement a with clause is used so we need only compare the field gender to male. The field gender has an ordinal or enumerated type at its type. If its value were not properly initialized somewhere else in the program this would cause no problem here because the type of the gender field is the same type as the constant male.

32.   **(A)**
    The size of an array cannot change during execution of a program if the program was written in Pascal. It may be that not all elements of the array are used, but space is reserved for every element of an array. If a parameter is a var parameter then space must be allocated for its address when the procedure is called. If a parameter is a value parameter then space must be allocated for a copy of the value of the parameter. In the case of an array, this means that space must be allocated for every element of the array if it is a value parameter.

33.   **(A)**
The number of elements in each array may be computed as follows
    (A) $3 * 5 * 5 = 75$
    (B) $10 - (-10) + 1 = 21$
    (C) $6 * 9 = 54$
    (D) $6 * 9 = 54$
    (E) $55 - 1 + 1 = 55$

34.   **(B)**
    The number of elements in an array is declared and allocated with no concern for the types of each element. Every element of an array must be of the same time, there is random access to array elements (Choice (C)), and once an array has been declared the size cannot change.

35.   **(A)**
A record may be a collection of objects of different types. That is one of the major distinctions between records and arrays. A field in a record is accessed by adding a constant (a different one for each field) to the base address of the record. So choice (B) is true. Records of the same type may not be compared directly in Pascal and functions must return a value of one of the simple types.

36.   **(D)**
(A) and (B) are meaningless because, among other things, *Items[PLAYER]* and *Items[BORIS]* are records and cannot be added. (C) copies all the items from BORIS to PLAYER, but in the process PLAYER's existing items are lost. (D) performs a union of PLAYER's and BORIS's items, which is the desired operation.

37.   **(D)**
Issuing this command would initiate a call to *GetItemNumber ("BORIS")*. Since no item with the name "BORIS" appears in the *Items* array, the *WHILE* loop would terminate with $i = NumItems + 1$. The statement *GetItemNumber := i* would then generate a range error since *NumItems+1* is outside the defined range of an *ItemNumber*.

38.   **(C)**
Since all the strings in *CommandStringTable* are in uppercase, the loop within *CommandToString* would continue executing until all entries have been checked. After checking the last command, *ATTACK*, the statement *i := SUCC(ATTACK)* would be executed. Since *ATTACK* has no successor, this statement would produce a range error.

39.   **(B)**
The symbols BORIS_SWORD and PLAYER_SWORD have different values (3 and 4). Adding BORIS_SWORD would have the effect of adding 4 to the player's item set, effectively giving the player two distinct swords.

40.   **(C)**
ProcessGo calls *InitialAction* and that procedure *(InitialAction)* would perform the desired function.

DETAILED EXPLANATIONS OF ANSWERS SECTION 2

1.

```
FOR ib := b TO u DO
BEGIN
    jt := t;
    WHILE ( jt < = u ) DO
    BEGIN
        FOR kx := x DOWNTO y DO
            n := ib + jt + kx;
        jt := jt + k;
    END;
END
```

A FOR Loop is either written as

```
FOR var := init TO final DO
    statement;
```

or

```
FOR var := init DOWNTO final DO
    statement;
```

where 'statement' represents any valid statement or statement block. In the first case the variable named var has one added to it after 'statement' is executed each time through the loop. **The variable var cannot be changed in any other way.** To write this type of FOR Loop as an equivalent WHILE Loop we would use

```
var := init;
WHILE( var < = final ) DO
BEGIN
    statement;
    var := var + 1;
END
```

In the second case the variable named var has one subtracted from it after 'statement' is executed each time through the loop. **The variable var cannot be changed in any other way.** To write this type of FOR Loop as an equivalent WHILE Loop we would use

```
var := init;
WHILE( var >= final ) DO
BEGIN
    statement;
    var := var − 1;
END
```

WHILE loops may be written as FOR loops only when the variable being tested is either increased or decreased by one each time through the loop.

In this case the variable jt is increased by 2 each time through the WHILE Loop which begins with the statement WHILE (jt < = u) DO.

2. Make the following changes:

Add *weight : INTEGER* to *ItemRecord*

Add a *weight* parameter to the *InitItem* and *InitWeapon* procedures

Add *maxweight : INTEGER* and *CurrentWeightCarried : INTEGER* to *CharacterRecord*.

Add a *maxweight* parameter to *InitCharacter* and add a statement that sets *CurrentWeightCarried* to zero.

Modify *AddItemToCharacter* as shown below:

PROCEDURE AddItemToCharacter(VAR character : CharacterRecord; number : ItemNumber);

```
BEGIN
  ItemWeight := Items[number].Weight;   ·
  NewWeight := character.CurrentWeightCarried + ItemWeight;
  IF NewWeight > character.MaxWeight THEN
    Writeln('Sorry, too heavy!')
  ELSE BEGIN
```

```
              character.CurrentWeightCarried := NewWeight;
              character.Items := character.Items + [number];
           END;
        END;
```

3.

   a.   student = record

```
                   name     :     pa30;
                   age      :     integer;
                   address  :     adrs;
                   gpa      :     real;
              end;
```

   b.   people = array[1 ..100] of student;

   c.   procedure sortstu(var A: people; B: integer);

```
           var i,j: integer;
                 tmp: student;

           begin
                 for i := 1 to B–1 do
                 begin
                       for j := i+1 to B do
                       begin
                             if( A[i].gpa > A[j].gpa ) then
                             begin
                                   tmp := A[i];
                                   A[i] := A[j];
                                   A[j] := tmp;
                             end;
                       end;
                 end;
           end;
```

a.   We use the specification for the record as given in the problem and use the types that have been defined previously.

b.   Here again we use the specification give that we are to define an array with 100 elements and each element must be of type student.

c.   Any sorting algorithm will work here. This demonstrates a bubble or exchange sort. The crucial parts are the use of a local variable named tmp which must be of type student to allow us to sort the records and the proper comparison of the records by the gpa field.

4.

a.   ```
function httocm(feet: integer; inches: integer): real;
CONST
      INTOCM = 2.54;
      FTTOIN= 12;
begin
      httocm := (FTTOIN*feet + inches) * INTOCM;
end;
```

b.    ```
function wttokg (weight: integer): real;
CONST
      KGTOLB = 2.2;
begin
      wttokg := weight * 1.0/KGTOLB;
end;
```

c.   ```
function sarea(feet: integer, inches: integer, weight:integer): real;
CONST
      FACTOR = 7.184;
      POW =   -3;
      FIRSTEXP= 0.452;
      SECONDEXP =   0.725;
var
      ht, wt: real;
begin
      ht := httocm(feet, inches);
      wt := wttokg(weight);
      sarea := exp(POW * (ln FACTOR)) * exp(FIRSTEXP * ln(wt))
             * exp(SECONDEXP * ln(ht));
end;
```

a.    We use the constants INTOCM and FTTOIN to set up the expression which multiplies the person's height converted to inches by the number of centimeters in an inch.
```

b.   Since one kilogram equals 2.2 pounds, one pound equals 1/2.2 kilograms.

c.   We use the formula given to compute the surface area. We also use the fact that to express x^y in Pascal we must write it as exp(y * ln(x));

5.

```
program bobo( inf, outf );
const
        Fail = 'E';
var
        inf, outf   :    text;
        sum         :    real;
        idnum       :    integer;
        grade       :    char;
        credits     :    integer;
        sumc        :    integer;
        num         :    integer;
        gpa         :    real;

        function rat( x: real; y:integer): real;
```

inf and outf are used as the first arguments to read and write and so should be of type text.

sum is initialized to 0.0 so it must be of type real.

idnum is set to round(gpa) and it is used in a read statement so it must be of type integer.

grade is compared to '$' so it must be of type char.

Fail is compared to grade and it gets no value in the executable block so it must be a constant of type char.

Credits may be of type integer or real but since it is used on the right of an expression which has sumc on the left it must be of the same type as sumc.

sumc is of type integer as it is initialized to 0. It may be of type real but it must be of the same type as credits.

num may of type integer or real but since it is used to hold the result of ord('E') – ord(grade) it makes most sense for it to be of type integer.

GPA should be type real since from the context it will hold a grade point average.

Rat is a function with two parameters. Using the declarations established so far its first parameter should be type real, its second of type integer, and the result should be type real as it is assigned to gpa.

ADVANCED PLACEMENT EXAMINATION IN
COMPUTER SCIENCE A

Test 2

ADVANCED PLACEMENT EXAMINATION IN
COMPUTER SCIENCE

Answer Sheet

1. Ⓐ Ⓑ Ⓒ Ⓓ Ⓔ   21. Ⓐ Ⓑ Ⓒ Ⓓ Ⓔ
2. Ⓐ Ⓑ Ⓒ Ⓓ Ⓔ   22. Ⓐ Ⓑ Ⓒ Ⓓ Ⓔ
3. Ⓐ Ⓑ Ⓒ Ⓓ Ⓔ   23. Ⓐ Ⓑ Ⓒ Ⓓ Ⓔ
4. Ⓐ Ⓑ Ⓒ Ⓓ Ⓔ   24. Ⓐ Ⓑ Ⓒ Ⓓ Ⓔ
5. Ⓐ Ⓑ Ⓒ Ⓓ Ⓔ   25. Ⓐ Ⓑ Ⓒ Ⓓ Ⓔ
6. Ⓐ Ⓑ Ⓒ Ⓓ Ⓔ   26. Ⓐ Ⓑ Ⓒ Ⓓ Ⓔ
7. Ⓐ Ⓑ Ⓒ Ⓓ Ⓔ   27. Ⓐ Ⓑ Ⓒ Ⓓ Ⓔ
8. Ⓐ Ⓑ Ⓒ Ⓓ Ⓔ   28. Ⓐ Ⓑ Ⓒ Ⓓ Ⓔ
9. Ⓐ Ⓑ Ⓒ Ⓓ Ⓔ   29. Ⓐ Ⓑ Ⓒ Ⓓ Ⓔ
10. Ⓐ Ⓑ Ⓒ Ⓓ Ⓔ   30. Ⓐ Ⓑ Ⓒ Ⓓ Ⓔ
11. Ⓐ Ⓑ Ⓒ Ⓓ Ⓔ   31. Ⓐ Ⓑ Ⓒ Ⓓ Ⓔ
12. Ⓐ Ⓑ Ⓒ Ⓓ Ⓔ   32. Ⓐ Ⓑ Ⓒ Ⓓ Ⓔ
13. Ⓐ Ⓑ Ⓒ Ⓓ Ⓔ   33. Ⓐ Ⓑ Ⓒ Ⓓ Ⓔ
14. Ⓐ Ⓑ Ⓒ Ⓓ Ⓔ   34. Ⓐ Ⓑ Ⓒ Ⓓ Ⓔ
15. Ⓐ Ⓑ Ⓒ Ⓓ Ⓔ   35. Ⓐ Ⓑ Ⓒ Ⓓ Ⓔ
16. Ⓐ Ⓑ Ⓒ Ⓓ Ⓔ   36. Ⓐ Ⓑ Ⓒ Ⓓ Ⓔ
17. Ⓐ Ⓑ Ⓒ Ⓓ Ⓔ   37. Ⓐ Ⓑ Ⓒ Ⓓ Ⓔ
18. Ⓐ Ⓑ Ⓒ Ⓓ Ⓔ   38. Ⓐ Ⓑ Ⓒ Ⓓ Ⓔ
19. Ⓐ Ⓑ Ⓒ Ⓓ Ⓔ   39. Ⓐ Ⓑ Ⓒ Ⓓ Ⓔ
20. Ⓐ Ⓑ Ⓒ Ⓓ Ⓔ   40. Ⓐ Ⓑ Ⓒ Ⓓ Ⓔ

Use a separate sheet of paper to answer the free-response questions.

COMPUTER SCIENCE A

TEST 2

SECTION 1

TIME: 1 hour, 15 minutes
40 Questions

DIRECTIONS: Choose the best answer and darken the corresponding oval on your answer sheet.

1. Which of the following three statements is (are) true about all for-loops?

    I.   If the body of a for-loop has no statements modifying the index variable, then that for-loop could still loop infinitely (i.e., indefinitely).

    II. For-loops are executed at least once.

    III. For-loops are the best structured programming constructs for searching in an array for one value.

    (A) Only I.

    (B) Only II.

    (C) Only III.

    (D) I and III.

    (E) Neither I, II, nor III.

2. The following code finds the minimal number in an array X:

    ```
    const SIZE = 100;
    type TABLE = array[1..SIZE] of integer;

    . . .

    function MIN( var X: TABLE; var TOP:integer): integer ;
    { MIN will return the smallest value in the array X }
    ```

```
            var LEAST, J : integer ;
            begin
                    { Initialize LEAST }
                    _____
                    for J:= 1 to TOP do
                            if _____ then
                                LEAST :=  X[J];
                end;
                MIN := LEAST
            end;
```

Which statement and which condition best fills in the two blank lines (respectively)?

	statement	condition
(A)	LEAST := 1;	LEAST > X[J]
(B)	LEAST := 1;	LEAST < X[J]
(C)	LEAST := TOP;	LEAST < X[J]
(D)	LEAST := maxint;	LEAST < X[J]
(E)	LEAST := maxint;	LEAST > X[J]

3. Which of the following is an illegal or bad array definition?

(A) TYPE COLOGNE = (LIME, PINE, MUSK, MENTHOL);
        VAR A : ARRAY[COLOGNE] OF REAL ;
(B) VAR A : ARRAY[1.1 .. 1.9] OF REAL ;
(C) VAR A : ARRAY['A' .. 'Z'] OF REAL ;
(D) VAR A : ARRAY[BOOLEAN] OF REAL ;
(E) VAR A : ARRAY[–10 .. –2] OF REAL ;

4. Call-by-value is preferable to call-by-address in

(A) a procedure which sorts an array.

(B) a procedure with massive amounts of data to be passed.

(C) a procedure which conducts input operations for the main program.

(D) a numerical function called with expressions for arguments, like:
Y := F(X+1) ;

(E) no case, since call-by-address is always preferable.

5. Which of the following is a random access device?

(A) Tape drive

(B) Printer

(C) Disk drive

(D) Modem

(E) Power supply

6. Which of the following arrays will be useful in counting the number of occurrences of each letter in a file containing only capital letters? Assume the file can be as long as 20000 characters.

(A) var FREQ : array['a'..'z'] of 'A'..'Z';

(B) var FREQ : array['A'..'Z'] of integer ;

(C) var FREQ : array['A'..'Z'] of 1..26 ;

(D) var FREQ : array[1..26] of text ;

(E) var FREQ : array[integer] of 'A'..'Z' ;

7. Which of the following codes should be placed inside a loop in order to compute frequency counts of characters, as described in problem 6? Assume we have the following declaration:

var X : char ;

(A) read(AFILE, X) ; FREQ[X] := SUCC(FREQ[X]) ;

(B) read(AFILE, FREQ[X]) ;

(C) read(AFILE, X); FREQ[X] := FREQ[X+1] ;

(D) read(AFILE, X); if ('A'<= X) and (X <= 'Z') then
SUCC(FREQ[X]);

(E) read(AFILE, X); X := X + 1 ;

8. Which of the following codes will read 20 numbers into an array and store them in the reverse order (i.e., the reverse of the input order)?

    So 21 44 13 93 ... will be stored as ... 93 13 44 21.

    (A) for J:=1 to 20 do readln(A[J]); for J:=1 to 20 do A[J]:=A[21–J];

    (B) for J:=1 to 20 do readln(A[21–J]);

    (C) for J:=1 to 20 do begin; readln(A[J]); A[J]:=A[21–J]; end;

    (D) for J:=1 to 20 do begin; readln(A[J]); A[21–J]:=A[J]; end;

    (E) for J:=1 to 20 do begin; readln(A[J]); J:=21–J; end;

9. Determine what the following recursive function F will compute when invoked by the call: Y := F(5) ?

```
function F(n:integer): integer;
begin
        if n<3 then
                F := 1
        else
                F := F(n–1) * F(n–2) + n
end ;
```

    (A) 16

    (B) 32

    (C) 35

    (D) 37

    (E) 64

10. Which program segment will exchange elements X[J] and X[K] in array X? Choose the best, most well-designed solution.

    (A) procedure SWAP(J,K:integer; X:array[1..N] of integer);
         var TEMP: integer;
         begin;   TEMP:= X[K];   X[K]:=X[J]; X[K]:=TEMP;
         end;

    (B) procedure SWAP(J,K:integer; var X:array[1..N] of integer);
         begin;   X[J]:= X[K]; X[K]:=X[J];
         end;

(C)   procedure SWAP(J,K:integer; var X:array[1..N] of integer);
       var TEMP: integer;
       begin;   TEMP:= X[K];   X[K]:=X[J]; X[J] :=TEMP;
       end;

(D)   procedure SWAP(J,K:integer; var X:array[1..N] of integer);
       var TEMP: integer;
       begin;   TEMP:= X[K];   X[J]:=X[K]; X[K]:= TEMP;
       end;

(E) procedure SWAP(J,K:integer; var X:array[1..N] of integer);
       begin   TEMP:= X[K];   X[K]:=X[J]; X[K]:= TEMP;
       end;

11.   An applications program must read an input text file of twelve paragraphs of character input into variable NewsReport.

```
var NewsReport : array[1..20000] of char;
begin; N:= 0;
      repeat ;
      N:= N+1;
      read(NewsReport[N]);
      if _____ then
            begin;
                  readln; N:=N+1; NewsReport[N]=' ';
            end;
      until ( _____ );
```

What should the "if" and "until" conditions be?

(A) <u>Missing If Condition:</u> eoln

     <u>Missing Until Condition:</u>   eof

(B) <u>Missing If Condition:</u> eoln

     <u>Missing Until Condition:</u>   not eof

(C) <u>Missing If Condition:</u> eof

     <u>Missing Until Condition:</u>   eoln

(D) <u>Missing If Condition:</u> not eoln

     <u>Missing Until Condition:</u>   not eof

(E) <u>Missing If Condition:</u> not eof

     <u>Missing Until Condition:</u>   eoln

12. A payroll file contains records with a single character field for type of employee. For instance, 'F' means full-time, 'P' means part-time, 'M' means manager, etc. Which aspect of PASCAL would best handle these categories in terms of computations involving pay-scales, overtime, and benefits which have differing formulas and rules from one category to the next? For example, 'P' employees get no overtime or health benefits but have certain stock options.

(A) set constructs

(B) if-then-else statements

(C) chr( ) and ord( ) functions

(D) case statements

(E) parameter passing

13. How many dimensions is array PIPE? In other words, how many indices are required to access an element in array PIPE?

```
type PROD ={ELECTRIC, WATER, HEATING, GAS, CABLE,
                TELEPHONE};
        CONDITION = { NEW, GOOD, FAIR, ROTTEN } ;
        PIPING = array[PROD] of CONDITION ;
        FLOORNUM = 1..10 ;
        ROOMNUM = 1..12 ;
    var PIPE : array[ FLOORNUM , ROOMNUM ] of PIPING ;
```

(A) 1

(B) 2

(C) 3

(D) 4

(E) 5

14. Which if-statement computes the graduated tax for the middle bracket (10,000–40,000)?

Income:	Bracket:
0 – 10,000	10%
10,001 – 40, 000	25%
40,001 – UP	40%

(A) if Income>10000 then Tax := ...

(B) if Income<10000 and Income>=40000 then Tax := ...

(C) if Income>10000 or Income<=40000 then Tax := ...

(D) if Income>10000 and Income<=40000 then Tax := ...

(E) if Income>10000 or Income<=40000 then Tax := ...

15. What are valid assertions about the variable A at the output statement (postcondition)?

```
var A,B,J : integer
begin
        readln(A,B);
        while (B <> 0) do
            if B > 0 then
                begin
                    B:=B–1; A:=A–1;
                end
            else begin
                    B:=B+1; A:=A+1;
                end;
        writeln(A);
```

Assume the initial input numbers were A=k and B=m.

(A) A equals k+m

(B) A equals k–m

(C) A equals 0

(D) A equals 2*k

(E) A equals 2*m

16. What is the most exact and encompassing description of the principle and goal of structured programming?

(A) Every block of code has one way in and one way out in terms of flow of execution.

(B) Do not use GO-TO statements.

(C) Code should be written bottom-up. The bottom layer is the structural foundation upon which higher layers are written.

(D) Use data structures to store data and then organize the use of them.

(E) Break a program into procedures, thereby giving the program a good structure.

17. Which is the most ethical and responsible use of information contained in a customer data base?

(A) Maximize the flow of information in society by providing all customer files to other firms.

(B) Provide loan companies with data on delinquent customers. This will help needy customers get loans and assistance.

(C) Distribute customer names and addresses to other companies, thereby providing customers with broader product knowledge.

(D) Periodically produce mass printouts of customized letters which appear personalized by repeated reference to name or township. Suggest they nearly won a sweepstake.

(E) Mail periodic advertising and billing reports to the respective customers but keep files internal.

18. Which is the legal and ethical view on software duplication?

(A) Software can always be duplicated and distributed to friends and associates freely, thereby maximizing the flow of information in society.

(B) Software should never be duplicated except by the original authors or the owning company.

(C) Software may be duplicated and in some cases distributed but only as the licensing and the nature of software permits.

(D) Software may be duplicated if it occurs in source code form.

(E) Software may be freely distributed by modem since the caller has access to the computer with the installed software.

19. Which of the following expressions will produce the same effect as round(X)?

(A) trunc(X+1)

(B) trunc(X+0.5)

(C)   trunc(X) + 0.5

(D)   trunc(X–0.5)

(E)   X – trunc(X)

20. Which of the following statements about the standard binary search is valid?

(A)   Insertion of a new element requires one step, a single array access, not a loop.

(B)   Deleting one element requires one step, an array access, not a loop.

(C)   In a search for one element X which is not in the array, every element in the array is accessed to determine if it equals X.

(D)   Finding the smallest element requires a loop through the array.

(E)   A nonrecursive implementation of binary search requires a single loop containing a conditional statement.

21. Which describes the best approach to writing a large program to solve a problem using the top-down approach?

(A)   Go immediately to the nearest monitor and without losing the initial momentum, start writing code. Time is valuable.

(B)   Start by drawing a single flowchart which describes the full program with the first line of code in the first box, the second line in the second box, ... Flowcharts are an infallible guide.

(C)   First formulate the problem definition, then write the code sequentially.

(D)   First formulate the problem definition, then break it down into logical steps, then construct modules, procedures, or blocks of pseudocode which would then be rewritten as code.

(E)   First formulate the problem, then design the user interface and the input/output routines, and finally, write the compute routines.

22. Which of the following is the most essential for ALL operating systems?

(A)   Maintaining a file system which is stable and supports the creation, copying, deletion, and editing of files

(B) Maintaining an environment for executing several programs simultaneously

(C) Maintaining an environment for multiple users to log on simultaneously without interference from each other

(D) Supporting graphical display devices

(E) Supporting networking with other computers

23. Which of the following is the best way to start a sort routine for an array X? Assume this declaration precedes it:

type ALIST = array[1..MAXNUM] of real;

(A) function SORT(var X:ALIST) : ALIST;

(B) function SORT(X:ALIST);

(C) procedure SORT(X:ALIST);

(D) procedure SORT(var X:ALIST);

(E) procedure SORT(X);

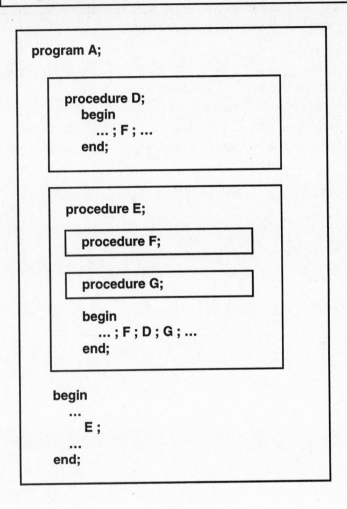

24. In what order are the procedures invoked (assuming no other calls, loops, gotos, etc.)?

    (A) A, D, E, F, G

    (B) A, D, F, E, F, D, G, E

    (C) A, E, F, D, F, G,

    (D) F, F, D, G, E

    (E) Invalid procedural calling structure

25. If variable Z is declared in a "var" statement in procedure D, then
_____.

(A) when D calls F, variable Z's scope will include F. As each procedure calls the next, the access to Z is passed until control returns to D and D is finished.

(B) Z is accessible in D but not in any internal subprocedure of D (if there were any).

(C) Z is accessible in D and in its super-procedure, namely A.

(D) Z is accessible in D and in all procedures textually after it like E, F, and G.

(E) Z is accessible only in D and any internal subprocedure of D.

26. What is printed out by the program below?

```
S:=0;
for J:= 1 to 10 do
        begin
                for K:= 1 to 10 do S:=S+1;
                S: = S+1;
        end;
```

(A) 10

(B) 11

(C) 110

(D) 101

(E) 111

27. The ACME Brush Company must keep information on its product lines such as the name of each brush type, its price, quantity, weight, etc. Assuming that new brush product lines with new names are continually being produced, what would be the best strategy for storing all the brush information?

(A) Use one big multidimensional array of integers.

(B) Use several arrays, one for name, one for price, ...

(C) Use an array of records, with one field being an enumerated (user-defined) data type for the brush names.

(D) Use an array of records, with one field being an array of characters for brush names.

(E) Use an array of records, with one integer field for a product number and then use a case statement in the program to convert a product number to a product name.

28. In what order should the following statements appear in a program?

(A) var X:TEXT ; begin; rewrite(X,REC); read(X);

(B) var X:TEXT ; begin; read(X REC); reset(X);

(C) var X:TEXT ; begin; write(X,REC); reset(X);

(D) var X:TEXT ; begin; reset(X); read(X,REC);

(E) var X:TEXT ; begin; reset(X); write(X,REC);

29. Which loop directly computes the following series?

$$\frac{1}{1+1} + \frac{1}{1+2} + \frac{1}{1+3} + \frac{1}{1+4} + \frac{1}{1+5} + \cdots + \frac{1}{1+50}$$

(A) SUM:=0 ; for J:= 1 to 50 do SUM:= 1/1+J ;

(B) SUM:=0 ; for J:= 1 to 50 do SUM:= SUM/(1+J) ;

(C) SUM:=0 ; for J:= 1 to 50 do SUM:= SUM + 1/1+J ;

(D) SUM:=0 ; for J:= 1 to 50 do SUM:= SUM + 1/(1+J) ;

(E) SUM:=0 ; for J:= 1 to 50 do SUM:= SUM + 1+ 1/J ;

30. Which of the following is true about program debugging?

(A) Logical errors are easier to debug than syntax errors.

(B) A program crashes at execution time on statement S in the code, so statement S must be modified.

(C) Debugging is best done at the design phase by prevention.

(D) Modularity does not affect debugging because two half-sized procedures have as much code as one long one.

(E) Fast unconventional code is always better than slower clearer code.

DIRECTIONS: For questions 31–32, assume the following code.

```
type
        VehicleType =(Scooter,Motorcycle,Car,Truck,Bus,SMV);
        OpticsType = (Blue, Brown, Green);
        HeightType = real ;
        WeightType = 80..700;
        PointsType = 0..19 ;
        NameType = array[1..50] of char;
        AddressType = array[1..50] of char;
var
        License : record
                LicenseNum      :       array[1..16] of char;
                SocSecNum       :       array[1..9] of 0..9;
                Vehicle         :       VehicleType;
                Eyes            :       OpticsType;
                Height          :       HeightType;
                Weight          :       WeightType;
                Points          :       PointsType;
                Name            :       NameType;
                Address         :       AddressType;
                Suspended       :       boolean;
        end;
```

31. Which of the following statements is illegal?

(A) License.Points:=Height;

(B) License.Suspended:= Points > 12 ;

(C) License.Eyes:= pred(Brown);

(D) License.Vehicle:=Scooter;

(E) Licence.Points:=10;

32. What is the value of: ord(Car) – ord(Scooter)?

(A) 0

(B) 1

(C) 2

(D) 3

(E) 4

33. In writing an exponentiation program for "A-to-the-B-power" we have

```
function Power(A,B:integer): integer;
var J : integer;
begin
        Power := 1;
        for J := B downto 1 do Power := Power * A ;
end;
```

What is wrong with this code and how should it be corrected?

(A) The for-loop should be: for J := A downto 1 do Power := Power * B ;

(B) The for-loop should count upward: for J:=1 to B do ...

(C) Apply the corrections from both choices (A) and (B)

(D) Use call-by-reference to return back numbers.

(E) Declare a local variable and use it for computing intermediate terms in the loop.

34. Which of the following is not a quadratic sort?

(A) Move the biggest element to the top and then reapply this rule repeatedly on the remaining array elements without the top element.

(B) Move the smallest element to the bottom and then reapply this rule successively on the remaining elements without the bottom element.

(C) Make successive passes through the array switching adjacent elements if they are not in order.

(D) In an outer loop, make one pass through the array but if a small number is encountered, use an inner loop to sequentially move that element down to its correct sorted position in the part of the array already covered by the outer loop.

(E)   Repeatedly split the array into successively halved subarrays and use comparisons and merging to place the subarrays into sorted order.

35.   Which of the following if-statements will cause the printing of all vowels in X, an array of only uppercase characters declared below?

```
        var X : array[1..70] of char ;
begin;

        . . . .
        for J := 1 to 70 do _____
```

(A)   if (X in [A,E,I,O,U]) then write(X) ;

(B)   if ('A'<=X[J] and X[J]<='U') then write(X[J]) ;

(C)   if (X[J] = 'A' or 'E' or 'I' or 'O' or 'U') then write(X[J]) ;

(D)   if ((X[J]='A') and (X[J]='E') and (X[J]='I') and (X[J]='O') and (X[J]='U')) then write(X[J]) ;

(E)   if (X[J] in ['A','E','I','O','U']) then write(X[J]) ;

Questions 36 through 40 are based on the case study provided at the back of this book.

---

36.   When the player enters a room or does a "LOOK" command, the program lists all of the characters in that room. What prevents the program from including the player himself in that list, since the player is a character and also in the room?

(A)   The player is not stored in the *Characters* array.

(B)   The *ProcessLook* procedure checks for this possibility.

(C)   The *PrintRoomDescription* procedure checks for this possibility.

(D)   The player's id number (1) is never actually added to the *Characters* field of a room.

(E)   Both (A) and (D).

37.   What would happen if the user entered the command "GET   SWORD" in the hallway? (There are three spaces after "GET".)

(A) The program would issue an "array subscript out of bounds" error and terminate.

(B) The program would get caught in an infinite loop.

(C) The program would issue an "unexpected input" error and terminate.

(D) The program would issue a "range" error and terminate.

(E) None of the above.

38. What would happen if the user misspelled the "INVENTORY" command?

(A) The program would issue an "array subscript out of bounds" error and terminate.

(B) The program would get caught in an infinite loop.

(C) The program would issue an "unexpected input" error and terminate.

(D) The program would issue a "range" error and terminate.

(E) None of the above.

39. Which type of definitions would have to be changed if we wished to add a "DROP *item*" command to the program?

(A) *CommandType* and *CommandStringTable*

(B) *CommandType* only

(C) *CommandType* and *CommandRecord*

(D) *CommandType*, *CommandStringTable*, and *CommandRecord*

(E) None of the above.

40. Notice that the procedure SetUpAdventure contains the following sequence:

```
AddItemToCharacter(BORIS, BORIS_SWORD);
SetWeapon(BORIS, BORIS_SWORD);
```

What would happen if this sequence were reversed?

```
SetWeapon(BORIS, BORIS_SWORD);
AddItemToCharacter(BORIS, BORIS_SWORD);
```

(A) This would generate a set inclusion error because you cannot set a weapon until the weapon has been added to the inventory.

(B) Nothing unusual would happen because the order of the statements doesn't matter.

(C) The effect would be unpredictable because variables are not automatically initialized.

(D) This would generate an "array out of bounds" error because you cannot set a weapon until the weapon has been added to the inventory.

(E) The program would get caught in an infinite loop.

SECTION 2

TIME: 1 hour, 45 minutes
5 Questions

DIRECTIONS: Give a detailed answer, written in standard Pascal, to each problem.

---

1.   The following code needs to be tested and debugged:

```
readln(X,Y) ;
if ( X < 10 ) then   ****
else  ++++ ;
if ( Y > 5 ) then    %%%%
else  $$$$ ;
```

Assume ****, ++++, %%%%, and $$$$ are blocks of code starting with "begin" and ending with "end." Determine the fewest values of X and Y (pairs) which are needed to test all the above code. Give a complete set of sample input values required to completely test this code. Explain why each step is necessary.

2.   A program can read two very large files (>1,000,000 records) of customers (call them A and B) and must produce a list of customers who are in both files. Which strategy/algorithms would best attack this problem? Assume only 2 megabytes of main memory are available. Also assume that the record structures of both files are identical.

3.   Write a program which will draw a picture of a circle using an array of 100 by 100 characters, using asterisks "*" and blanks " ". The equation for a circle is $R*R = X*X + Y*Y$ where R is a constant. Make sure the circle fills most of the 100x100 grid and be sure to print it.

4.   Variable length character strings (called the "string" type) are a useful feature of Turbo Pascal but not Standard Pascal.

    a.   Write a type definition in Standard Pascal which would meet the following defining characteristics. String variables must be capable of storing an ordered sequence of characters. Assume the maximum possible string length is eighty characters but keep track of the length of the string (i.e. the number of actual characters in the string).

b.   Write a function called CONCAT which will concatenate STRING2 to the ending of string STRING2, returning string STRING3. Use the string type created in part (a) above.

Question 5 is based on the case study provided at the back of this book.

---

5.   An obvious command that is missing from this system is one that allows the user to drop an item from his/her inventory. Show the changes you would make to the program to implement this command.

COMPUTER SCIENCE A
TEST 2

ANSWER KEY

1.	(E)		21.	(D)
2.	(E)		22.	(A)
3.	(B)		23.	(D)
4.	(D)		24.	(E)
5.	(C)		25.	(E)
6.	(B)		26.	(C)
7.	(A)		27.	(D)
8.	(B)		28.	(D)
9.	(D)		29.	(D)
10.	(C)		30.	(C)
11.	(A)		31.	(A)
12.	(D)		32.	(C)
13.	(C)		33.	(E)
14.	(D)		34.	(E)
15.	(B)		35.	(E)
16.	(A)		36.	(D)
17.	(E)		37.	(D)
18.	(C)		38.	(D)
19.	(B)		39.	(C)
20.	(E)		40.	(B)

DETAILED EXPLANATIONS
OF ANSWERS

COMPUTER SCIENCE A
TEST 2
SECTION 1

1.   **(E)**
        (I) is false since the index variable is compared to the upper bound value of the loop at the top of the loop. This prevents infinite loops since the index variable increments closer to the upper bound each time through the loop. This holds true provided no index modifying statements are in the body of the loop (bad style).
        (II) is false since the index variable is tested at the top of the loop, the loop could be bypassed immediately, as in:

    for J:= 9 to 3 do ...

        (III) is false since a search could end in the middle of an array but the for-loop is inflexible. For-loops always continue to the end of the array, generally wasting much compute time. The unstructured GOTO statements are not permitted.
        So (E) is the answer since none are true.

2.   **(E)**
        Assume variable LEAST is initialized to the largest possible integer value. It would be replaced by any other integer in the array since any other integer would be smaller. To make the "if" statement correct, note that a new low is reached if a given array element is smaller than our present minimum held in variable LEAST. So "LEAST > X[J]" is the valid condition to modify LEAST, hence choose (E).
        The conditions in (B), (C), and (D) are wrong because they state that larger elements in the array should become the new minimum in variable LEAST, contradicting the definition of minimum.
        To see why (A) is false, assume the array has only large numbers (e.g.

numbers larger than 1000); since LEAST starts as 1, no element in the array will be smaller. So LEAST will remain as one, a value not even in the array!

3.   **(B)**

Choice (B) uses real numbers as the index to the array. This is not possible since real numbers are not an ordinal type. There is no such thing as "the next real number" (i.e., no consecutiveness).

(A) uses an enumerated type to access an array. This is valid since the compiler converts the items to integer. (C) and (E) are fine since a subrange type of an ordinal type is also ordinal. (D)'s BOOLEAN is ordinal, too.

4.   **(D)**

(D) is correct since an expression argument can be sent to the procedure as a single numerical value. Call-by-address tries to return parameters back to the arguments calling them. Returning a number to the address of an expression is impossible since expressions have no permanent address. (E) is false since this example demonstrates a case for preferring call-by-value.

Call-by-value cannot return parameter values to the arguments in the main program. (C) fails since input operations must return data from the input stream. Since sort routines must return the ordered array back to the main program, (A) is false.

Likewise, passing masses of data is best achieved by sending a few addresses. Call-by-value sends data one number at a time, an unacceptably slow approach. Hence (B) is false.

5.   **(C)**

Disk drives allow the access of any data element without sequentially passing over all prior data zones. They can read/write at any position on disk in approximately the same time as any other position, ignoring minor head movement differences. So (C) is true.

Tape drives are sequential access devices. Accessing any one byte requires moving past all previous bytes, so (A) is false. Printers, modems, and power supplies are not data storage devices and data transmission is a sequential stream on both devices.

6.   **(B)**

Choices (B) and (C) have an index range that consists of capital letters. Choices (A), (D), and (E) fail in this respect. However, (C) is rejected because the number of characters in the file is 20000 while (C) offers a count of up to 26 for each letter at most. As a minimum, each letter's counter should be capable of storing counts near or exceeding 20000. Note also that the element type for choices (A), (D), and (E) are not appropriate counting types.

7.   **(A)**

Choice (A) reads a character and, using that character as an index to its counter, increments that counter using the SUCC function. Choice (B) is reading a numeric counter value from the text input stream of letters which is incorrect. Choice (C) reads correctly but then does not increment a counter but instead attempts to copy the counter of the next letter, using index X+1. Choice (D) reads correctly, even checks the data's validity with a range test, but fails by calling SUCC as a procedure and not storing the new value in FREQ. Choice (E) attempts to increment the letter just read, not its counter.

8.   **(B)**

Choice (B) reads each number and places it in the opposite end of the array, since 21–J has values 20, 19, 18, ... Choice (A) reads the array in the correct order and even attempts to copy the letters to the opposite end of the array but fails since that copying process overwrites the half of the array, producing a palindrome of numbers. Choice (C) clobbers each number just as it is read. Choice (D) also produces a palindrome, also losing half the array. Choice (E) reads in the array in the original order and even computes the opposite position in J but never uses it. Even worse, (E) modifies the index variable of a for-loop, a bad programming practice.

9.   **(D)**

The path of recursive calls and returns is:

$$Y := F(5) = F(4) * F(3) + 5 ;$$
$$F(4) = F(3) * F(2) + 4 ;$$
$$F(3) = F(2) * F(1) + 3;$$

$F(1)$ and $F(2)$ go to the stopping rule (since n<3), so $F(1)$ and $F(2)$ return back 1. Plugging backward, $F(3) = 1 * 1 + 3 = 4$ and $F(4) = 4 * 1 + 4 = 8$ and finally, $F(5) = 8 * 4 + 5 = 37$ (D). Most recursion questions involve a conditional with two possible rules, a stopping rule and a recursive call rule. Expect at least one power, factorial, or fibonacci problem but make sure to practice tracing the evaluation of arbitrary recursive functions (above) to understand the mechanism of recursion. Avoid the lengthier standard textbook recursions (e.g., towers of hanoi and fractal curves) since they are unlikely candidates for SAT-AP type A tests. Sometimes, simple loop-programs will appear as recursive procedures, notably binary-search programs may be implemented as such. Understand the basics of recursive sorts.

10.   **(C)**

Choice (A) passes array X by value which is very inefficient and logically wrong because the effect of the swap will not be returned to the main program. Call by address "var" is needed to return the modified X values. Choice (B) does the swap incorrectly, losing the original value in X[J] and overwriting it with X[K]'s value. Choice (C) is correct, saving X[K] in local variable TEMP, moving X[J] into X[K], and completing the move of X[K]'s original value to X[J]'s position. Choice (D) loses the value of X[J].

Choice (E) looks good but TEMP is not declared. A non-local variable can affect other segments of code, reducing procedure reusability and modularity.

11.　**(A)**
Choice (A) loops until eof is true. The outermost "read" loop should terminate when the end-of-file is encountered. Reminder: "until" tests for a terminate condition whereas "while" tests for permission to keep looping. Inside this loop, the end-of-line condition may be handled in the if statement by substituting ' ' for the eoln-symbol.

Choice (B) falls out of the loop on the opposite of the desired until condition. (B) would have been fine if a while-loop was being used. Choices (C) and (E) fall out of the loop upon encountering the first eoln-symbol, ignoring most of the input. Choice (D) will fall out of the loop upon encountering the first non-eof-symbol, which loses all of the input text.

12.　**(D)**
Sets are great for collecting cases but splitting into single cases is not their strong point, so choice (A) is wrong. Choice (B) can handle conditionals but is not the best solution for splitting into many categories based on the value of one byte. In fact, the case structure of choice (D) matches this criterion exactly. We can have:

```
case EmployeeCategory of
    'F' :  ... { handle full-time benefits, pay-scale, etc.}
    'P' :  ... { part-time case }
    end;
```

Choice (C) is for ASCII-decimal conversion and (E) is totally irrelevant.

13.　**(C)**
There are three dimensions to PIPE, specifically FLOORNUM, ROOMNUM, and by composition PROD. The CONDITION is not an index to the element but the type of the element. Semantically, this array records the conditions of a pipe, such as the water pipe in room 11 on the second floor. Other examples of three dimensional arrays are the temperatures of any point in a room, warehouse inventories of 50 products over 12 months during a 10

year period, or student grades for 9 sections of a course, each with 25 attending students, and three exams during the semester. Another common question involves determining how many elements are in the array. For PIPE, we have 10*12*6 = 720 elements.

14.   **(D)**
First note that Income must be greater than 10000 and less than 40000, so we need two conditions. So choice (A) is wrong. Both conditions must hold simultaneously, so "and" is the desired boolean operator, removing choices (C) and (E). Choice (B) has two conflicting conditions, Income being less than 10000 but simultaneously greater than 40000. So (D) is left, with Income exceeding 10000 but not exceeding 40000.

15.   **(B)**
Each time through the loop, we decrement both A and B by one. So A becomes A–1, A–2, A–3, ... This is repeated until B becomes 0, so the loop is executed B times, essentially resulting in a total effect of A:=A–B; so, A will finally have k–m as its value. In the "else" case, where B is negative, each time through the loop, A and B are incremented until B is zero. So, B times we can subtract –1 from A, which is also conventionally written A:=A–B when B is negative. Therefore, the "then" and the "else" case give the same assertion, choice (B). By renaming a few variables, we could have easily made choices (A), (C), (D), or (E) correct by computing k+m as A–B, 0 as A–A, 2*k as A–A, and 2*m as B–B.

16.   **(A)**
Choice (A) is correct, matching the concept of preconditions and postconditions, having execution flow simply between the basic building blocks of code, single statements, sequential compositions, conditionals, loops, and procedures. Choice (B) is very close but just describes one method for avoiding unstructured code. If choice (A) did not exist, (B) would be the closest answer. GOTO's should be avoided. (C) is wrong since Top-Down more closely matches good structured design but neither Top nor Bottom is the core issue. Data structures and program structures are independent issues, so (D) is wrong. (E) describes modularization but not structure; procedures could have bad GOTO's.

17.   **(E)**
Ethical use of customer data involves correct accounting and privacy issues. Choice (A) assumes that privacy and confidentiality are nonexistent. Choice (B) sounds like the customer is being helped but violates privacy with a presumption of need and providing credit information to third parties.

Choice (C) assumes customers want to be flooded by advertisements. Junk mail irritates many rather than informs. While not harassment, public pressure against such practices is mounting. Choice (D) customizes junk mail. While not fraudulent, it is misleading and hardly responsible. Choice (E) keeps customer data confidential and responsibly maintains accounts and produces advertising report generation.

18.   **(C)**
    Choice (A) ignores all concepts of copyright and intellectual property. The production costs and ownership of software are valid justification for restricting duplication and distribution. Purchasing software does not give free duplication rights. Choice (B) is incorrect since most software needs to be backed up. Also, public domain software, shareware, and specially licensed software (under site licenses and some instructional software agreements) legally may be duplicated. Choice (C) best expresses this. In choice (D), software may be sold as source code to help in customization but freely copying may be illegal. In choice (E), the caller may use the software but not duplicate it. Crimes by modem are a rising statistic.

19.   **(B)**
    Choice (B) is the correct answer. If X has a fractional part larger than or equal to 0.5, then X+0.5 will move up to or above the next integer, and trunc( ) will return that integer. If X has a fractional part smaller than 0.5, then X+0.5 remains below the next integer and trunc gives the integer part of X. Choice (A) is wrong since trunc(7.2+1)=8 but round(7.2)=7. Choice (C) is wrong since it always gives a number with a fractional part of .5 but the function round( ) always gives an integer. Choice (D) is wrong since trunc(7.2−.5)=6 while round(7.2)=7. Choice (E) is always either 0 or the fractional part of X, as in 7.2−trunc(7.2)=0.2

20.   **(E)**
    (A) and (B) neglect the fact that insertion or deletion requires moving approximately half the array to make one space for insertion or close one gap for deletion, either of which requires a loop. (C) is really how a linear search works. Binary searches repeatedly bisect an array, so a missing element requires checking log(N) elements to be sure of absence. (D) requires one step, since the smallest element is in the first position in the array. (E) is true since binary search is best expressed as a loop which repeatedly bisects a range of elements in a sorted array, with an if statement at each iteration testing to determine which of the two bisected sub-arrays is the feasible range for the next iteration.

21.   **(D)**

Choice (A) is fine for quickly writing short programs which have a short life cycle, since it may be buggy, poorly designed, and hard to maintain and modify. The use of quick coding means longer debugging sessions. Choice (B), a common mistake, assumes that flowcharts are a panacea. Flowcharts are useful but are neither infallible, nor a substitute for top-down thinking. Worse still, a flowchart with each line of code as a box is not much better than a code. (C) starts fine but returns to sequential coding rather than breaking down into logical subproblems. (D) divides a problem (top) into subproblems, then converts it to pseudocode, and eventually produces code (bottom), so it is correct. (E) assumes that programs have an input-compute-output design, a bit simplistic. Large projects are rarely attacked in that way and top-down programming does not place such stress on user-interface as a design phase.

22.   **(A)**

(A) is correct; without files and these basic operations over them, computers cannot support any user activities, except as control devices (as in cars and thermostats) and games. While multiprogramming is a nice feature, many microcomputer operating systems do not provide it. Multiple users are common in mainframe and minicomputers but is not necessary nor prevalent in most microcomputers. Graphics and windowing is commonplace but not required; many older small computers and mainframes exist with little to no pixel-oriented graphics support. Networking and operating system support of data communications is also a growing trend but many computers are stand-alone systems. Communications is often an application package; operating systems would provide low-level support.

23.   **(D)**

Choice (A) is wrong since functions cannot return an array as their value. (B) and (C) use call-by-value, preventing the return of the sorted array. (E) is syntactically wrong, missing a type specification. (D) uses call-by-address, so the sorted array can be returned to the main procedure unlike the other choices.

24.   **(E)**

Choice (E) is correct. Procedure D cannot call procedure F because it is an invalid calling procedure. The calling structure, while valid in some programming languages, is not valid in PASCAL.

25.   **(E)**

(E) is correct since Z is accessible only in D and all its internal subprocedures (of which there are none). Choice (A) assumes scope can be passed dynamically by procedure calls which is false. Scope in Pascal is not dynamic but depends on the source code's organization. Choice (B) negates the internal subprocedure rule. Choice (C) is false, since A never has access to Z. Choice (D) is ridiculous. Warning: good program design does not depend on scope to pass variables to subprocedures; explicit argument-parameters passing is recommended.

26.   **(C)**

Choice (C) is correct. The K loop produces the net result of S:=S+10. Each time through the J loop, the net result is S:=S+11. The J loop is executed 10 times, so we have 10*11=110. An alternate analysis is that the inner K loop code is executed 100 times (as counted in S) and the outer J loop is executed 10 times (also counted in S) resulting in 110.

27.   **(D)**

Choice (A) incorrectly assumes that all the data is numeric. (B) ignores the significance of record-types in keeping related items together. (C) is close but changing brush names requires rewriting the enumerated data type. Continually rewriting code for new data is a bad practice. Also, (C) makes output difficult. Choice (D) combines the structure of records with the effective storage of strings in a modifiable way and with direct output capabilities. Product numbers are fine but storing product names in a program is bad design. Worse, using a case-statement to store data mixes program and data. New products means code modification.

28.   **(D)**

In (A), "rewrite" will blank the file, defeating the intention of a "read." In (B), "reset" is needed to open the file by setting the file pointer to the beginning, prior to any "read" statement. (C) intends to output data and then overwrite it., which is bad. (D) follows the proper order, first opening the file for reading and then reading. (E) uses the wrong command to open a file for writing; "rewrite" is needed to clear the file.

29.   **(D)**

(A) and (C) appears correct as an immediate choice but a more careful inspection shows 1/1+J+SUM produces I+J+SUM because division has precedence over addition. (A) also does not accumulate any terms but has only one term. (B) would build a complicated fraction by repeatedly dividing into a sum. Continued fractions or repeated products could occur on an SAT-

AP exam but series addition is far more common, so expect a statement like:

SUM:= SUM + an expression

in the body of the loop. (E) is false but shows a common algebraic mistake of reducing 1/(1+J) to 1/1 + 1/J.

If time permits, try computing SUM for the first two values of J and the last value of J. (D) computes 1/(1+J) using the proper parentheses and then accumulating terms properly.

30.   **(C)**

Choice (A) is false since syntax errors are located by compiler and often involves small spelling errors, grammatical mistakes, or type mismatches. Debugging logical errors requires meticulous analysis and understanding the computation. Erroneous values can go undetected. (B) is false since the seeds of disaster are often sown long in advance. For example, variable A may be set to or left at zero in many ways but a ZERO-DIVIDE crash may occur many lines later in the code. Erroneous input can cause trouble later.

(C) is true since debugging can require much time and effort which is easily avoided by proper, careful methodology during the design phase. Rethinking poorly designed code and catching subtle errors due to initial lack of thought is exhausting and wasteful. (D) is false since large programs have more variables and more complex interactions between statements. Modularity means procedures are isolated for easier bug location and fixing. (E) encourages using tricks and complex programs at the expense of clarity, reliability, maintenance, and especially debugging time and effort.

31.   **(A)**

In (A), an ordinal type is assigned a real value which is illegal. Reals are not ordinal. (B) is valid; it assigns a boolean variable the truth value of a comparative expression. (C) is assigning an enumerated-type variable the value Blue. (D) and (E) are straightforward assignments.

32.   **(C)**

Scooter is the first vehicle while Car is the third, so the ord-function returns back numeric assignments, say 1 and 3 respectively. The difference will always be 3–1 = 2.

33.   **(E)**

Power is not a variable and so cannot appear on the right of the ":=" sign except as a recursive call. Choice (E) suggests that we create a local variable by including:

33.   **(E)**
Power is not a variable and so cannot appear on the right of the ":=" sign except as a recursive call. Choice (E) suggests that we create a local variable by including:

    var Prod : integer ;

then setting variable Prod to 1 and replacing the multiplication assignment statement with:

    Prod := Prod * A ;

and then assign Power:=Prod;.
Choice (A) will compute B-to-the-power-A, the wrong exponentiation. Choice (B) suggests counting upward but this does not affect the final result. (C) is wrong since (A) is wrong. No parameter changes occurred, so (D) is irrelevant.

34.   **(E)**
(A), (B), (C), and (D) define insertion sorts, bubble sorts, and exchange sorts, all prime examples of simple nested loop quadratic sorts. (E) suggests a divide-and-conquer strategy which is quite distinct and faster than quadratic approaches. The halving of the array requires logarithmically many passes and each pass is a "simple" loop.

35.   **(E)**
Choice (E) loops through array X and at each point J, checks if X[J] occurs as an element in the set of vowels and prints accordingly. Choice (A) syntactically misuses array X (only one element of X is permitted) and also leaves out quotation marks on the vowels so that we have five variables in the set. (B) sounds correct and will handle correct cases well but erroneous cases like X[J]='M' will also print. (C) attempts to use the set concept using "or" operators in a commonly mistaken fashion. (D) shows another common mistake, using "and" where "or" would have given a correct answer.

36.   **(D)**
Notice that *SetUpAdventure* does not include a statement adding PLAYER to HALLWAY, and *ProcessGo* also does not call *AddCharacterToRoom*. Thus, PLAYER is never added to any room's character set. Instead, the global variable *CurrentLocation* is used to record the room the player is in.

37.   **(D)**

Issuing this command would initiate a call to *GetItemNumber(" SWORD")*. Since no item with the name " SWORD" appears in the *Items* array, the *WHILE* loop would terminate with *i = NumItems + 1*. The statement *GetItemNumber := i* would then generate a range error since *NumItems+1* is outside the defined range of an *ItemNumber*.

38.   **(D)**

The loop within *CommandToString* would continue executing until all entries have been checked. After checking the last command, *ATTACK*, the statement *i := SUCC(ATTACK)* would be executed. Since *ATTACK* has no successor, this statement would produce a range error.

39.   **(C)**

A DROP symbol would have to be added to *CommandType* and *CommandRecord* would be modified to read *GET, DROP : (item : ItemNumber)*. *CommandStringTable* would also have to be modified but this is a variable not a data type.

40.   **(B)**

SetWeapon does not check to see if the specified item is in the character's inventory so the order doesn't matter.

DETAILED EXPLANATIONS OF ANSWERS SECTION 2

1.   The minimal number of data pairs required to test this code is four. The fundamental rule is to test all paths through the flowchart. The following table shows the four paths and the corresponding data values for testing those paths:

	Paths	X and Y
#1	**** followed by %%%%	8 and 7
#2	**** followed by $$$$	8 and 2
#3	++++ followed by %%%%	13 and 7
#4	++++ followed by $$$$	13 and 2

For example, X being 8 reaches the code **** and then Y=7 guarantees that %%%% is executed afterwards.

A common mistake is to test only two paths like #1 and #4, hoping that #1's covers **** and %%%% while #4 hits the other two blocks of code. This is insufficient and erroneous. In testing only paths #1 and #4, we would ignore the bugs cropping up from the effect of **** on $$$$. For example, if **** sets a variable M to zero and if $$$$ has code which divides an number by M, then a bug would result. This bug would have gone undetected if test #2 was ignored. Bugs like this are commonplace and become extremely difficult to detect or fix as programs lengthen.

2.   To compute this "intersection" of two files, one approach would involve sorting each file separately and then run a program which linearly goes down both lists in parallel, with customer keys (or names) "at" both file pointers being the closest ones (or equal at an intersection). This parallel comparator is essentially a merge program (from the merge-sort) but with output being only those records common to both files.

Since disk sorts are common and a parallel comparator requires the memory-space for only one record in each file, this strategy will easily fit in the memory- and disk-space specified in this question.

(ALTERNATE ANSWER to #2)
An alternate strategy is to tag each record of both files. Tag those records in file 1 with 'A' and file 2 with 'B'. Next, append file 1 to file 2, giving file 3. Sort file 3. Next, make one pass of file 3. During this pass, if two

sequentially read records have the same customer id. and different tags, then that customer is in both the original file and that customer should be written to the output file. Again, the disk and memory constraints are met.

Unacceptable solutions would be:
1.　　　load both files entirely into memory (insufficient memory)
2.　　　make one pass through the file and for each record read, do a linear search on disk in the other file. This fails because it is unfeasibly time consuming, requiring (1,000,000 * 1,000,000) input-commands.

3.
```
program DrawCircle;
const N = 50;
var GRID : array[-N..N,-N..N] of char;
      L, M, X, Y : integer :
begin
      { Clear the array }
      for L:= -N to N do for M:= -N to N do GRID[L,M]:=' ';
      { Loop to fill GRID with circle's plot points }
      for X := -N to N do
            begin
                  { Compute <X,Y> coordinates for circle, radius N}
                  { Formula given in problem is solved for Y }
                  Y := trunc( sqrt( N*N – X*X ) ) ;
                  GRID[X, Y] := '*' ; { plot this point }
                  GRID[X,-Y] := '*' ; { this point below x-axis }
            end; { end of array filling }
      for L:= -N to N do { loop over lines to print }
            begin
                  writeln ; { print one line of plot }
                  for M:= -N to N do write(GRID)L,M]);
            end ; { end printing loop }
end. { end of program }
```

4. a.　　To declare variable length character string, use the following record type to form a composite of array and number of elements.

```
const MAXLEN = 80 ;
      type STRRANG = 1..MAXLEN : { String Range 1..80 }
            STRING = record
                  STR : array[STRRANG] of char;
                  LEN : STRRANG ;
            end;
```

b.

```
procedure CONCAT(var STRING1, STRING2, STRING3 : STRING ) ;
var K : STRRANG :
begin { copy STRING1 to STRING3 first }
    for K:= 1 to STRING1.LEN do
        STRING3.STR[K] = STRING1.STR[K] ;
    STRING3.LEN := STRING1.LEN ; { Upgrade length }
    { copy STRING2 to STRING3 }
    for K:= 1 to STRING2.LEN do
        STRING3.STR[ STRING3.LEN + K ] = STRING2.STR[K] ;
    STRING3.LEN := STRING2.LEN ; { Upgrade length }
end;
```

Note that the above program is essentially two sequential array-copy-loops, each followed by two length upgrades.

Always include comments in your code or explanations outside the code describing the basic algorithm so as to get at least some partial credit.

5. Add DROP to *CommandType* and the statement CommandStringTable[DROP] := 'DROP' to *InitializeTables*. Add DROP to the *GET, USE* case in *GetCommand* and in *CommandRecord*. Add the case *DROP : ProcessDrop(Command.item)* to *ProcessCommand* and add the following procedure:

```
PROCEDURE ProcessDrop(item : ItemNumber);
BEGIN
  Characters[PLAYER].Items := Characters[PLAYER].Items - [item];
  Rooms[CurrentLocation].Items := Rooms[CurrentLocation].Items + [item];
END;
```

ADVANCED PLACEMENT EXAMINATION IN
COMPUTER SCIENCE AB

Test 3

ADVANCED PLACEMENT EXAMINATION IN
COMPUTER SCIENCE

Answer Sheet

1. Ⓐ Ⓑ Ⓒ Ⓓ Ⓔ   21. Ⓐ Ⓑ Ⓒ Ⓓ Ⓔ

2. Ⓐ Ⓑ Ⓒ Ⓓ Ⓔ   22. Ⓐ Ⓑ Ⓒ Ⓓ Ⓔ

3. Ⓐ Ⓑ Ⓒ Ⓓ Ⓔ   23. Ⓐ Ⓑ Ⓒ Ⓓ Ⓔ

4. Ⓐ Ⓑ Ⓒ Ⓓ Ⓔ   24. Ⓐ Ⓑ Ⓒ Ⓓ Ⓔ

5. Ⓐ Ⓑ Ⓒ Ⓓ Ⓔ   25. Ⓐ Ⓑ Ⓒ Ⓓ Ⓔ

6. Ⓐ Ⓑ Ⓒ Ⓓ Ⓔ   26. Ⓐ Ⓑ Ⓒ Ⓓ Ⓔ

7. Ⓐ Ⓑ Ⓒ Ⓓ Ⓔ   27. Ⓐ Ⓑ Ⓒ Ⓓ Ⓔ

8. Ⓐ Ⓑ Ⓒ Ⓓ Ⓔ   28. Ⓐ Ⓑ Ⓒ Ⓓ Ⓔ

9. Ⓐ Ⓑ Ⓒ Ⓓ Ⓔ   29. Ⓐ Ⓑ Ⓒ Ⓓ Ⓔ

10. Ⓐ Ⓑ Ⓒ Ⓓ Ⓔ   30. Ⓐ Ⓑ Ⓒ Ⓓ Ⓔ

11. Ⓐ Ⓑ Ⓒ Ⓓ Ⓔ   31. Ⓐ Ⓑ Ⓒ Ⓓ Ⓔ

12. Ⓐ Ⓑ Ⓒ Ⓓ Ⓔ   32. Ⓐ Ⓑ Ⓒ Ⓓ Ⓔ

13. Ⓐ Ⓑ Ⓒ Ⓓ Ⓔ   33. Ⓐ Ⓑ Ⓒ Ⓓ Ⓔ

14. Ⓐ Ⓑ Ⓒ Ⓓ Ⓔ   34. Ⓐ Ⓑ Ⓒ Ⓓ Ⓔ

15. Ⓐ Ⓑ Ⓒ Ⓓ Ⓔ   35. Ⓐ Ⓑ Ⓒ Ⓓ Ⓔ

16. Ⓐ Ⓑ Ⓒ Ⓓ Ⓔ   36. Ⓐ Ⓑ Ⓒ Ⓓ Ⓔ

17. Ⓐ Ⓑ Ⓒ Ⓓ Ⓔ   37. Ⓐ Ⓑ Ⓒ Ⓓ Ⓔ

18. Ⓐ Ⓑ Ⓒ Ⓓ Ⓔ   38. Ⓐ Ⓑ Ⓒ Ⓓ Ⓔ

19. Ⓐ Ⓑ Ⓒ Ⓓ Ⓔ   39. Ⓐ Ⓑ Ⓒ Ⓓ Ⓔ

20. Ⓐ Ⓑ Ⓒ Ⓓ Ⓔ   40. Ⓐ Ⓑ Ⓒ Ⓓ Ⓔ

Use a separate sheet of paper to answer the free-response questions.

COMPUTER SCIENCE **AB**

TEST 3

SECTION 1

TIME: 1 hour, 15 minutes
          40 Questions

DIRECTIONS: Choose the best answer and darken the corresponding oval on your answer sheet.

1. Which of the following statements is NOT true?

    (A) Top-down programming facilitates implementing a complex program in stages.

    (B) Decomposing the problem into subproblems is essential to stepwise refinement.

    (C) High-level programming languages facilitate transporting programs to different hardware platforms.

    (D) Software documentation is intended to assist in maintenance and modification.

    (E) The practice of designing programs as a sequence of clearly separated layers is called modular programming.

2. All of the following are advantages of modular program design EXCEPT

    (A) allowing several people to work on the program.

    (B) making the problem intellectually simple.

    (C) several transfers between secondary and main modules.

    (D) decomposing problems into logical subproblems.

    (E) proceeding from the general to the particular with each module solving an individual task.

3. Which of the following errors can be detected by a compiler?

    I)   stack overflow
    II)   undeclared variables
    III) passing illegal parameters to standard functions

    (A) I only

    (B) II only

    (C) III only

    (D) II and III only

    (E) I, II, and III

4. The function F is recursively defined as follows:

$$F(x) = x/2 \quad \text{if x is even}$$
$$= F(F(3x + 1)) \text{ otherwise}$$
If $x = 2^k + 1$, then $F(x) =$

    (A) $3*2^k + 1$

    (B) $3*2^k + 4$

    (C) $3*2^{k-1} + 1$

    (D) $3*2^{k-2} + 1$

    (E) $3*2^{k-3} + 1$

5. Given the program statement:

    IF a > b THEN x:= a;

and the assertion that x = a after the statement, which of the following represents the weakest (least restrictive) condition that must be satisfied before the execution of the statement.

    (A) x = a AND a > b

    (B) a > b

    (C) x = a

    (D) x = b

    (E) x = a OR a > b

6. Consider the following program fragment:

```
a:= x;
b:= Y;
c:= 0;
while a > 0 do
        begin
        {label 1}
                c:= c + b;
                a:= a - 1
end;
```

Which of the following would represent a valid assertion at {label 1} in the program?

(A) c = c + b

(B) c = a * b

(C) a * b = c + x * y

(D) c = x * y − a * b

(E) a = a − 1

7. Consider the following statement:

IF a = b THEN c = d;

Which of the following would represent a valid assertion after the execution of this statement?

(A) a = b OR c = d

(B) c = d

(C) a = b OR c <> d

(D) c = d OR a <> b

(E) a = b AND c = d

8. Given the following syntax diagram for WORD, indicate which of the following is NOT a valid WORD?

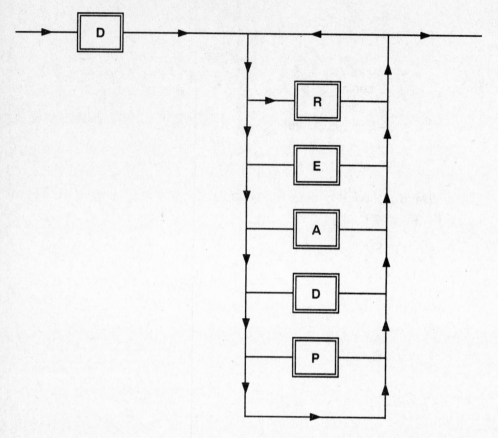

(A) DREAD

(B) DRAPE

(C) DEAR

(D) READ

(E) DEEP

9. Which of the following statements is NOT true?

(A) not A and B or C is equivalent to (((not (A) and (B) or (C)

(B) not (A and (B) is equivalent to not A or not B

(C) round(−x) is equivalent to −round(x)

(D) 12 mod −3 is equivalent to −12 mod 3

(E) 6 + 4 div 10 is equivalent to 1

Questions 10–13 are based on the following program.

```
program XYZ;
var X, Y: real;

procedure ABC(X: real);
var Y: real;
begin
        Y:= 1.0;
        X:= Y;
end; { ABC }

begin { XYZ }
        ABC(X);
end.
```

10. What are the values of main program variables X and Y after the execution of the program?

    (A) X = 1.0 and Y = 1.0

    (B) X = 1.0 and Y is undefined

    (C) X is undefined and Y = 1.0

    (D) X is undefined and Y is undefined

    (E) X = 0.0 and Y = 0.0

11. Assume parameter X of ABC is a variable parameter. What are the values of main program variables X and Y after the execution of the program?

    (A) X = 1.0 and Y = 1.0

    (B) X = 1.0 and Y is undefined

    (C) X is undefined and Y = 1.0

    (D) X is undefined and Y is undefined

    (E) X = 0.0 and Y = 0.0

12. Assume parameter X of ABC is a variable parameter and the local declaration for Y is removed from ABC. What are the values of main program variables X and Y after the execution of the program?

    (A) X = 1.0 and Y = 1.0

    (B) X = 1.0 and Y is undefined

    (C) X is undefined and Y = 1.0

    (D) X is undefined and Y is undefined

    (E) X = 0.0 and Y = 0.0

13. Assume parameter X of ABC is a variable parameter, Y is a local variable in ABC, and the procedure call statement is changed to ABC(Y). What are the values of main program variables X and Y after the execution of the program?

    (A) X = 1.0 and Y = 1.0

    (B) X = 1.0 and Y is undefined

    (C) X is undefined and Y = 1.0

    (D) X is undefined and Y is undefined

    (E) X = 0.0 and Y = 0.0

14. Given the declarations:

    var A: char;

    and the following input line from the keyboard:

    123 4 56

    what will be output by: readln(A); writeln(A);?

    (A) 123

    (B) 1

    (C) 56

    (D) 6

    (E) 123 4 56

15. Random access means

   (A) any record in the file can be retrieved by beginning the search of the records in the file at the midpoint and searching forwards and backwards depending on the key.

   (B) any record in the file can be retrieved without reading any other record in the file.

   (C) any record stored in a file can be retrieved by searching the keys of each of the records in the file.

   (D) any record in the file can be retrieved by searching the keys of each of the records in the file in either ascending or descending sequence.

   (E) any record in the file can be retrieved by a random algorithm.

16. Consider the recursive procedure P(N,A,B,(C) defined by:

```
if N <> 0 then do begin
            P(N–1,A,B,(C);
            writeln;
            P(N–1,C,B,(A)
      end;
```

   How many lines will result from the writeln statement during the invocation of P(4,a,b,c)?

   (A) 4

   (B) 8

   (C) 15

   (D) 20

   (E) 24

17. If symbol – is used for both unary and binary minus in polish notation, then which of the following is NOT ambiguous?

   I) abc*– –
   II) ab*–c–
   III) ab–c*–

(A) I only

(B) II only

(C) III only

(D) All three are not ambiguous.

(E) All three are ambiguous.

18. A stack as a data structure is NOT typically used in a program for:

(A) binary search.

(B) evaluating arithmetic expressions in compilers.

(C) tree traversal.

(D) recursion.

(E) a stack data structure is needed for all of the above.

19. An important property of a doubly (two-way) linked list over a singly (one-way) linked list is the ease of determining the predecessor of any item in the list. Which of the following operations utilizes the capacity to determine the predecessor of any item to its greatest advantage?

(A) Locating an item in the list

(B) Copying the list

(C) Merging two sorted lists

(D) Sorting the list

(E) Recovering (correcting) a lost pointer

20. Each record of the Student data file shown below consists of the following fields: SID, Name, Major, Year, Sex, GPA, and a pointer to the next record sharing the same value for field Sex. That is, the records of female students (Sex = F) form a linked list and the records of male students (Sex = M) form another linked list. (As usual, the end of a list is indicated by a null pointer.)

DATA FILE

Record Address	SID	Name	Major	Year	Sex	GPA	pointer to next record with same value for Sex
1	S12	JONES	MIS	1	M	3.45	??
2	S11	SMITH	ACC	2	F	3.25	4
3	S07	ABLE	ACC	2	M	4.00	null
4	S32	GARY	MGT	3	F	3.75	null
5	S19	SCHAD	MGT	G	M	3.00	???
6	S15	CYRUS	MIS	G	M	3.50	5

The missing pointers denoted by ?? and ??? are respectively:

(A) 3, 6

(B) 3, 5

(C) 6, 4

(D) 5, 3

(E) 6, 3

Questions 21–23 are based on the following array of records called Class.

Name	Score	Grade
Jones	98	A
Quincy	72	C
Philips	65	D
Austin	86	B

21. Which of the following could be a possible declaration for Class? (Assume type String is defined as packed array[1..12] of char.)

(A) type Student = record
              Name: String;
              Score: integer;
              Grade: char;
        end;
      var Class: array of Student;

(B) type Student = record
              Name: String;
              Score: integer;
              Grade: char;
      end;
var Class: array[1..4] of Student;

(C) type Student = record
              Name: String;
              Score: integer;
              Grade: char;
      end;
var Class: array[1..4, 1..3] of Student;

(D) type Student = record
              Name: String;
              Score: integer;
              Grade: char;
      end;
var Class: array[1..3, 1..4] of Student;

(E) type Student = record
              Name: String;
              Score: integer;
              Grade: char;
      end;
var Class: array[3, 4] of Student;

22. Which of the following is going to determine the average score? (Assume Sum, I, and Average are declared properly.)

(A) Sum:= 0;
      for I:= 1 to 4 do Sum:= Sum + Score[I];
      Average:= Sum/4;

(B) Sum:= 0;
      for I:= 1 to 4 do Sum:= Sum + Class.Score[I];
      Average:= Sum/4;

(C) Sum:= 0;
      for I:= 1 to 4 do Sum:= Sum + Class[I];
      Average:= Sum/4;

(D) Sum:= 0;
      for I:= 1 to 4 do Sum:= Sum + Class[I].Score;
      Average:= Sum/4;

(E) Sum:= 0;
         for I:= 1 to 4 do Sum:= Sum + Class[I].Score[I];
         Average:= Sum/4;

23. Which of the following is going to sort the array elements based on Name?
     (Assume I, J are declared properly and that the procedure Swap is as
     follows:

```
procedure Swap(A, B: Student);
var Temp: Student;
begin
        Temp:= A; B:= A; B:= Temp;
end;
```

(A) for I:= 1 to 3 do
         for J:= I+1 to 4 do
              if Class[I] > Class[J] then Swap(Class[I], Class[J]);

(B) for I:= 1 to 3 do
         for J:= I+1 to 4 do
              if Name[I] > Name[J] then Swap(Class[I],
     Class[J]);

(C) for I:= 1 to 3 do
         for J:= I+1 to 4 do
              if Class[I].Name > Class[J].Name
                    then Swap(Class[I], Class[J]);

(D) for I:= 1 to 3 do
         for J:= I+1 to 4 do
              if Class.Name[I] > Class.Name[J]
                    then Swap(Class[I], Class[J]);

(E) None of the above.

24. The maximum number of nodes at level h of a binary tree is:

(A) $2^h - 1$

(B) $2^{h-1} - 1$

(C) 2^h

(D) $2^h - 1$

(E) 2^{h+1}

25. Let x be a character string. Define the following operations:

Head(x)   the first character of x; undefined if x is the empty string

Tail(x)   the character string without the head; the empty string if x is a single character

Join(x,y)   concatenation of character strings x and y

Which of the following functions gives the reverse of character string x?

(A)   Reverse(x) = Join(Tail(x),Head(x))

(B)   Reverse(x) = Reverse(Join(Tail(x),Head(x)))

(C)   Reverse(x) = Join(Reverse(Tail(x)),Head(x))

(D)   Reverse(x) = Join(Reverse(Head(x)),Reverse(Tail(x)))

(E)   Reverse(x) = Join(Head(x),Tail(x))

26. What is the minimum number of direct comparisons between the keys of two records in order to sort 128 records?

(A) 0

(B) 7

(C) 64

(D) 128

(E) 256

27. Which of the following statements is NOT true?

(A) A bubble sort compares adjacent elements in a list and switches them when necessary.

(B) A selection sort iteratively passes through a list to exchange the first element with any element less than it and then repeats with a new first element.

(C) The worst case that could be presented to the quicksort would be a list in correct order.

(D) The worst case that could be presented to the straight insertion sort would be a list in reverse order.

(E)   The number of comparisons required to bubble sort a list of length N is $O(N \log_2 N)$.

28.   Which of the following statements is NOT true?

(A)   Binary search takes advantage of the order of the list while linear search does not.

(B)   Worst case performance of linear search on a list of length N is $O(N)$.

(C)   Worst case performance of binary search on a list of length N is $O(\log_2 N)$.

(D)   Worst case performance of hash coded search on a list of length N is not dependent on N.

(E)   All of the above statements are true.

29.   Which of the following sorts a ten element array of integers in descending order?

(Assume that variables used are declared properly.)

(A)   for I:= 1 to 9 do
```
        begin
                Max:= I;
                for J:= I+1 to 10 do if A[J] > A[Max] then Max:= J;
                Temp:= A[I]; A[I]:= A[Max]; A[Max]:= Temp;
        end;
```

(B)   for I:= 1 to 9 do
```
        begin
                Max:= I;
                for J:= I+1 to 10 do if A[J] < A[Max] then Max:= J;
                Temp:= A[I]; A[I]:= A[Max]; A[Max]:= Temp;
        end;
```

(C)   for I:= 1 to 9 do
```
        begin
                Max:= I;
                for J:= I+1 to 10 do if A[J] < A[Max] then Max:= J;
                Temp:= A[I]; A[Max]:= A[I]; A[I]:= Temp;
        end;
```

(D)   for I:= 1 to 9 do

```
        begin
            Max:= I;
            for J:= I+1 to 10 do if A[J] < A[Max] then Max:= J;
            Temp:= A[Max]; A[Max]:= A[I]; A[I]:= Temp;
        end;
```

(E)   none of the above.

30.   In the following nested loop:

```
    for I:= 2 to 5 do
        for J:= I+1 to 6 do
            writeln;
```

the writeln procedure is invoked a total of:

(A)   30 times

(B)   24 times

(C)   18 times

(D)   11 times

(E)   10 times

31.   Consider the program fragment:

```
    IF a > b THEN a[i] := f(i) ELSE IF b > c THEN a[i] := g(i);
```

Suppose a > b for 75% of times and b > c for 25% of times. In 10,000 executions of the above program statement how many times will functions f and g be evaluated?

(A)   7500 and 2500

(B)   7500 and 1375

(C)   7500 and 625

(D)   2500 and 2500

(E)   2500 and 1375

32. Consider the real function f partially defined as follows:

    x: -2   0   2   4
    f(x): -4   1   3   7

    What is f(2.5) by interpolation of two closest values?

    (A) 4

    (B) 4.5

    (C) 5

    (D) 6

    (E) 6.5

33. The ASCII code for the character E is 01000101. What is the decimal value of the ASCII code for E?

    (A) 1,000,101

    (B) 138

    (C) 74

    (D) 69

    (E) 42

34. The hexadecimal number system is also a positional number system which uses the number 16 as its base. That is, the weight of each position is a power of 16. It has 16 digits (often called HEX digits) which are denoted by: 0, 1, 2, 3, 4, 5, 6, 7, 8, 9, A, B, C, D, E, and F. (The value of hex digit A in decimal is 10, B is 11, C is 12, D is 13, E is 14, and F is 15.)

    What is the decimal value of the hexadecimal number 1A7?

    (A) 117

    (B) 267

    (C) 423

    (D) 439

    (E) 3184

35. Exactly how many bytes are in 64K bytes?

    (A) 64

    (B) 64000

    (C) 64536

    (D) 65536

    (E) 66536

Questions 36 through 40 are based on the case study provided at the back of this book.

---

36. In *SetUpAdventure*, What would happen if the statement SetWeapon (BORIS, SWORD) was used instead of SetWeapon(BORIS, BORIS_SWORD)?

    (A) This would generate a set inclusion error.

    (B) No errors would be generated.

    (C) No errors would occur until combat began.

    (D) This would generate an "array out of bounds" error because *SWORD* is already owned by the player.

    (E) The program would get caught in an infinite loop.

37. Suppose we wanted to add the additional complication that every time the player enters the study there is a 50 percent chance that he will be hit by a loose ceiling tile and take two points of damage. Which of the following describes how to make this change?

    (A) Add the statement

    IF random(2) = 1 THEN DeductHealth(PLAYER, 2) to *InitialAction*.

    (B) Add the statement

    IF random(2) = 1 THEN DeductHealth(Player.Health, 2) to *ProcessCommand*.

    (C) Add the statement

    IF random(0.5) = 1 THEN DeductHealth(Player.Health, 2) to *ProcessCommand*.

(D) Add the statement

IF random(2) = 0.5 THEN DeductHealth(PLAYER, 2) to *InitialAction*.

(E) None of the above.

38. Which of the following best explains why the author chose to use an IF statement in the *CanEnter* function rather than a CASE statement?

(A) A CASE statement must include a branch for all possible rooms, and in this example only the bedroom has an entry precondition.

(B) IF statements are always more efficient than CASE statements.

(C) A CASE statement will not work for the *RoomNumber* type because it is a subrange of integers.

(D) IF statements are preferred over CASE statements because they are easier to read.

(E) Both (A) and (B).

39. Which procedures would have to be modified if we wanted to add a "DROP *item*" command to the program? Assume that the symbol DROP would be defined as the successor to GET.

(A) *ProcessCommand, GetCommand,* and *StringToCommand*

(B) *ProcessCommand, GetCommand, StrngToCommand,* and *SetUpAdventure*

(C) *ProcessCommand* and *SetUpAdventure*

(D) *ProcessCommand* and *GetCommand*

(E) None of the above.

40. If we wanted to add an extra room to the north of the study, which procedures would have to be modified?

(A) *StringToDirection, PrintRoomDescription,* and *ProcessGo*

(B) *StringToDirection* and *ProcessGo*

(C) *StringToDirection* only

(D) *StringToDirection* and *PrintRoomDescription*.

(E) None of the above.

SECTION 2

TIME: 1 hour, 45 minutes
             5 Questions

DIRECTIONS: Give a detailed answer, written in standard Pascal, to each problem.

1.   A lotto ticket consists of six distinct numbers from 1 to 44. Complete the following Pascal procedure intended to print a random lotto ticket.

```
procedure Lotto;
. . .
begin
. . .
for I:=1 to 44 do if Lotto[I] then writeln(I);
end;
```

Assume the availability of the integer function RANDOM(N) which would return a random integer between 0 and N–1 (inclusive).

2.   Consider the following declarations for a linked list:

```
type ListPtr = ^Node;
     Node = record
                 Item: ItemType;
                 Next: ListPtr
          end;
```

where ItemType is a user-defined type.

(A)   Write a recursive function with header statement:
             function Size(L: ListPtr): integer;
      • whose value is the number of items in the list.

(B)   Write a recursive procedure with header statement:
             procedure CopyList1(var L1: ListPtr; L2: ListPtr);
             to produce a copy of list L2.

(C)   Write a non-recursive procedure with header statement:
             procedure CopyList2(var L1: ListPtr; L2: ListPtr);
             to produce a copy of list L2.

3. Consider the following declarations for a binary tree:

```
type TreePtr = ^Node;
     Node = record
                   Left: TreePtr;
                   Item: ItemType;
                   Right: TreePtr
          end;
```

where ItemType is a user-defined type.

(A) Write a recursive procedure with header statement:
     procedure CopyTree(var T1: TreePtr; T2: TreePtr);
     to produce a copy of tree T2.

(B) Write a recursive function with header statement:
     function CountLeaves(T: TreePtr): integer;
     to count the number of leaves in tree T.

Question 4 is based on the case study provided at the back of this book.

---

4. With regard to the sample four-room adventure that is implemented here, suppose that there was a troll that attacked as soon as the player entered the bedroom. Show the additions you would make to the program to add this extra twist to the adventure.

5. A special deck of playing cards consists of only Aces, Kings, Queens, Jacks, and Tens in 4 different suits for a total of 20 cards. The program shown below is intended to simulate a random dealing of all 20 cards, with the output from the program being in the format:

```
Ace of Hearts
Ten of Diamonds
etc.
```

(The integer function RANDOM(N) is assumed to return a random integer between 0 and N–1 (inclusive).)

As noted by ??????, three fragments of the correct program have been deleted below. Complete those fragments so that the program would indeed accomplish the intended task.

```
program Deal;
type   Suits = (Spades, Hearts, Diamonds, Clubs);
       Ranks = (Ace, King, Queen, Jack, Ten);
       Cards = record
                    Rank: Ranks;
                    Suit: Suits
              end;

var    Deck: array[Suits, Ranks] of boolean;
       Card: Cards;
       S: Suits;
       R: Ranks;
       N: integer;

procedure Display(C: Cards);
begin
       ??????
end;

begin { main program }

       ??????

N:= 0;
repeat
       S:= Suits(random(4));
       R:= Ranks(random(5));
       if not Deck[S,R] then begin
                    ??????
                              Display(Card);
                              N:= N + 1;
                end;
until N = 20;
end.
```

COMPUTER SCIENCE AB
TEST 3

ANSWER KEY

1.	(E)	21.	(B)
2.	(C)	22.	(D)
3.	(D)	23.	(E)
4.	(D)	24.	(C)
5.	(E)	25.	(C)
6.	(D)	26.	(A)
7.	(D)	27.	(E)
8.	(D)	28.	(E)
9.	(E)	29.	(A)
10.	(D)	30.	(E)
11.	(B)	31.	(C)
12.	(A)	32.	(A)
13.	(C)	33.	(D)
14.	(B)	34.	(C)
15.	(B)	35.	(D)
16.	(C)	36.	(B)
17.	(B)	37.	(A)
18.	(A)	38.	(A)
19.	(E)	39.	(D)
20.	(E)	40.	(D)

DETAILED EXPLANATIONS
OF ANSWERS

COMPUTER SCIENCE AB
TEST 3
SECTION 1

1.   **(E)**
     The practice of designing programs as a sequence of clearly separated
layers is called stepwise refinement.

2.   **(C)**
     A program designed in top-down fashion would consist of a main
module that calls other modules to accomplish its task. The secondary
modules, in turn, would comprise of procedure calls such that each procedure
solves a single task. As such, during the execution, the program incurs the
overhead of switching control and transferring parameters back and forth to
the subprocedures.

3.   **(D)**
     A compiler can detect undeclared variables. It can also determine
whether or not the parameters passed to standard functions are of the required
data type. But, stack overflow is a runtime error.

4.   **(D)**
     $F(2^k + 1)$

$= F(F(3*(2^k + 1)+1))$	since 2^k+1 is odd
$= F((3*(2^k + 1)+1)/2)$	since $3*(2^k+1)+1$ is even
$= F(3*2^{k-1} + 2)$	after simplification
$= (3*2^{k-1} + 2)/2$	since $3*2^{k-1} + 2$ is even
$= 3*2^{k-2} + 1$	after simplification

5.   **(E)**
      For x = a to be true after execution of the IF statement, it must be either the case that x = a before the IF statement or that a > b so that x will be assigned the value a by the IF statement.

6.   **(D)**
      The while loop computes the product c = a * b by adding b a total of a times. At label 1 in the program, c holds the running sum and a holds the number of times the repeated addition must be continued. Therefore, c + a * b must be equivalent to the final product which is x * y.

7.   **(D)**
      Before the IF statement, one of the following conditions must be true:

      a = b AND c = d
      a = b AND c <> d
      a <> b AND c = d
      a <> b AND c <> d

Of the 5 answers listed, the only assertion that would be true, after the execution of the IF statement, under every one of the above possibilities is c = d OR a <> b.

8.   **(D)**
      The syntax diagram indicates that valid WORDs must start with the letter D and can be followed by any combination of letters R, E, A, D, and P.

9.   **(E)**
      6 + 4 div 10 = 6 + (4 div 10) = 6 + 0 = 6

10.   **(D)**
      The assignments to X and Y remain local to procedure ABC.

11.   **(B)**
      The assignment to Y remains local to procedure ABC, but because X is now a variable parameter, the assignment to it is seen by the main program.

12.   **(A)**
      Y is now a global variable, and because X is a variable parameter, the assignment to it is seen by the main program.

13.   **(C)**

The procedure call ABC(Y) passes the address of main program variable Y to procedure ABC to serve as the variable parameter X. Therefore, the assignment statement X:= Y; in procedure ABC, assigns the value of local variable Y to memory position addressed by X, i.e., the main program variable Y.

14.   **(B)**

The readln A statement reads the entire line and assigns to char variable A the first character in the line read.

15.   **(B)**

In a random access file, any record can be retrieved directly either by a key to address transformation process or through consulting an index.

16 .   **(C)**

Let F (K) stand for the number of times the writeln statement gets executed during the procedure call P(K,x,y,z). We have:

$$F(0) = 0$$

$$F(1) = 1$$

$$F(2) = 2 * F(1) + 1 = 3$$

$$F(3) = 2 * F(2) + 1 = 7$$

$$F(K) = 2 * F (K-1) + 1$$

So, $F(4) = 15$

17.   **(B)**

abc*– – can be interpreted as either –(a–(b*c)) or (a–(–b*c)).
ab*–c– can only be interpreted as ((–(a*b))–c)
ab–c*– can be interpreted as either –((a–b)*c) or (a–(–b*c))

18.   **(A)**

A stack is typically used for backtracking. In the binary search algorithm, there is no need to keep track of past history. The middle element of a sorted list is compared against the search key and if there is no match the search proceeds to the appropriate half. Although binary search can be written as a recursive algorithm, it would be more efficient to program the binary search by iteration.

19.   **(E)**

Locating an item in a linked list, or copying the list can easily be accomplished by a forward traversal of the list. Although in sorting a linked list, or merging two sorted linked lists the ability to locate the predecessor of any item is necessary, it however can be accomplished by keeping track of the pointer to the previous element as we move forward in the lists. However, if, for example, the forward pointer fields in one or more elements of a linked list are corrupted, the capacity to determine the predecessor element is absolutely essential to correcting the errors.

20.　**(E)**
Since no information is provided about which record is the head of the linked list, the correct answer must be determined by a process of elimination. Choice C is obviously incorrect as it would link record #4, a female student, to the linked list intended for male students. Choices B and D are not correct as they include a pointer to record #5 which is already being pointed to by record #6. Choice A is incorrect as it will create a cycle with record #5 pointing to record #6 and record #6 pointing to record #5. The correct answer is thus E resulting in the following linked list of male student records: 1 –> 6 –> 5 –> 3 –> null

21.　**(B)**
Class is a one-dimensional array of Student records.

22.　**(D)**
Class[I] references the I-th element of Class array, which would be a Student record. And, the correct way to reference the Score field of that record is: Class[I].Score

23.　**(E)**
None of the choices will be able to sort the Class array because the necessary switching of out of order elements will not take place! This is because the parameters of the Swap procedure which is called to accomplish the switching are not variable parameters.

24.　**(C)**
The maximum number of nodes at level h is 2^h. When h = 0, the tree would consist of a single root node at level 0. When h = 1, the tree would consist of root and two leaves at level 1. When h = 2, the tree would consist of root, two internal nodes at level 1, and two leaves for each internal node for a total of 4 nodes at level 2. Etc.

25.　**(C)**
Reversing a string is defined recursively by reversing its tail and concatenating to its end the original head of the string.

26.   **(A)**

There are several sorting algorithms that do not require any direct comparisons between the keys of two record. One such sorting algorithm is the radix or digital sort.

27.   **(E)**

In bubble sort, there are N–1 passes with N–1 comparisons in each pass. Therefore, the number of required comparisons is $O(N^2)$.

28.   **(E)**

Binary search assumes an ordered list and divides the search space in half in every probe resulting in $O(\log_2 N)$ performance. In linear search, all N items need to be examined before it is discovered that the search item is not in the list – resulting in $O(N)$ worst case performance. An important advantage of a hashed table is that search time is independent of the number of elements in the table.

29.   **(A)**

A selection sorting algorithm is employed to order the items in descending order.

30.   **(E)**

When I = 2, J will assume 4 values (i.e., 3,4,5, and 6). When I = 3, J will assume 3 values. When I = 4, J will assume 2 values. When I = 5, J will assume 1 value. Therefore, the writeln procedure is invoked a total of 4+3+2+1=10 times.

31.   **(C)**

Since a > b for 75% of times, the THEN part (i.e., a[i]:= f(i);) will be executed 7500 times. The remaining 2500 times, the ELSE part will be executed, and since b > c for 25% of times, the assignment a[i]:= g(i); will be executed 2500/4=625 times.

32.   **(A)**

The closest x values to 2.5 are 2 and 4 with f(2) = 3 and f(4) = 7. We have by interpolation:

$$
\begin{aligned}
f(2.5) \ &= f(2) + \{2.5 - 2\} * \{(f(4) - f(2))/(4 - 2)\} \\
&= 3 \ + \ \ .5 \ \ *\{ \ (7-3) \ / \ 2\} \\
&= 3 \ + \ 1 \\
&= 4
\end{aligned}
$$

33. **(D)**

$01000101 = 1 * 2^6 + 1 * 2^2 + 1 * 2^0 = 64+4+1 = 69$

34. **(C)**

$1A7 = 1 * 16^2 + 10 * 16^1 + 7 * 16^0 = 256+160+7 = 423$

35. **(D)**

Each Kbyte is 1024 bytes.

36. **(B)**

SetWeapon does not check to see if the specified item is in the character's inventory so the order doesn't matter.

37. **(A)**

(B) and (C) are nonsensical since the first argument to *DeductHealth* should be a character number not an integer. Since the random function returns an integer, (D) is also incorrect.

38. **(A)**

IF statements are not inherently more efficient or easier to read than CASE statements, and there is no reason why a CASE statement using room numbers could not be constructed. However, since it is tedious to specify initial actions for every possible room in a game, even if no initial actions apply, a CASE statement was not used.

39. **(D)**

As long as DROP is added after GET and before ATTACK, there is no reason to change *StringToCommand*. *GetCommand* must be modified to read *GET, USE, DROP : BEGIN*, and an appropriate CASE label must be added to *ProcessCommand*.

40. **(D)**

These are the only procedures where direction values are used. Note that *StringToDirection* would have to be substantially modified since directions no longer differ by their first character.

DETAILED EXPLANATIONS OF ANSWERS SECTION 2

1.
```
procedure Lotto;
var Lotto: array [1..44] of boolean;
     I, J, K: integer;

begin
for I:= 1 to 44 do Lotto[I]:= false;
K:= 0;
repeat
     J:= random(44) + 1;
     if not Lotto[J] then begin
                  Lotto[J]:= true;
                  K:= K + 1;
             end;
until K = 6;
for I:=1 to 44 do if Lotto[I] then writeln(I);
end;
```

2.   A)
```
     function Size(L: ListPtr): integer;
     begin
          if L = nil
                  then Size:= 0
                  else Size:= Size(L^.Next) + 1
     end;
```

   B)
```
   procedure CopyList1 (var L1: ListPtr; L2: ListPtr);
   begin
          if L2 = nil
          then L1:= nil
          else
                  begin
                        new(L1);
                        L1^.Item:= L2^.Item;
```

```
                          CopyList1 (L1^.Next, L2^.Next)
                 end
      end;


C)    procedure CopyList2(var L1: ListPtr; L2: ListPtr);
      var P: ListPtr;
      begin
           if L2 = nil
           then L1:= nil
           else
                begin
                     new(L1);
                     L1^.Item:= L2^.Item;
                     P:= L1;
                     L2:= L2^.Next;
                     while L2 <> nil do
                          begin
                               new(P^.Next);
                               P^.Next^.Item:= L2^.Item;
                               P:= P^.Next;
                               L2^:= L2^.Next
                          end;
                     P^.Next:= nil
                end
      end;


3.    A)    CopyTree(var T1: TreePtr; T2: TreePtr);
            begin
                 if T2 = nil
                 then T1:= nil
                 else
                      begin
                           new(T1);
                           T1^.Item:= T2^.Item;
                           CopyTree(T1^.Left, T2^.Left);
                           CopyTree(T1^.Right, T2^.Right)
                      end
            end;
```

B) function CountLeaves(T: TreePtr): integer;
    begin
        if T = nil
        then CountLeaves:= 0
        else if (T^.Left = nil) and (T^.Right = nil)
            then CountLeaves:= 1
            else
                CountLeaves:= CountLeaves(T^.Left) +
                            CountLeaves(T^.Right)
    end;

4.   Add the constants TROLL = 3. The troll will need a weapon, so also add CLUB = 4. Change *NumCharacters* to 3 and *NumItems* to 4. Assuming the troll has health of 20 and the club has damage potential of 20, add the following statements to *SetUpAdventure:*

InitCharacter(TROLL, 'Troll', 20);

InitWeapon(CLUB, 20);

AddItemToCharacter(TROLL, CLUB);

SetWeapon(TROLL, CLUB);

AddCharacterToRoom(BEDROOM, TROLL);

Modify *InitialAction* as follows:

```
PROCEDURE InitialAction(room : RoomNumber);
BEGIN
  IF room = DiningRoom THEN BEGIN
   Writeln('A troll attacks you!');
   ChooseWeapon;
   Fight(TROLL, PLAYER);
   IF (GetHealth(PLAYER) <= 0) THEN
     Writeln('You are dead!')
   ELSE BEGIN
     RecordDeath(TROLL);
     PrintRoomDescription(CurrentLocation);
   END;
```

```
      END;
      END;

5.    program Deal;
          type  Suits = (Spades, Hearts, Diamonds, Clubs);
                Ranks = (Ace, King, Queen, Jack, Ten);
                Cards = record
                            Rank: Ranks;
                            Suit: Suits
                      end;

          var  Deck: array[Suits, Ranks] of boolean;
               Card: Cards;
               S: Suits;
               R: Ranks;
               N: integer;

          procedure Display(C: Cards);
          begin
              case C.Rank of
                      Ace:       write('Ace');
                      King:      write('King');
                      Queen:     write('Queen');
                      Jack:      write('Jack');
                      Ten:       write('Ten')
              end;
              case C.Suit of
                      Spades:        writeln(' of Spades');
                      Hearts:        writeln(' of Hearts');
                      Diamonds:      writeln(' of Diamonds');
                      Clubs:         writeln(' of Clubs')
              end
          end;

          begin { main program }
              for S:= Spades to Clubs do
                  for R:= Ace to Ten do
                      Deck[S, R]:= false;
```

```
            N:= 0;
            repeat
                    S:= Suits(random(4));
                    R:= Ranks(random(5));
                    if not Deck[S,R] then begin
                                Deck[S,R]:= true;
                                Card.Suit:= Suits(S);
                                Card.Rank:= Ranks(R);
                                Display(Card);
                                N:= N + 1;
                        end;
                until N = 20;
        end.
```

Test 4

ADVANCED PLACEMENT EXAMINATION IN
COMPUTER SCIENCE

Answer Sheet

1. Ⓐ Ⓑ Ⓒ Ⓓ Ⓔ
2. Ⓐ Ⓑ Ⓒ Ⓓ Ⓔ
3. Ⓐ Ⓑ Ⓒ Ⓓ Ⓔ
4. Ⓐ Ⓑ Ⓒ Ⓓ Ⓔ
5. Ⓐ Ⓑ Ⓒ Ⓓ Ⓔ
6. Ⓐ Ⓑ Ⓒ Ⓓ Ⓔ
7. Ⓐ Ⓑ Ⓒ Ⓓ Ⓔ
8. Ⓐ Ⓑ Ⓒ Ⓓ Ⓔ
9. Ⓐ Ⓑ Ⓒ Ⓓ Ⓔ
10. Ⓐ Ⓑ Ⓒ Ⓓ Ⓔ
11. Ⓐ Ⓑ Ⓒ Ⓓ Ⓔ
12. Ⓐ Ⓑ Ⓒ Ⓓ Ⓔ
13. Ⓐ Ⓑ Ⓒ Ⓓ Ⓔ
14. Ⓐ Ⓑ Ⓒ Ⓓ Ⓔ
15. Ⓐ Ⓑ Ⓒ Ⓓ Ⓔ
16. Ⓐ Ⓑ Ⓒ Ⓓ Ⓔ
17. Ⓐ Ⓑ Ⓒ Ⓓ Ⓔ
18. Ⓐ Ⓑ Ⓒ Ⓓ Ⓔ
19. Ⓐ Ⓑ Ⓒ Ⓓ Ⓔ
20. Ⓐ Ⓑ Ⓒ Ⓓ Ⓔ

21. Ⓐ Ⓑ Ⓒ Ⓓ Ⓔ
22. Ⓐ Ⓑ Ⓒ Ⓓ Ⓔ
23. Ⓐ Ⓑ Ⓒ Ⓓ Ⓔ
24. Ⓐ Ⓑ Ⓒ Ⓓ Ⓔ
25. Ⓐ Ⓑ Ⓒ Ⓓ Ⓔ
26. Ⓐ Ⓑ Ⓒ Ⓓ Ⓔ
27. Ⓐ Ⓑ Ⓒ Ⓓ Ⓔ
28. Ⓐ Ⓑ Ⓒ Ⓓ Ⓔ
29. Ⓐ Ⓑ Ⓒ Ⓓ Ⓔ
30. Ⓐ Ⓑ Ⓒ Ⓓ Ⓔ
31. Ⓐ Ⓑ Ⓒ Ⓓ Ⓔ
32. Ⓐ Ⓑ Ⓒ Ⓓ Ⓔ
33. Ⓐ Ⓑ Ⓒ Ⓓ Ⓔ
34. Ⓐ Ⓑ Ⓒ Ⓓ Ⓔ
35. Ⓐ Ⓑ Ⓒ Ⓓ Ⓔ
36. Ⓐ Ⓑ Ⓒ Ⓓ Ⓔ
37. Ⓐ Ⓑ Ⓒ Ⓓ Ⓔ
38. Ⓐ Ⓑ Ⓒ Ⓓ Ⓔ
39. Ⓐ Ⓑ Ⓒ Ⓓ Ⓔ
40. Ⓐ Ⓑ Ⓒ Ⓓ Ⓔ

Use a separate sheet of paper to answer the free-response questions.

COMPUTER SCIENCE AB
TEST 4

SECTION 1

TIME: 1 hour, 15 minutes
40 Questions

> **DIRECTIONS:** Choose the best answer and darken the corresponding oval on your answer sheet.

1. The tree to the right is transversed using inorder traversal, and each time a node is visited, the label for that node is printed. Which of the following would be the resulting output?

   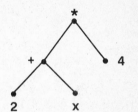

   (A) * 4 + 2 x

   (B) 2 + x * 4

   (C) 4 * + 2 x

   (D) * + 2 x 4

   (E) 2 x + 4 *

2. Given the binary tree shown to the right, which of the following 6 x 3 arrays presents the correct left child-right child representation of the tree. Column 1 indicates the node. Column 2 denotes the left child and Column 3 denotes the right child. A zero indicates a nil pointer.

   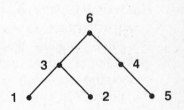

   (A)   4   0   0
            2   4   5
            6   0   0
            3   0   6
            5   0   0
            1   2   3

(B)

3	1	2
2	0	0
1	0	0
6	3	4
5	0	0
4	0	5

(C)

6	3	4
2	1	3
5	0	0
4	0	5
1	0	0
3	4	5

(D)

1	2	5
2	0	0
3	6	0
4	2	5
5	0	0
6	3	4

(E)

3	6	4
2	0	0
1	0	0
6	3	4
5	0	0
4	0	5

DIRECTIONS: Questions 3-4 refer to the following information concerning a string of integers. Consider a string of integers that are an even number of characters in length, where half of the characters are positive and the other half are zeros. Suppose the string is processed through a stack as follows: As we read from left to right, the "push" instruction is applied to the stack for any nonzero integer, and a zero causes the "pop" instruction to be applied to the stack. The result of the "popped" integers is printed. Only the topmost item on the stack is accessible at any moment. The stack is initially empty.

---

3. Using the above procedure, what is the output for the following string
1 2 0 3 0 0 0 4 0 ?

(A) 1   2   3   4

(B) 2   3   4   1

(C) 2   3   1   4

(D) 4   3   2   1

(E) 2   1   4   3

4.   Using the above procedure, what is the output for the following string
     1 0 0 2 0 3 4 0 ?

     (A) 1   2   3   4

     (B) 1   3   4   2

     (C) 1   4   2   3

     (D) 0

     (E)   Impossible to handle

5.   Given the graph to the right, what is its adja-
     cency matrix?

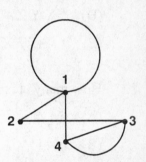

(A)
$$\begin{bmatrix} 1 & 1 & 0 & 1 \\ 1 & 0 & 1 & 0 \\ 0 & 1 & 0 & 2 \\ 1 & 0 & 2 & 0 \end{bmatrix}$$

(B)
$$\begin{bmatrix} 1 & 1 & 0 & 1 \\ 1 & 0 & 1 & 0 \\ 0 & 1 & 0 & 1 \\ 1 & 0 & 2 & 0 \end{bmatrix}$$

(C)
$$\begin{bmatrix} 1 & 1 & 0 & 1 \\ 1 & 1 & 1 & 0 \\ 0 & 1 & 1 & 2 \\ 1 & 0 & 2 & 1 \end{bmatrix}$$

(D)
$$\begin{bmatrix} 0 & 1 & 0 & 1 \\ 1 & 0 & 1 & 0 \\ 0 & 1 & 0 & 2 \\ 1 & 0 & 2 & 0 \end{bmatrix}$$

(E)
$$\begin{bmatrix} 1 & 1 & 0 & 1 \\ 1 & 0 & 1 & 0 \\ 1 & 1 & 0 & 2 \\ 1 & 0 & 2 & 0 \end{bmatrix}$$

6. Given the expression a + (b * c – d), which of the following would correctly represent it in prefix notation?

   (A) + a – * b c d

   (B) * a + – b c d

   (C) a b c * d – +

   (D) * b c d + a –

   (E) * – + a b c d

7. Given the expression W + (X * Y – Z), which of the following would correctly represent it in postfix notation?

   (A) + W – * X Y Z

   (B) * W + – X Y Z

   (C) W X Y * Z – +

   (D) * X Y Z + W –

   (E) * – + W X Y Z

8. How many arcs are in a tree structure with n nodes?

   (A) n * n

   (B) n – 1

   (C) n + 1

   (D) 2n

   (E) n

9. Given the graph to the right, which arc(s) must be removed to make the graph a tree structure?

   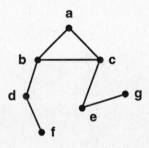

   (A) (a,b)

   (B) (e,g)

   (C) (b,c)

   (D) (d,f)

   (E) both A and C

10. An engineer wants to design a network which will connect all the computer nodes, given in the scaled graph to the right, in an efficient manner, starting with node 1. The arcs in the graph indicate weights between nodes. Let N denote a set which initially contains node 1 but grows as nodes are added to the set in a particular order so as to obtain a minimal spanning tree for the graph. A spanning tree for the graph connects all the nodes of the graph with no excess arcs. A minimal spanning tree is a spanning tree with minimial weight, for a given weighted, connected graph. Which of the following sets represents the set N for a minimial spanning tree for the given weighted, connected graph?

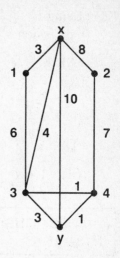

(A) (1, x, y, 2, 4, 3)

(B) (1, 3, y, 4, 2, x)

(C) (1, x, 2, 4, y, 3)

(D) (1, x, y, 4, 3, 2)

(E) (1, x, 3, 4, y, 2)

11. Using the properties of Boolean algebra, which of the following expression can be obtained from

$$x_1 x_2 x_3 \quad + \quad x_1 x_2' x_3 \quad + \quad x_1 x_2' x_3' \quad + \quad x_1' x_2' x_3 \quad + \quad x_1' x_2' x_3',$$

if the symbol ' denotes the unary operation NOT, + denotes OR, and no operation between two variables denotes AND?

(A) $x_1 x_2 + x_3'$

(B) $x_1' x_2 + x_3$

(C) $x_1' x_2' + x_3$

(D) $x_1 x_3 + x_2'$

(E) $x_1' x_3 + x_2'$

12. Using Boolean algebra properties, which expression is a result of the expression x + x'y?

(A) y

(B) x + y

(C) x + x'

(D) x

(E) 1 + y

DIRECTIONS: The following information is applicable for Questions 13 – 15.

Suppose that pointer types are defined as follows in Pascal:

```
type  IntPtr : ^integer;
      CharPtr : ^integer;
var   Point1, Point2 : IntPtr;
      Point3 : CharPtr;
```

13. What is the result of the following statement?

(A) It creates an integer Point1 to reference.

(B) It creates a point for Point1 to reference.

(C) It creates a variable for Point1 to reference.

(D) It creates an integer for IntPtr to reference.

(E) It creates an IntPtr value for Point1 to reference.

14. If the following segment is executed, what will be the output?

```
New(Point1);
writeln(Point1);
```

(A) The value of Point1 will be displayed.

(B) The value of Point1 points to another displayed value of Point1.

(C) The display value will be 0.

(D) The value of Point1 is displayed as a pointer.

(E) It is not possible to display the value of Point1.

15. If new(Point2) has been executed, what is the result of the following statement?

    Point2 := Point2 + 3

(A) The variable created for Point2 will be given a new name, Point2 + 3.

(B) The variable created for Point2 will reference a location 3 units from Point2.

(C) The value of the variable created for Point2 is increased by 3.

(D) No arithmetic is allowed involving this variable.

(E) The variable created for Point2 will reference an arbitrary pointer.

16. If a stack consists of the following string of integers, 9 5 1 7 3, in which the left side of the string is at the bottom of the stack, what is the result of applying Pop procedure once?

(A) 9   5   1   7   0

(B) 3   7   1   5   0

(C) 9   5   1   7

(D) 9   7   5   1

(E) 1   5   7   9

17. A programmer is to design a software program for a beauty supply company which will allow the company to search, manipulate, and display values of various supply items in a table. Of the following, which gives the BEST design of a Pascal procedure that performs the task of displaying information about a particular item upon receiving a specification for the item? The Pascal procedure

(A) searches the table for the specified item and then calls a procedure P to display the information about that item.

(B) searches the table for the specified item and then displays the information about that item.

(C) calls a procedure Q to search the table for the specified item and then itself displays the information about that item.

(D) calls a procedure R to search the table for the specified item and then calls a procedure S to display the information about that item.

(E) displays the entire table of items and the user searches for the desired information about that item.

18. Which of the following data structures would be MOST appropriate for use in a Pascal program that simulates the waiting line in a popular doctor's office who has reportedly found the cure for the common cold?

(A) An array

(B) A binary tree

(C) A string

(D) A linked list

(E) A queue

19. Suppose that 60 percent of all cars approaching a certain intersection go straight; 30 percent turn right; and 10 percent turn left. Using the function Rnd in the code below, which of the following pair of statements, when inserted at the indicated point in the program segment

```
X := Rnd;
if ( INSERT A HERE ) then
            writeln (' Straight ')
else if ( INSERT B HERE ) then
            writeln (' Right ')
      else
            writeln (' Left ');
```

will cause the program segment to simulate the traffic?

	(Insert A)	(Insert B)
I.	X > 0.6,	(X >= 0.6) and (X < 0.9)
II.	X < 0.3,	(X > 0.3) and (X < 0.9)
III.	X < 0.6,	(X >= 0.6) and (X < 0.9)
IV.	X < 0.1,	(X > 0.6) and (X < 0.9)

The CORRECT answer is:

(A) I only.

(B) II only.

(C) III only.

(D) I and III.

(E) IV only.

20. A function that returns to the calling program the total shown on the uppermost faces of a pair of dice when tossed is given in the segment below. Which of the following statement when inserted in the appropriate place in the procedure

```
function DiceTol : integer;
var Die1, Die2 : integer;

begin
        ( INSERT A ) ;
        ( INSERT B ) ;
        DieTol := Die1 + Die2
end;
```

will cause the procedure to provide the appropriate total to be returned to the calling program?

(Insert A)	(Insert B)

I. $Die1 := Trunc(6*Rnd + 1)$ $Die2 := Trunc(6*Rnd + 1)$

II. $Die1 := Round(Rnd + 1)$ $Die2 := Round(6*Rnd + 1)$

III. $Die1 := Trunc(2*Rnd)$ $Die2 := Trunc(12*Rnd + 1)$

IV. $Die1 := Trunc(2*Rnd + 1)$ $Die2 := Trunc(12*Rnd + 1)$

The CORRECT answer is:

(A) I only

(B) II only

(C) III only

(D) IV only

(E) II and IV

21. Let Rnd be a function that returns a real number between 0 and 1. Which of the following expressions, when selected as indicated in the Pascal program segment.

```
Num := 0;
for i := 1 to n do
        if ( INSERT EXPRESSION HERE ) then
                Num := Num + 1;
Pi := 4 * Num/n
```

will cause the program segment to approximate the number $Pi = 3.14159...$by a Monte Carlo technique?

I.   Rnd * Rnd + Rnd * Rnd < 1

II.   sqr(Rnd) + sqr(Rnd) < 1

III. Rnd + Rnd < 1

(A) I only

(B) II only

(C) III only

(D) I and II

(E) II and III

22. If list A contains the integers in the set (3, 7, 8, 10, 18, 22, 35) and if a binary search routine is to be used to determine whether the number 25 is in the list, how many comparisons are needed to make the correct comparison?

(A) 8

(B) 7

(C) 6

(D) 3

(E) 1

23. If there are 8 internal nodes in a full binary tree, at MOST how many leaves can there be?

    (A) 8

    (B) 4

    (C) 16

    (D) 1

    (E) 15

24. If a list A contains 32 distinct numbers arranged in ascending order and a binary search is to be used to determine whether some number x occurs in this list, what is the number of comparisons that must be made by the search in the WORST case?

    (A) 5

    (B) 26

    (C) 13

    (D) 8

    (E) 4

25. Given the following program segment in Pascal, where all the variables are assumed to be properly declared,

    ```
    N := 1;
    while N < > 1000 do
            begin
                    writeln(N);
                    N := N + 2
            end.
    ```

    which of the following statements BEST describes this program segment?

    (A) It prints just the positive integers less than 1000.

    (B) It prints just the positive odd integers less than 1000.

    (C) It contains an infinite loop.

    (D) It contains a finite loop.

    (E) It produces no output.

26. Consider the following recursive function

```
function ABC(M : integer): integer;
var VALUE : integer;

begin
        if M := 0 then VALUE := 3
                else VALUE := ABC(M – 1) + 5;
        ABC := VALUE
        writeln ('Current values of M and VALUE are ', M, VALUE)
end;
```

What output is produced by the following statement: writeln(ABC(3));

(A) 8

(B) 18

(C) 13

(D) 5

(E) 3

27. Given the following function in Pascal

```
function Sum(Limit : integer) : integer;
var Total, Incr : integer;

begin
        Total := 0
        for Incr := 1 to Limit do
                Total := Total + Incr;
        Sum := Total
end;
```

which of the following is being calculated by the function?

(A) 1 + 2 + ... + Total

(B) 1 + 2 + ... + Sum

(C) 1 + 2 + ... + Incr

(D) 1 + 2 + ... + Limit

(E) 1 + 2 + ... + Limit + ...

28. Given the following function Recur in Pascal in which one of the numbered statements as written will cause a problem in the program:

```
function Recur(Y : integer) : integer;
var Temp : integer;

begin
      if Y < 0 then
              Temp := 1                    [ 1 ]
      else
              Temp := Recur(Y)             [ 2 ]
end;
```

which of the following statements, when substituted for the numbered statement, will correct the problem in the program?

(A)   [2] Temp := Recur(Y + 1)

(B)   [1] Temp := 0

(C)   [1] Temp := Y

(D)   [2] Temp := Recur(Y) + 1

(E)   none of the choices

29. If the integers X1, X2, X3, …, X32 were placed on a stack in that order and the following TYPE and VAR declarations for constructing the stack data structure are given below

```
type Ptr = ^SkElement;
       SkElement = Record
                        Structure : integer;
                        P : Ptr
              end;
       var SkPtr : Ptr;
```

which stack data structure is represented?

(A)   A record

(B)   Files

(C)   Pointers

(D)   Queue

(E)   One-dimensional array of 32 integers

30. The following set of TYPE and VAR declarations in Pascal

```
type XPtr : ^XEntry;
        XEntry : record
                data : integer;
                next : XPrt
                    end;

var Front, Back, Entry : Prt;
```

represents which type of dynamic data structure?

(A) Queue

(B) Stack

(C) Graph

(D) Binary tree

(E) Doubly linked list

31. The intent of the following algorithm is to delete the last node from a singly linked list. The variable First points to the first node in the list, if there is one, and otherwise has the value Nil.

```
type Node = record
                    DatVal : integer;
                    Link : ^ Node
            end;

var X, Y, First : ^Node;

X := First
Y := X^.Link
while Y^.Link < > Nil do
        begin
                X:= Y;
                Y := Y^.Link
        end;
    X^.Link := Nil
```

Which of the following statements correctly describes the class of all linked lists for which the algorithm works?

(A) The empty list and all linked lists with more than one entry

(B) All doubly linked lists

(C) All nonempty linked lists

(D) All linked lists with more than one entry

(E) No linked lists

DIRECTIONS: Questions 32 and 33 refer to the following procedure that sorts integers from smallest to largest by performing a selection sort.

```
Procedure Selectsort(Var item : list; itemnum : integer);
Var
        min : ,integer; (*smallest value in the sublist*)
        minpos          (*position index for min*)
        i,j : integer;    (*running indices*)

BEGIN
        FOR  i := 1 to itemnum –1 DO
              BEGIN
                      minpos := i;
                      min   := item[minpos];
                      FOR  j := i + 1 itemnum  DO
                             IF item[j] < min  THEN
                                    BEGIN
                                          minpos := j ;
                                          min    := item[j]
                                    END;  (*End IF*)
                             item[minpos] := item[i];
                             item[i]        := min
              END (*End for i*)
        END (*End Procedure*)
```

32. If the ArraySize is 6, how many passes are required to sort the entries into ascending order?

   (A) 6

   (B) 12

   (C) 7

   (D) 5

   (E) 4

33. Which of the following expressions indicates the number of passes P required to sort a list of M elements in increasing order?

    (A) 2 * M

    (B) M − 1

    (C) M + 1

    (D) M

    (E) 2^M

34. Suppose that the items X1, X2, X3, X4, and X5 are pushed, in that order, onto an initial empty stack S, that S is then popped four times, and that as each Xi is popped off S, it is inserted into an initially empty queue. If one Xi is then deleted from the queue, what is the NEXT item that will be deleted from the queue?

    (A) X4

    (B) X1

    (C) X3

    (D) X5

    (E) X2

35. Consider the following sequence of procedure calls:

    ```
    Push(X);
    Push(Y);
    Add;
    Push(Z);
    Push(W);
    Mult;
    Add;
    ```

    A Push invoked causes its argument to be pushed onto a stack. The procedure Add or Mult causes (1) the stack to be popped twice, (2) the two popped items to be added or multiplied, and (3) the result to be pushed onto the stack. If X = 5, Y = 10, Z = 15 and W = 20, and the stack is empty initially, then at the end of the sequence of procedure calls, which of the following values does the stack contain?

(A) 220

(B) 705

(C) 0

(D) 315

(E) empty

Questions 36 through 40 are based on the case study provided at the
back of this book.

---

36. Logically, an item can only be picked up by the player if that item is in
    the room currently occupied by the player. Which of the following
    statements would correctly test for this? The test would appear as the
    first statement in the procedure *ProcessGo*.

    (A) IF NOT (item IN Rooms[CurrentLocation].Items) THEN

    (B) IF item NOT IN Rooms[CurrentLocation].Items) THEN

    (C) IF Rooms[CurrentLocation].Items <= Characters[PLAYER].Items
         THEN

    (D) IF NOT (item IN CurrentLocation) THEN

    (E) None of the above.

37. Assume FUNCTION Opposite(d : DirectionType) : DirectionType has
    been added to the program. This function returns the opposite of a
    specified direction. For example, *Opposite(NORTH) = SOUTH*. This
    function would be useful in modifying the *EstablishConnection* proce-
    dure so that it established a two-way connection between two rooms.
    Which of the statements below would be added to *EstablishConnection*
    to accomplish this?

    (A) Rooms[Opposite(Start)].Exits[Opposite(Direct)] := Finish;

    (B) Rooms[Finish].Exits[Opposite(Direct)] := Start;

    (C) Rooms[Finish].Exits[Direct] := Opposite(Start);

    (D) Rooms[Start].Exits[Opposite(Direct)] := Finish;

    (E) None of the above.

38. If we wanted to modify the command interface so that it would allow multiple spaces before and after commands, which of the following techniques would be effective?

(A) Modify *ReadWord* so that it reads as follows:
```
REPEAT
Read(c);
UNTIL c <> ' ';
i := 1;
WHILE c <> ' ' DO BEGIN
  s[i] := c;
  Read(c);
  i := i + 1;
END;
FOR j := i TO StringSize DO
  s[j] := ' ';
```

(B) Modify *ReadWord* so that it reads as follows:
```
i := 1;
WHILE c <> ' ' DO BEGIN
  s[i] := c;
  Read(c);
  i := i + 1;
END;
REPEAT
Read(c);
UNTIL c <> ' ';
FOR j := i TO StringSize DO
  s[j] := ' ';
```

(C) Modify *ReadWord* so that it reads as follows:
```
i := 1;
WHILE c <> ' ' DO BEGIN
  s[i] := c;
  Read(c);
  i := i + 1;
END;
WHILE c <> ' ' DO Read(c);
FOR j := i TO StringSize DO
  s[j] := ' ';
```

(D) (B) and (C) will both work, but (A) will not.

(E) (A) and (B) will work, but not (C).

39. Someone might argue that using an enumerated *CommandType* introduces needless complexity to this program since the command string read from the user must always be converted to the corresponding enumerated type. Which of the statements below best explains why an enumerated *CommandType* was adopted?

   (A) Strings cannot be used as array indices.

   (B) Strings cannot be used as CASE statement labels.

   (C) Using an enumerated type makes it easier to add new commands to the program.

   (D) Enumerated types can be checked for equality.

   (E) Both (A) and (D).

40. Rather than use the index of the room itself to indicate that there is no exit in a given direction, why is it not possible to set the value of the *Exits* array to zero to indicate this?

   (A) Because zero is not a legitimate room number.

   (B) Because zero is not a legitimate direction type.

   (C) Because there would be no matching CASE lable in the *ProcessCommand* procedure.

   (D) Because this would require an additional array location in the *Exits* array.

   (E) All of the above.

SECTION 2

TIME: 1 hour, 45 minutes
5 Questions

DIRECTIONS: Give a detailed answer, written in standard Pascal, to each problem.

---

1. Suppose that the declarations for a stack of integers is given by

    ```
    type   StackPtr : ^StackEntry;
           StackEntry : record
                           Data : integer;
                           Next : StackPtr
                        end;
       var   Top, NewEntry : StackPtr;
    ```

    Assume that a procedure which adds an entry (Push procedure) exists. Use standard Pascal to write a procedure with header statements

    ```
    procedure Pop(var Top : StackPtr;
                  var Value : integer
                  var Error : Boolean);
       var   Ptr : StackPtr;
    ```

    that guard against the stack being empty before applying Pop. The error is called Stack Underflow. Use a parameter Error which will be set equal to true if Pop is called when the stack is empty, and will also output the error message "Stack Underflow." Otherwise, Error will be set to false.

2. Consider the sum of the first N positive integers: $1 + 2 + \ldots + N$. Write a program in Pascal, using the following header statements, to find the first value of N for which the sum exceeds 10,000.

    ```
    program SumN(Input, Output);

       var Sum, NumTerms : integer;
    ```

3. Write a Pascal program which will create a file containing the integers 1, 2, 3, ..., 1000. Use the following header/declarations:

```
program CreateFile( Input, Output);

type IntFile = file of integer;

var Nums : IntFile;
      K : integer;
```

Questions 4 and 5 are based on the case study provided at the back of this book.

4. Most "real" text adventure games offered a sense of atmosphere by having long detailed descriptions of the rooms as players would enter them. The implementation described here does not allow for this, since it is not practical to store lengthy stretches of text within a Pascal record. Suggest a technique whereby this feature can be added to the program. (Hint: Consider how *CanPass* and *InitialAction* are used.)

5. Show the code additions you would make to add a closet to the north of the bedroom. The closet contains a treasure chest.

COMPUTER SCIENCE AB
TEST 4

ANSWER KEY

1.	(B)		21.	(B)
2.	(B)		22.	(D)
3.	(C)		23.	(A)
4.	(E)		24.	(A)
5.	(A)		25.	(C)
6.	(A)		26.	(B)
7.	(C)		27.	(D)
8.	(B)		28.	(E)
9.	(E)		29.	(C)
10.	(E)		30.	(A)
11.	(D)		31.	(D)
12.	(B)		32.	(D)
13.	(C)		33.	(B)
14.	(E)		34.	(A)
15.	(D)		35.	(D)
16.	(D)		36.	(A)
17.	(D)		37.	(B)
18.	(E)		38.	(A)
19.	(C)		39.	(B)
20.	(A)		40.	(A)

DETAILED EXPLANATIONS OF ANSWERS

COMPUTER SCIENCE AB
TEST 4
SECTION 1

1.   **(B)**
To do an inorder traversal of the above tree, we must first process the leftmost subtree. This leads down to node 2, which has no subtrees. Therefore, we can first write out 2 and back up to the next node which is the binary operation addition, +. The result of processing the left subtree yields the printed results 2 +. From this point we lead to the next node, x, down the right subtree which has no further subtrees. So, we can now write out x next to 2 + to obtain 2 + x. The next step is to back up to the next node which is the operation symbol, *, and write out * next to 2 + x to obtain 2 + x *. From this point proceed down the right subtree from node * to node 4 and write out the node value 4 next to * in 2 + x *. The result is now 2 + x * 4. Note that since the two operation symbols appear between two operands, it is often necessary to put in some parentheses to determine the order of operations. Thus, 2 + x * 4 would be (2 + x) * 4.

Answer choice A indicates that the node labeled * is the leftmost subtree which is to be processed first. This is false because the node has another left subtree, namely, 2. So the first printed result in the traversal must be 2. Thus, it is impossible for the results of choice A to be correct.

Since the inorder traversal process requires that the leftmost subtree is always processed first, it is easy to conclude that 4 * + 2 x, answer choice (C), is impossible to obtain. Note that the first value in the output is a right subtree node.

Instead of answer choice (D) addressing an inorder traversal process it addresses a classic preorder traversal. Note that for a preorder traversal, we must first write the root node, *, and then proceed to do a preorder on the left subtree, +, from the root node. A similar process is done for the right subtree from the root node. Answer choice (E) addresses a classic postorder transversal instead of an inorder traversal process. Note that for a postorder traversal, we must first write out the leftmost node, 2, followed by writing out the right node for the operation node + in the graph to obtain 2 x +. Next we are led to write out node 4, which is the subtree for operation *. This is followed by a write out of the operation *. The final results is 2 x + 4 *.

2.   **(B)**

As a result of observing the construction of the given binary tree notice that node 6 has both a left and a right child given by nodes 3 and 4, respectively. This is shown in row 4 of the array in response (B). From node 3 observe that there is a left and right child given by 1 and 2, respectively, shown in row 1 of the array. Node 4 has only a right child which is given in row 6 of the array. Finally observe that nodes 1, 2 and 5, respectively, do not have children. This is given in rows 3, 2 and 5, respectively, of the array.

Answer choice A is incorrect because none of the rows in the array represents any part of the given binary tree. Observe that row 1 in the array for answer choice C indicates correctly that node 6 has left and right children (nodes 3 and 4); row 4 shows correctly that node 4 has only a right child; and, rows 3 and 6 show that nodes 1 and 5 have nil pointers. However, notice that row 2 in the array shows that node 2 has left and right children (nodes 1 and 3) which is not true.

After observing the array for answer choice D, notice that row 1 indicates that node 1 has a left child (node 2) and a right child (node 5) which is not correct. Hence, this choice is incorrect. Finally, observe that row 1 in answer choice E indicates that node 3 has a left and a right child at nodes 6 and 4, respectively. This is not true. Hence, answer choice E is incorrect.

3.   **(C)**

In accordance with the above procedure, the first integer, 1, in the string is pushed onto the stack, followed by 2 (the second integer in the string) which is now the topmost integer in the stack. The third or next digit encountered in the string is 0 which evokes a "pop" from the stack of the topmost integer which is 2. Thus, 2 is the first character to be printed in the output. The fourth digit encountered in the string is 3 which is pushed onto the track above 1. The fifth and sixth digits in the string, 0 and 0, respectively, each envokes a pop from the stack. Thus, 3 and 1, respectively, are popped from the stack. So, the printed output at this point is 2 3 1. The seventh digit, 4, in the string is pushed onto the stack and the eighth digit, 0, in the string pops the 4 out of the stack. Thus, the final printed output is 2 3 1 4.

To understand the reason why answer choice A is incorrect one should again consider the same approach to the procedure for the given string, 1 2 0 3 0 0 4 0. In particular, note that the first two integers in the string are pushed onto the stack, that is, 1 followed by 2. The third integer, 0, in the string pops 2 from the stack and thus 2 is the first digit in the printed output. Since the first digit in answer choice A is 1, and the first digit to be popped from the stack is 2, it is impossible for this answer choice to be correct.

For answer choice B notice again that the first two integers in the given string, 1 followed by 2, are pushed onto the stack, while the third integer, 0, causes the 2 to be popped from the stack. So 2 is the first digit in the output. The fourth integer, 3, in the string is pushed onto the stack, but the next two digits, 0 and 0, cause the 3 and 1, respectively to be popped from the stack. At this point notice that the output is 2 3 1, whereas answer choice B for the first three digits is 2 3 4. Hence, this choice cannot be correct.

Using the reasoning stated for answer choice A, notice that the first digit in the output for the given string is 2, whereas the first digit in answer choice D is 4. Thus, answer choice D cannot be correct. Finally, if the string given in answer choice E is compared with the correct answer string one can easily note that they differ at the second digit. Hence, answer choice E cannot be correct.

4.   **(E)**

In accordance with the above procedure, the first digit to be pushed onto the stack is 1. Then, the next digit invokes a pop routine which means that the 1 is now an output value. The third integer, 0, envokes a second pop but there is nothing in the stack to be popped. The stack is empty. Hence, the procedure on the string is terminated or it impossible to handle the given string. So, answer choice E is correct.

Answer choices A, B, C, and D are all incorrect because it is impossible to achieve either of these results from the procedure given for the problem.

5.   **(A)**

The adjacency matrix of the given graph is a 4 x 4 matrix where the entry (i,j) is the number of arcs (or edges) between nodes n(i) and n(j). Observe that entry (1,1) is a 1 due to the loop at node 1. All other entries along the main diagonal [(2,2), (3,3), (4,4)] are 0 because there are no loops at the nodes 2, 3, and 4. Entry (2,1) is a 1 because there is one arc between node 2 and node 1, which also means that entry (1,2) is a 1. Entry (3,1) is a 0 because there is no arc between node 3 and node 1, which means that entry (1,3) is 0. Entry (4,1) is a 1 because there is one arc between node 4 and node 1, which also means that entry (1,4) is a 1. Entry (3,2) is 1 and entry (2,3) is also 1 because there is only one arc between their respective nodes. Entry (4,3) is 2 and entry (3,4) is also 2 because there are two arcs between their respective nodes. Finally, entry (4,2) is 0 and (2,4) is also 0 because there is no arc between their respective nodes. Thus, answer choice A is correct.

A careful examination of the matrix given for answer choice B indicates that it only differs from the matrix given for the correct answer at entry (3,4). This entry indicates a 1 which means that there is only 1 arc between node 3 and node 4. The graph indicates that there are 2 arcs. Hence, answer choice B is incorrect.

For answer choice C observe that the entries along the diagonal are all 1's. The graph indicates that only one entry, (1,1) along the diagonal of the matrix should have a value of 1 because of the loop at node 1. Hence, this answer choice is incorrect. For answer choice D observe that the entries along the diagonal are all 0's. The graph indicates that each of the entries along the diagonal should be 0 except for entry (1,1), which should have a value of 1 because of the loop at node 1. Hence, answer choice D is not correct. Finally, for answer choice E observe that the entries in column 1 are all 1's. The graph indicates that entry (3,1) has a value of 0 because there is no arc between node 3 and node 1. Hence, choice E is incorrect.

6.   **(A)**
To form an expression for a + (b * c) − d in prefix notation requires the following action. First, we can write the operation symbol + before its operand a. The prefix notation allows the operation symbol − to be written out before any action on the expression, b * c, or d. Then, the prefix notation allows the operation symbol *, which occurs between b and c, to be written after the − symbol. This is true because when the expression in prefix notation is executed the operation symbol in front of an operand is placed after the operand unless another symbol has been previously placed there. In that case, the operation symbol is placed later in the next available position. Finally, the prefix notation allows the operands b, c and d to be written in that order in the expression. Thus, the prefix notation for the given expression is given by + a − * b c d.

Answer choices B, D and E are incorrect because the prefix notation in each case requires that the operation symbol + for "a" be written first. Choice C is the postfix notation for the given expression.

7.   **(C)**
To form an expression for W + (X * Y − Z) in postfix notation requires the following action. First, the postfix notation allows one to write the operands W, X and Y before the first operation symbol *, and follow this with the operand Z. The reason for this can be seen when the postfix expression is executed. Here the operation * is placed in post order between X and Y. The

final step in the postfix notation allows the two operation symbols – and + to be placed in that order in the expression after the operand Z. This is true because the execution of the postfix expression places, in post order, the – symbol in front of Z and the + symbol in front of X since the * symbol would have already been placed. Thus, the final postfix notation for the given expression is given by W X Y * Z – +.

Answer choices B, D and E are incorrect because the postfix notation requires that the operand W, X and Y be written first. Neither of these choices meets this requirement. Answer choice A is the prefix notation for the given expression.

8.   **(B)**
If n = 1 node, then the tree structure consists of a single node and no arcs, so the number of arcs is 1 less than the number of nodes. That is, the number of arcs is given by 1 – 1 = 0 or no arc. Let n = 2 nodes. Then, the tree structure consists of two nodes and one arc. So the number of arcs is still 1 less than the number of nodes. That is, 2 – 1 = 1 arc. This process can be generalized using mathematical induction, so that one can easily see that there are n – 1 arcs in any tree structure with n nodes.

Answer choice A is incorrect since it states that the number of arcs for a tree structure with n nodes is squared. This is impossible by considering any simple example of a tree structure. Using other simple examples it can be easily shown that answer choices C, D and E, respectively, are not possible.

9.   **(E)**
The graph is not a tree structure since it is not acyclic. That is, the graph has a cycle at (b,c) or (c,b). Thus, if we remove this cycle or the one at (a,b), then the graph becomes acyclic. Hence, the graph will then be a tree structure.

Answer choices B, D and E do nothing to transform the graph into an acyclic structure. Thus, each of these choices is incorrect.

10.   **(E)**
Let node 1 be the initial node in set N. Next consider all the nodes adjacent to any given node in N, that is, all nodes adjacent to node 1, and select the closest one with smallest distance-weight (3 units), which is node x. So, N = (1, x), and consider all nodes not in N that are adjacent to either 1 or x. The closest such node is 3, 4 units away from x. For N = (1, x, 3), the next closest node is node 4, 1 unit away from node 3. The remaining nodes are added in a similar fashion. Thus, node y is added to N, followed by node 2. Finally, the minimial spanning tree is given by the set N = (1, x, 3, 4, y, 2).

The set given in answer choice A, B, C and D, respectively, will not yield a tree structure with minimal weight.

11.   **(D)**

The key procedure for reducing the given expression is to observe that an additional term, namely, x x' x , must be added to the expression. This is
$$\underset{1\ \ 2\ \ 3}{}$$
possible by using the Boolean property, idempotent, which states that x + x = x. Thus, we can write the original expression with the additional term included as follows:

$$\underset{1\,2\,3}{x\,x\,x} + \underset{1\,2\,3}{x\,x'\,x} + \underset{1\,2\,3}{x\,x'\,x} + \underset{1\,2\,3}{x\,x'\,x'} + \underset{1\,2\,3}{x'\,x'\,x} + \underset{1\,2\,3}{x'\,x'\,x'},$$

where the second and third terms represent a replacement for the second term in the original expression by the idempotent property. Using the appropriate grouping, factoring and the Boolean complement property we can obtain,

$$\underset{1\,3\,2\quad2}{x\,x\,(x+x')} + \underset{1\,2\,3\quad3}{x\,x'\,(x'+x)} + \underset{1\,2\,3\quad3}{x'\,x'\,(x+x')}$$

$$= \underset{1\,3}{x\,x\,(1)} + \underset{1\,2}{x\,x'\,(1)} + \underset{1\,2}{x'\,x'\,(1)}$$

$$= \underset{1\,3}{x\,x} + \underset{2\,1\,1}{x'(x'+x')}$$

$$= \underset{1\,3}{x\,x} + \underset{2}{x'\,(1)} = \underset{1\,3}{x\,x} + \underset{2}{x'}$$

None of the other answer choices satisfy the conditions of the given expression.

12.   **(B)**

First, write the given expression as follows and replace 1 with 1 + y, where 1 = 1 + y in Boolean algebra. Thus, we get

$$x + x'y = x\,(1) + x'y$$
$$= x\,(1 + y) + x'y$$

Then, we expand, factor appropriately, and replace x + x' with 1 to get the desired expression.

$$= x + xy + x'y = x + y(x + x') = x + y$$

Answer choices A, C, D, and E cannot be obtained from the given expression.

13.   **(C)**
        Notice that IntPtr is defined as a pointer type data structure that points to a variable of type integer. Also note that the declared pointer variable, Point1, is a variable containing the address of a variable of integer type. The statement new(Point1) creates a variable for Point1 to reference.
        The NEW procedure does not create an integer (see answer choices A and D), nor does it create a point or pointer value (see answer choices B and E).

14.   **(E)**
        Observe that Point1 is declared as an integer pointer. In Pascal, the value of a pointer cannot be displayed. Thus, writeln(Point1) in the program segment will not display the results of New(Point1). Usually, a run-time error will occur. None of the other answer choices is possible for the given set of statements.

15.   **(D)**
        Observe that Pointer2 is an integer pointer. In Pascal, no arithmetic is allowed involving pointer variables. Thus, the given statement will usually cause a run-time error. None of the other answer choices is possible for the given statement.

16.   **(D)**
        Since the string of integers 9 5 1 7 3 is arranged on the stack such that 9 is at the bottom and 3 is at the top, a Pop procedure will eliminate the 3 from the stack. Thus, the result after the pop is the string given by 9 5 1 7. None of the other answer choices will yield an appropriate result after the Pop procedure.

17.   **(D)**
        Recall that a procedure is a section of a program that performs a specific task, whenever the programs encounter the procedure name. When the program calls procedure, it assigns a value to each parameter. When the second procedure, S, is called the information from procedure R is appropriately passed. Top-down design approach, ease of passing parameters, and ease of testing procedures are among the reasons choice D is the BEST.
        All of the other answer choices can work in finding the information desired about an item in the table. However, no other choice represents the BEST, efficient approach.

18.   **(E)**

A queue grows by inserting new entries at one end (the rear of the queue) and shrinks by deleting new entries from the other end (the front of the queue). Since the waiting line in the doctor's office adds patients to the end of the line, while deleting from the beginning of the line those patients who have seen the doctor, the process is an example of a queue structure.

The structure listed in each of the other answer choices does not simulate a deleting process. Hence, the structure in choices A, B, C, and D fail to be appropriate for the waiting line simulation.

19.   **(C)**

Since the Rnd function returns a real number in the interval from 0 to 1.0, it is desirable to divide the real line in this interval in tenths. Then, the distance from 0 to 0.6 will be 60 percent of the distance from 0 to 1.0; 0.6 to 0.9 will be 30 percent of the distance; and, 0.9 to 1.0 will be 10 percent of the distance. This suggests, from the information given in the problem, that 'Straight' should correspond to a value of Rnd between 0 and 0.6, 'Right' corresponds to a value between 0.6 and 0.9, and 'Left' be a value between 0.9 and 1.0. Hence, only choice III will satisfy the missing information in the given segment.

Answer choices A, B, D and E will not satisfy the missing information in the program segment.

20.   **(A)**

Observe that the smallest integer value for DiceTo1 is 2 and the largest integer value is 12. When Trunc(6 * Rnd + 1) is executed for either Die1 or Die2, an integer is returned with a value in the interval from 1 to 6. Thus, the sum of Die1 and Die2 will yield a total in the interval from 2 to 12. Thus, Option I is the only one among the four that is correct. None of the other answer choices will make the program segment complete.

21.   **(B)**

Observe that the function sqr produces a value that is the square of its argument and the value produced is also the same type as its argument. In expression II, each of the sqr(Rnd) terms involves a two-step action before the addition operation occurs. First, the function Rnd is called and it returns a real number value between 0 and 1 to the argument of the function sqr. Then, the sqr function is called and it returns a real number that is the square of its argument. If the sum of the sqr(Rnd) and sqr(Rnd) is less than 1, then the Num variable is increased by 1. The procedure, when completed will have simulated a Monte Carlo technique in the approximation of Pi. Thus, choice B is correct.

Expression I appears at first glace to yield the same result as expression II. However, the problem is that expression I will usually give a run-time error because of the operation involved. Hence, answer choices A, C, D and E are incorrect.

22.　　**(D)**
Since there are $n = 7$ items in the list, the items are in ascending order, and a binary search is to be used, the first step in the search is to start with the middle item ($n/2 = 3$) which is the third item, namely 18. Compare the middle item with $x = 25$. Because $x > 18$, the search commences on the second half of the list, namely the items, 22, 34. This time the number of items has been reduced to 2, so the location of the middle item is at 22. Because $x > 22$, the middle item, search the second half of this list, namely the item 34. Now the middle item is located at 22. Because $x > 22$, the search commences with the second half of this list, namely 34. This is a 1-element list, in which the middle item is the only item. Now compare 34 with x. Because $x < 34$, search the first half of this list, but the first half is empty. Thus, the process is done and we know that x is not in the list. There were three comparisons required in all. None of the other answer choices satisfy the conditions of the problem.

23.　　**(A)**
A node with no children is said to be a leaf of the binary tree. Thus, all nonleaves are internal nodes of the tree. As a result of this there are at most 8 leaves on a full binary tree that has 8 internal nodes. Use an example to verify this result. None of the other answer choices work if the full binary tree has only 8 internal nodes.

24.　　**(A)**
In the worst case using a binary search the total number of comparisons, c, is given by the expression $2^{\wedge}c = n+1$, where n is the number of items in the list. Observe that $2^{\wedge}5 = 32$. Thus, the number of comparisons is $c = 5$. None of the other answer choices satisfy the conditions of the problem.

25.　　**(C)**
Observe that for $N = 1$ the first printout in the while...do loop is 1. Then, N is incremented by 2 in the loop so that the next printed output is 3. This process is continued and will yield an infinite loop since N will never equal 1000. Thus, answer choice C is the BEST description of the program segment. None of the other answer choices will completely describe what happens in the program segment.

26.   **(B)**
When the current value of M has the value 0, the variable VALUE has the value 3. When M has the value 1, VALUE has the value 8. When M has the value 2, VALUE has the value 13. Finally, when M has the value 3, VALUE has the value 18. Thus, writeln(ABC(3)) will output the value 18. None of the other answer choices meet the requirements of the recursive function.

27.   **(D)**
Observe that a sum of integers is being calculated. The variable Total accumulates the sum which is initially set equal to 0. The number of loops with the variable Incr depends on the value of Limit passed to the function Sum. On each Incr repetition or loop, Incr is added to Total. Finally, Total is assigned to Sum. Hence, answer choice D, 1 + 2 + ... + Limit, is the correct sum being evaluated. None of the other answer choices satisfy the conditions of the function given in the problem.

28.   **(E)**
Observe that if the value of Y is positive, then the function Recur will recurse infinitely using the same value of Y. Thus, the current structure of statement [2] sets up an infinite recursive call. This is a recursive call that never ends. To fix this problem one needs to place Y − 1 in the argument of the function Recur to obtain Recur(Y−1). This move will eventually reduce the computation of Recur(Y−1) to computing Recur(0), (when Y = 1), which will halt the procedure. None of the answer options will satisfy the conditions of the problem.

29.   **(C)**
The stack data structure, represented in the TYPE and VAR declarations, is stack pointers. This is indicated in the TYPE statements as follows: The name Ptr is defined as a dynamic data type whose pointers will point to objects of the indicated name "SkElement." In the VAR statement the variable SkPtr is a reference variable or pointer variable that is bound to an integer value. Thus, answer choice C is correct. None of the other choices will satisfy the given TYPE and VAR declarations.

30.   **(A)**
Note that a queue has a front and a back, and so the two pointers, Front and Back, are required to point to these entries. The queue entries themselves are records similar to those used in a linked list. The defined type statement XPtr is a dynamic data type whose pointers will point to objects of the

indicated XEntry. Note again that the Front and Back variables are pointer variables to be used in the queue process. Thus, a queue is the correct dynamic data structure given in the declarations. None of the other answer choices satisfy the requirements given in the declarations.

31. **(D)**
Observe that X^.Link in the algorithm points to the node to be deleted. To make the deletion of the node in the singly linked list, the algorithm allows for the value of the X^.Link pointer to be adjusted. If the node to be deleted is the last entry in the list, then X^.Link will be set to Nil. Otherwise, the algorithm will let the X^.Link pointer point to the entry node. Thus, the algorithm will work correctly with all singly linked lists with more than one entry. The algorithm will not satisfy the conditions given by the other answer choices.

32. **(D)**
Observe that the algorithm operates as a sequence of passes. The number of passes is determined by the positioning of the integers in order. Note that each pass may or may not require an interchange of entries to establish the correct position of the entry in the ordering. An interchange of entries is required unless the entry is already in the correct position. Thus, only 5 passes is required to order the integers. None of the other answer choices satisfy the conditions given in the algorithm.

33. **(B)**
The procedure first determines the smallest entry among the array of entries and interchanges it with the first entry if the first entry is not the smallest. This process continues until the Pth pass places the last element in the ordering. The total number of passes is given by $P = M - 1$. That is, the number of passes P is the total number of elements M to be sorted less 1. None of the other answer choices satisfy the conditions given in the algorithm.

34. **(A)**
Observe that the five items are already onto the stack S with X5 at the top. The popping action four times will cause the items to be removed from the stack in the following order: first X5, followed by X4, X3, X2. As each Xi is popped from the stack it is placed into the queue in the order X5, X4, X3, X2. The one Xi deleted from the queue will be the first one placed into it, that is, X5. Hence, X4 is the NEXT Xi that will be deleted from the queue. None of the other answer choices will satisfy the conditions given in the problem.

35.   **(D)**
Push(X) and Push(Y) place 5, followed by 10 onto the stack. Add pops 10 and 5 off the stack, adds them to get 15 and push the results or sum onto the stack. Push(Z) and Push(W) place 15 and 20, respectively, onto the stack. Thus, the stack contains 15, 15, and 20 in that order. Mult pops 20 and 20 off the stack, multiply them to get the product 400 and pushes the product onto the stack. Thus, the stack contains 15 and 300 in that order. Finally, the Add pops 300 and 15 from the stack, adds them to get 315 and then pushes the sum onto the stack. Thus, the stack contains 315 at the end of the sequence of procedure calls. None of the other answer choices will yield this result.

36.   **(A)**
(B) is syntactically incorrect. (D) is nonsensical since *CurrentLocation* is not a set. (C) tests to see if the items in the room are a subset of the items in the player's inventory, which is not relevant to the question.

37.   **(B)**
(A) and (C) are incorrect since the argument to *Opposite* must be a direction, not a room number. (D) is incorrect since it establishes an incorrect connection from *Start* to *Finish*. (B) is the only statement that specifies a connection from *Finish* to *Start*.

38.   **(A)**
(B) and (C) will cause the first letter of the next word typed to be skipped.

39.   **(B)**
(A) is a true statement but not relevant to this design decision since *CommandStringTable* would not be needed if an enumerated type for definitions was not used. (D) is also true, but not relevant since the program also contains a mechanism for comparing strings for equality. (C) is incorrect since using an enumerated type for commands actually increases the number of modifications that must be done when a new command is entered. (A) is the only true, relevant, statement.

40.   **(A)**
(B) and (C) are nonsensical. (D) would be true if one created an additional room corresponding to "nowhere," but since none is defined or postulated (A) is the only correct answer.

DETAILED EXPLANATIONS OF ANSWERS SECTION 2

1.

```
begin                                            (1)
    if Top = nil then                            (2)
    begin
            Error := true;                       (3)
            writeln('Stack Underflow')           (4)
        end                                      (5)
    else
      begin                                      (6)
        Ptr := Top                               (7)
        Value := Top^.Data;                      .
        Top := Top^.Next                         .
        dispose(Ptr);                            .
        Error := false                          (10)
    end
end;                                            (11)
```

Statement (1) begins the Pop routine. Statement (2) is an if statement in the error checking routine which acts to begin the next segment of the program if a nil value is stored in Top. Statement (3) actually makes the Error variable true if Top of the stack has a nil value. Statement (4) writes the message "Stack Underflow" as a result of the previous statement being true. Then, statement (5) ends the procedure. On the other hand, statement (6) is executed only if Top does not equal to a nil value. In statements (7) – (10) the program entries sequentially check the integer values from Top of the stack, disposes Ptr, and stores "false" in Error for each non-nil integer. Statement (11) ends Pop routine.

2.

```
begin                                            (1)
    Sum := 0;                                    (2)
    NumTerms := 0;                               (3)
    while Sum <= 10000 do                        (4)
```

```
                begin
                        NumTerms := NumTerms + 1        (5)
                        Sum := Sum + NumTerms           (6)
                end;                                    (7)
            writeln('It takes ', NumTerms ,
                    ' terms to exceed 10000.')          (8)
    end.                                                (9)
```

Statement (1) begins the SumN program. Statements (2) and (3) initialize the accumulator variable Sum and the counter variable NumTerms. Statements (4) – (7) represent a while...do loop to calculate the various sums, by continually adding one more term. For each sum, the program checks the value and stops the loop when the sum exceeds 10000. Then, statement (8) outputs the required number NumTerms. Statement (9) terminates the program.

3.

```
    begin                                               (1)
            rewrite(Nums);                              (2)
            for K := 1 to 1000 do                       (3)
                begin                                   (4)
                        Nums^ := K                      (5)
                        put(Nums);                      (6)
                end                                     (7)
    end.                                                (8)
```

Statement (1) begins the CreateFile routine. Statement (2) invokes the Rewrite procedure which erases the current contents of the file and positions the file pointer to component 0 (that is, the beginning of the file). Statements (2) – (7) is a for...do loop designed to place the integers into the IntFile. Statements (5) and (6) within the loop write each value of K to the file as follows: Each value of K is assigned to the buffer variable Nums^ and then put(Nums) writes each value of the file buffer variable into the file. Statement (8) concludes the program.

4.   Add the line De*scribe(room)* as the first statement inside the IF statement of *ProcessGo*. Create the procedure below:

```
PROCEDURE Describe(room : RoomNumber);
BEGIN
  CASE room OF
```

```
      HALLWAY : BEGIN
        Writeln('The hallway is long and dark.  The only light');
        Writeln(' comes from a broken window above the door.')
        END;
      DINING_ROOM : BEGIN
        { ... appropriate write statements ...}
        END;
      {create cases for all the other rooms}
      END;
    END;
```

5.   Add the constants CLOSET = 5 and CHEST = 4. Change NumRooms and NumItems to 5 and 4. Add the following lines to *SetUpAdventure*:

```
      InitRoom(CLOSET, 'Closet');
      InitItem(CHEST, 'Chest');
      EstablishConnection(BEDROOM, NORTH, CLOSET);
      EstablishConnection(CLOSET, SOUTH, BEDROOM);
      AddItemToRoom(CHEST, CLOSET);
```

Case Study

CASE STUDY

1   SPECIFICATION

1.1   Text Adventure Games

In a text adventure game, the player assumes the role of a character wandering through an adventure world which may be a dungeon, a haunted house, an enchanted forest, or the like. The player operates the game by issuing commands within a text-based interface. These commands typically allow the user to pick up items, move around in the world, and interact with the denizens of the game world.

This case study concerns the construction of a program which provides the basic functionality of a text adventure program. The program developed herein will be designed for easy expansion. Thus, the goal of the case study is not to develop a particular adventure, but to provide data types and functions that would form the basis from which an adventure game could be constructed.

1.2   Case Study Problem Description

The program will accept the commands listed below. Each command must be typed on a single line.

GO *direction*

where *direction* is one of NORTH, SOUTH, EAST, or WEST. This command moves the player to the next "room" in the specified direction. The user may specify the entire word ("NORTH") for the direction, or only the first letter ("N").

GET *item*

where *item* is a reference to some item in the room occupied by the player. This command adds the specified item to the player's "inventory," which is a list containing all the items the player has picked up in the course of the adventure.

INVENTORY

Prints out a list of all the items in the player's inventory.

USE *item*

where *item* is a reference to an item within the player's inventory, or within the room occupied by the player. The effect of this command varies depending upon the item being used and where it is being used. For example, if the player uses a healing potion, it may restore his health, or using a key in a particular room may unlock a door.

LOOK

Prints out a description of the room that the player is currently in.

ATTACK *character*

where *character* is a reference to a character in the room occupied by the player. This command initiates a combat between the player and the specified character.

EXIT

Exits the user from the program.

When a user enters a room, or issues a *LOOK* command, a list of the items and characters in the room is printed, as illustrated below.

You are in: The Hallway.
There are doors: NORTH, EAST.
You see the following items:
SWORD
PAINTING
You see the following characters:
BORIS
Enter command: GET SWORD
Enter command: ATTACK BORIS

When the player initiates combat, he or she is asked to select a weapon from the inventory. Potentially, any item could be used as a weapon, but items vary in the amount of damage they may inflict on an opponent. (A sword, for example, would have a higher damage potential than a stick.) Combat proceeds by turns, with each combatant striking the other until one combatant suffers a fatal amount of damage. Whichever character initiates the combat always strikes the first blow. The amount of damage inflicted by a blow should be a random number between zero and the damage potential of the weapon used.

If the player loses the combat, the game is effectively over. If the player wins, then the opponent is removed from the game, and all the items owned by that combatant are placed in the room where the combat took place. The player may then pick up these items or ignore them, as desired.

As is typical with these games, access to some rooms may be blocked due to locked doors or some similar contrivance. Thus, the following interaction may occur:

```
You are in: The Hallway.
There are doors: NORTH, EAST.
You see the following items:
SWORD
PAINTING
You see the following characters:
BORIS
Enter command: GO NORTH
Sorry, Boris won't let you go that way.
Enter command:
```

As another potential complication, some "rooms" in an adventure may be programmed with actions that occur automatically when the player enters them. For example, the following may occur, after which a combat action ensues:

```
Enter command: GO WEST
You are in: The Hallway.
There are doors: NORTH, EAST.
You see the following items:
SWORD
PAINTING
You see the following characters:
BORIS
BORIS attacks you!
```

2   PROBLEM ANALYSIS AND SOLUTION DESIGN

2.1   Data Types

Analysis reveals that the abstract types described below would be present in any implementation of a text adventure game.

Item.

A type identifier used to represent any concrete item that appears within the text adventure world, such as a sword, a key, a book, and so forth. Associated with every item is the name of the item and the amount of damage inflicted by the item when used as a weapon

Character.

A type identifier used to represent any character, including the player, that may be present in the text adventure. Associated with every character is the character's name, the weapon the character is currently armed with, the character's current "health," and a collection of items that comprise the characters inventory. A character's health value is used in combat. When a character is struck by an opponent the character's health is decreased by the amount of damage inflicted. A character "dies" when its health value becomes less than or equal to zero.

Room.

A type identifier used to represent a "room" within the text adventure world. (The word "room" is used here in a general sense. For a particular game, a "room" may be a section of a forest, or a tunnel, but conceptually they are "rooms.") Associated with every room is a name, a collection of items in the room, a collection of characters in the room, and four values corresponding to the other rooms located to the north, south, east, and west of the room (some of these may be "empty" if there is no exit in a particular direction).

Associated with each of these types are the following operations, grouped according to the abstract type to which they are most relevant.

Item Operations.

PROCEDURE InitializeItem

Given: An item and its name
Purpose: Set the name information for the specified item. Sets the damage value of the item to zero.

PROCEDURE InitializeWeapon

Given: An item, its name, and its damage value

Purpose: Sets the name and damage information for the specified item.

Character Operations.

PROCEDURE InitializeCharacter

Given: A character, its name, and health
Purpose: Set the name and health information for the specified character.

PROCEDURE AddItemToCharacter

Given: An item and a character
Purpose: Record the fact that the specified item is in the inventory of the specified character.

PROCEDURE RemoveItemFromCharacter

Given: An item and a character
Purpose: Record the fact that the specified item is not in the inventory of the specified character.

PROCEDURE SetWeapon

Given: An item and a character
Purpose: Record the fact that the specified player is now using the specified item as a weapon.

FUNCTION GetDamage

Given: A character
Purpose: Return the amount of damage that the player inflicts on an opponent. (According to the specification, this would be a random number.)

FUNCTION GetHealth

Given: A character
Purpose: Return the current health of the character.

PROCEDURE DeductHealth

Given: A character and an amount
Purpose: Deduct the specified amount from the player's current health level.

Room Operations.

PROCEDURE InitializeRoom

Given: A room and its name

Purpose: Set the name for the specified room. Record that the room contains no items and no characters. Record that there are no exits (neither north, south, east, nor west) from the room.

PROCEDURE PrintRoomDescription

Given: A room
Purpose: Print out a narrative detailing the name of the room and its contents (items, characters, and exits).

PROCEDURE AddItemToRoom

Given: A room and an item
Purpose: Record the fact that the specified item is in the specified room.

PROCEDURE RemoveItemFromRoom

Given: A room and an item
Purpose: Record the fact that the specified item is not in the specified room.

PROCEDURE AddCharacterToRoom

Given: A room and a character
Purpose: Record the fact that the specified character is in the specified room.

PROCEDURE RemoveCharacterFromRoom

Given: A room and a character
Purpose: Record the fact that the specified character is not in the specified room.

PROCEDURE EstablishConnection

Given: Two rooms and a direction (north, south, east, or west)
Purpose: Record the fact that moving from the first room in the specified direction will lead the player to the second room.

2.2 Global Values

It will be necessary to have available at all points in the program variables holding all the items, characters, and rooms used in the program. (In the implementation, these will be arrays, i.e., an array of characters, an array of items, and an array of rooms.) It will also be necessary to have a global variable identifying the room currently occupied by the player.

2.3   Command Interface

The key type abstraction used in the implementation of the command interface will be a *CommandRecord* which is to encapsulate all the information contained within a single command entered by the player. For the simple user interface described in the problem specification, a *CommandRecord* would contain at most two values: one specifying the command action selected by the user (GO, GET, etc.) and the other specifying the referent of the command (a direction, an item, or a character for instance.) With this in mind, the following two operations are central to the command interface:

PROCEDURE GetCommand

Given: A CommandRecord (presumably empty)
Purpose: Read a command from the user and fill the CommandRecord with appropriate values.

PROCEDURE ProcessCommand

Given: A CommandRecord (presumably produced by a call to GetCommand)
Purpose: Perform appropriate actions based on the values in the CommandRecord.

To make the program modular and increase the ease with which new commands can be added to the system, a procedure will be defined for each of the possible user commands. Thus, the implementation of the *ProcessCommand* procedure will involve checking the appropriate value in its *CommandRecord* parameter and calling one of these procedures. It is not necessary to list each of these since they correspond directly to the user commands described in the problem specification. However, three are given below for the purposes of illustration.

PROCEDURE ProcessGo

Given: A direction
Purpose: Perform all actions required when the user enters a GO command specifying the given direction. These are: (1) Check that the player meets the necessary preconditions for moving into the room (has the key, etc.), (2) record that the player is in the room, (3) print a description of the room, and (4) perform any automatic actions associated with moving into the room.

PROCEDURE ProcessGet

Given: An item

Purpose: Perform all actions required when the user enters a GET command specifying the given item. These are: (1) remove the item from the room currently occupied by the player, and (2) add the item to the player's inventory.

PROCEDURE ProcessAttack

Given: A character

Purpose: Perform all actions required when the user initiates combat with the specified character. These are: (1) have the player select a weapon, (2) execute a loop that deducts damage from the two combatants until one "dies," (3) if the player wins the combat then remove the other character from the room and add all of its inventory items to the room.

The USE command cannot be implemented in the same way as the GET and ATTACK commands. Since the effect of the USE command will depend upon the particular item being used, or upon where it will be used, the details of the procedure that implements USE will be different for each adventure game. (Notice that this is not true for ProcessGet, for example. This procedure will be the same for all adventure games.)

The same also applies to the procedures which implement the preconditions and automatic actions that apply when the player executes a GO command. These will be different for every room. To handle these elements of the specification, the following two procedures will be defined:

FUNCTION CanPass

Given: A room the player wishes to move into

Purpose: Return TRUE if the player is able to move into the room, FALSE otherwise. If FALSE, print some appropriate message.

PROCEDURE InitialAction

Given: A room the player is moving into

Purpose: Perform actions, if any, that happen automatically when the user enters the specified room.

Given these procedures, the main activity of an adventure game program can be described by the following algorithm:

Setup the adventure world by executing the procedures *InitializeItem*, *InitializeCharacter*, *EstablishConnection*, and so forth, as required for every item, character, and room in the game.

REPEAT

    Execute the *GetCommand* procedure

    Execute the *ProcessCommand* procedure

UNTIL the user has entered the EXIT command OR the user has died.

3   IMPLEMENTATION

3.1   Primitive Data Types and Utility Procedures

Reference the program listing in section 4 and note that a string data type and enumerated types for the four directions and each of the user commands are defined. Functions are needed to convert character strings to these enumerated types. Two techniques are used here. Read the *StringToDirection* function and notice that it simply checks the first letter of the specified string and returns the appropriate enumerated value. This technique will not work for converting strings to command types, however, since commands are not unique in their first character. Thus, to perform this function an array called *CommandStringTable* is defined in the global variables section and initialized in the *InitializeTables* procedure. This array has the property that *CommandStringTable[GO] = 'GO'*, *CommandStringTable[GET] = 'GET'*, and so forth. With this in mind, notice that the function *StringToCommand* works by performing a search for the specified command in *CommandStringTable*. This technique makes it easy to add additional commands to the adventure program.

Throughout the program it will be convenient to refer to individual items, characters, and rooms by an identification number. (These numbers will correspond to an object's index within the relevant global array.) Thus, subrange types for items, character, and room numbers are defined.

Finally, note that a random number function and a function to compare two strings for equality are defined. These are lacking in some Pascal implementations.

3.2   Abstract Data Types and Global Variables

The three abstract data types described in section two are implemented as records. Notice that the *SET* construct is used to implement the idea of a collection. Thus, a character contains a *SET OF* items, a room contains a *SET OF* characters, and so forth.

In the global variables section of the program, arrays are defined to store all the characters, items, and rooms in the adventure world. It is very important to understand that the index locations of objects within these arrays are used as the identification numbers for those objects. These identification numbers are what are stored in the *SET* fields of the character and room records. As an illustration, suppose there is a room called "The Hallway" which contains an item called "SWORD". We decide that "The Hallway" will be stored as the first item in the rooms array and that "SWORD" will be stored as the first item in the items array. To this end, the following statements could be written:

```
Rooms[1].Name := 'The Hallway';
Items[1].Name := 'SWORD';
```

To indicate that the sword is contained in the hallway, the following statement could be written, since 1 corresponds to item one, i.e., the sword, and Rooms[1] corresponds to the hallway:

```
Rooms[1].Items := [1]
```

With this in mind, notice that the implementation of the *AddItemToRoom* procedure involves adding the specified item number to the Items set of the specified room. The "Remove" and the other "Add" procedures are implemented similarly.

It will be necessary to find the identification number associated with the name of a particular item or character. For example, if the user enters the word "SWORD" in a command, it is necessary to know that he or she is referring to item number one. This functionality is provided by the *GetItemNumber* and *GetCharacterNumber* functions. Both are given a character string and return the index of the record containing that string as a name.

Finally, notice the implementation of the *Exits* field within *RoomRecord*. For some *RoomRecord, R, R.Exits[NORTH]* specifies the index of the room to the north of *R, R.Exits[EAST]* specifies the index of the room to the east of *R*, and so forth. Some mechanism is required to indicate that there is no exit in a particular direction. This will be indicated by putting the index of the room itself in the *Exits* array. For example, if there is no exit to the north of room number one, then *Rooms[1].Exits[NORTH]* will equal 1. Observe how this convention is used in the implementation of the *ProcessGo* procedure to tell the user that he or she cannot move in the specified direction.

3.3   User Interface Procedures

A *CommandRecord* as described in section 2.3 is implemented using the variant record construct of Pascal. Every *CommandRecord* contains an *Action* field specifying the type of command described by the record. Based on the value of this field, a *CommandRecord* may contain an additional field representing an item, character, or direction.

The GetCommand procedure uses a procedure called *ReadWord* which reads a character string terminated by a blank. *GetCommand* reads the first word typed by the player and converts this to a *CommandType*. It may then read additional words and fill in the appropriate fields of the *CommandRecord*, depending upon the type of command entered.

The procedure *RunAdventure* executes *GetCommand* and *ProcessCommand* in a loop, as described in section 2.3. The implementations of the various command procedures requires little explication, provided one understands how the various data types and variables described in the previous sections interact with one another.

3.4   A Sample Game

To test the game types and functions, a simple adventure game that involves four rooms—a hallway, a dining room, a study, and a bedroom—is implemented. A map of the game world is shown on the next page.

The player begins in the hallway and must make his way to the bedroom. The door from the study to the bedroom is locked, however. Boris, who resides in the dining room, holds the key. There is a sword in the hallway. The player must pick up the sword, defeat Boris, and take the key. After the key has been retrieved, the player can enter the bedroom. The procedure *SetUpAdventure* is used to encapsulate all the procedure calls necessary to set up this adventure. Notice that symbolic constants are used to represent the various objects in the game. Also note how the "key" condition on the entrance to the bedroom is implemented in *CanEnter*.

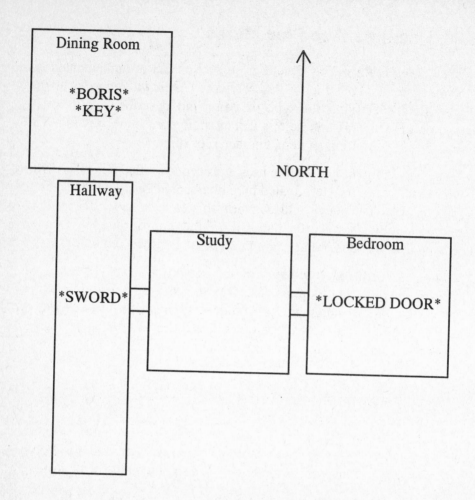

4 THE TEXT ADVENTURE PROGRAM

```
PROGRAM Adventure(input, output);
CONST
      StringSize = 32;
      NumRooms = 4;
      NumItems = 4;
      NumCharacters = 2;
{== Symbolic Constants for the Sample Adventure =}
      PLAYER = 1;
      BORIS = 2;                    KEY = 1;
      BORIS_SWORD = 2;              PLAYER_SWORD = 3;
      HALLWAY = 1;                  DINING_ROOM = 2;
      STUDY = 3;                    BEDROOM = 4;
```

```
TYPE
      String = PACKED ARRAY [1..StringSize] OF CHAR;
      DirectionType = (NORTH, SOUTH, EAST, WEST);
      RoomNumber = 1..NumRooms;
      ItemNumber = 1..NumItems;
      CharacterNumber = 1..NumCharacters;
      CharacterRecord = RECORD
          Name : String;
          Items : SET OF ItemNumber;
          Weapon : ItemNumber;
          Health : INTEGER;
  END;
      ItemRecord = RECORD
          Name : String;
          Damage : INTEGER;
      END;
      RoomRecord = RECORD
          Name : String;
          Exits : ARRAY [DirectionType] OF RoomNumber;
          Items : SET OF ItemNumber;
          Characters : SET OF CharacterNumber;
      END;
      CommandType = (GO, EXIT, USE, INVENTORY, LOOK, GET, ATTACK);
      CommandRecord = RECORD
          CASE Action : CommandType OF
              GO : (Direction : DirectionType);
              GET, USE : (Item : ItemNumber);
              ATTACK : (Character : CharacterNumber);
      END;

VAR
      Rooms : ARRAY [RoomNumber] OF RoomRecord;
      Items : ARRAY [ItemNumber] OF ItemRecord;
      Characters : ARRAY [CharacterNumber] OF CharacterRecord;
      CommandStringTable : ARRAY [CommandType] OF String;
      CurrentLocation : RoomNumber;
      seed : REAL;
```

```
{=========================}
{====  Utility Procedures =====}
{=========================}


FUNCTION random(n : integer) : INTEGER;
BEGIN
    seed := sqr(seed + 3.1415927);
    seed := seed - trunc(seed);
    random := trunc(n * seed) + 1;
END;


FUNCTION StringEqual(s1, s2 : String) : BOOLEAN;
VAR
    i : INTEGER; Equal : BOOLEAN;
BEGIN
    Equal := TRUE;
    i := 1;
    WHILE (Equal) AND (i <= StringSize) DO
        IF (s1[i] <> s2[i]) THEN
            Equal := FALSE
        ELSE
            i := i + 1;
    StringEqual := Equal;
END;


FUNCTION StringToCommand(s : String) : CommandType;
VAR
    i : CommandType; Found : BOOLEAN;
BEGIN
    Found := FALSE;
    i := GO;
    WHILE (NOT Found) DO BEGIN
        IF StringEqual(CommandStringTable[i], s) THEN
            Found := TRUE
        ELSE
            i := SUCC(i);
    END;
    StringToCommand := i;
END;
```

```
FUNCTION StringToDirection(s : String) : DirectionType;
BEGIN
    CASE s[1] OF
        'S': StringToDirection := SOUTH;
        'N': StringToDirection := NORTH;
        'E': StringToDirection := EAST;
        'W': StringToDirection := WEST;
        END;
END;


FUNCTION GetItemNumber(s : String) : ItemNumber;
VAR
    i : INTEGER; Found : BOOLEAN;
BEGIN
    Found := FALSE;
    i := 1;
    WHILE (NOT Found) AND (i <= NumItems) DO
        IF StringEqual(Items[i].Name, s) THEN
            Found := TRUE
        ELSE
            i := i + 1;
    GetItemNumber := i;
END;


FUNCTION GetCharacterNumber(s : String) : CharacterNumber;
VAR
    i : INTEGER; Found : BOOLEAN;
BEGIN
    Found := FALSE;
    i := 1;
    WHILE (NOT Found) AND (i <= NumCharacters) DO
        IF StringEqual(Characters[i].Name, s) THEN
            Found := TRUE
        ELSE
            i := i + 1;
    GetCharacterNumber := i;
END;
```

```
{=========================}
{==== Room Procedures =====}
{=========================}


PROCEDURE PrintRoomDescription(number : RoomNumber);
VAR
    I :INTEGER;
BEGIN
    WITH Rooms[number] DO BEGIN
        Writeln('You are in ', Name);
        Write('There are exits to the: ');
        IF Exits[NORTH] <> number THEN Write('NORTH ');
        IF Exits[SOUTH] <> number THEN Write('SOUTH ');
        IF Exits[EAST] <> number THEN Write('EAST ');
        IF Exits[WEST] <> number THEN Write('WEST ');
        Writeln;
    END;
        Writeln('In this room you see the following items:');
    FOR i := 1 TO NumItems DO
        IF i IN Rooms[number].Items THEN
            Writeln(Items[i].Name);
        Writeln('In this room you see the following characters:');
    FOR i := 1 TO NumCharacters DO
            IF i IN Rooms[number].Characters THEN
            Writeln(Characters[i].Name);
END;


PROCEDURE AddItemToRoom(room : RoomNumber; item : ItemNumber);
BEGIN
    WITH Rooms[room] DO
        Items := Items + [item];
END;


PROCEDURE RemoveItemFromRoom(room : RoomNumber; item :
        ItemNumber);
BEGIN
    WITH Rooms[room] DO
        Items := Items - [item];
END;
```

```
PROCEDURE AddCharacterToRoom(room : RoomNumber; character :
        CharacterNumber);
BEGIN
    WITH Rooms[room] DO
        Characters := Characters + [character];
END;

PROCEDURE RemoveCharacterFromRoom(room : RoomNumber; character
        : CharacterNumber);
BEGIN
    WITH Rooms[room] DO
        Characters := Characters - [character];
END;

PROCEDURE InitRoom(room : RoomNumber; s : String);
VAR
    i : DirectionType;
BEGIN
    WITH Rooms[room] DO BEGIN
        FOR i := NORTH TO WEST DO
            Exits[i] := room;
        Name := s; Characters := [ ]; Items := [ ];
    END;
END;

PROCEDURE EstablishConnection(Start, Finish : RoomNumber; Direct :
        DirectionType);
BEGIN
    Rooms[Start].Exits[Direct] := Finish;
END;

{========================}
{==== Item Procedures ======}
{========================}

PROCEDURE InitItem(item : ItemNumber; s : String);
BEGIN
    WITH Items[item] DO BEGIN
        Name := s;
```

```
            Damage := 0;
        END;
    END;


    PROCEDURE InitWeapon(item : ItemNumber; s : String; d : INTEGER);
    BEGIN
        WITH Items[item] DO BEGIN
            Name := s;
            Damage := d;
        END;
    END;


{===========================}
{==== Character Procedures ====}
{===========================}


    FUNCTION GetHealth(character : CharacterNumber) : INTEGER;
    BEGIN
        GetHealth := Characters[character].Health;
    END;


    PROCEDURE ReduceHealth(character : CharacterNumber; amount : INTEGER);
    BEGIN
        WITH Characters[character] DO
            Health := Health - amount;
    END;


    PROCEDURE SetWeapon(character : CharacterNumber; item : ItemNumber);
    BEGIN
        Characters[character].Weapon := item;
    END;


    PROCEDURE AddItemToCharacter(character : CharacterNumber;   item :
            ItemNumber);
    BEGIN
        WITH Characters[character] DO
            Items := Items + [item];
    END;
```

```
PROCEDURE RemoveItemFromCharacter(character : CharacterNumber;
        item : ItemNumber);
BEGIN
    WITH Characters[character] DO
        Items := Items - [item];
END;

PROCEDURE RecordDeath(character : CharacterNumber);
{
    This procedure assumes that the character is in the
    same room as the player, ie, CurrentLocation.
}
VAR
    i : ItemNumber;
    BEGIN
    FOR i := 1 TO NumItems DO
        IF i in Characters[character].Items THEN BEGIN
            RemoveItemFromCharacter(character, i);
            AddItemToRoom(CurrentLocation, i);
    END;
    RemoveCharacterFromRoom(CurrentLocation, character);
END;

PROCEDURE InitCharacter(character : CharacterNumber; s : String;  h :
        INTEGER);
BEGIN
    WITH Characters[character] DO BEGIN
        Health := h;
        Name := s;
        Items := [ ];
    END;
END;

FUNCTION GetDamage(character : CharacterNumber) : INTEGER;
BEGIN
    GetDamage := random(Items[Characters[character].Weapon].Damage);
END;
```

```
{=========================}
{=== Command Procedures ===}
{=========================}

PROCEDURE ProcessLook;
BEGIN
    PrintRoomDescription(CurrentLocation);
END;
PROCEDURE ProcessInventory;
VAR
    i : ItemNumber;
BEGIN
    FOR i := 1 TO NumItems DO
        IF i IN Characters[PLAYER].Items THEN
            writeln(Items[i].name);
END;


FUNCTION CanEnter(room : RoomNumber): BOOLEAN; FORWARD;
PROCEDURE InitialAction(room : RoomNumber); FORWARD;
PROCEDURE ProcessGo(Where : DirectionType);
VAR
    NewLocation : INTEGER;
BEGIN
    NewLocation := Rooms[CurrentLocation].Exits[Where];
    IF CanEnter(NewLocation) THEN
        IF NewLocation = CurrentLocation THEN
            Writeln('There is no exit that way!')
        ELSE BEGIN
            CurrentLocation := NewLocation;
            PrintRoomDescription(NewLocation);
            InitialAction(NewLocation);
        END;
END;


PROCEDURE ProcessGet(item : ItemNumber);
BEGIN
    RemoveItemFromRoom(CurrentLocation, item);
    AddItemToCharacter(PLAYER, item);
END;
```

```
PROCEDURE ProcessUse(number : ItemNumber);
BEGIN
{
    Implementation of this procedure will be different for every
    adventure
}
END;

PROCEDURE ReadWord(VAR s : String); FORWARD;
PROCEDURE ChooseWeapon;
VAR
    s : String;
BEGIN
    ProcessInventory;
    Write('Choose your weapon: ');
    ReadWord(s);
    SetWeapon(PLAYER, GetItemNumber(s));
END;

PROCEDURE Fight(initiator, opponent : CharacterNumber);
VAR
    damage : INTEGER;
    attacker, defender, temp : CharacterNumber;
BEGIN
    attacker := initiator;
    defender := opponent;
    REPEAT
        damage := GetDamage(attacker);
        ReduceHealth(defender, damage);
        Writeln(Characters[defender].Name, 'is hit for ',
            damage, ' amount!');
        temp := attacker;
        attacker := defender;
        defender := temp;
    UNTIL (GetHealth(defender) <= 0) OR (GetHealth(attacker) <= 0);
END;

PROCEDURE ProcessAttack(opponent : CharacterNumber);
BEGIN
    ChooseWeapon;
```

```
            Fight(PLAYER, opponent);
            IF (GetHealth(PLAYER) <= 0) THEN
                    Writeln('You are dead!')
            ELSE BEGIN
                RecordDeath(opponent);
                PrintRoomDescription(CurrentLocation);
            END;
    END;


    {===================}
    {==== User Interface ====}
    {===================}


    PROCEDURE ProcessCommand(Command : CommandRecord);
    BEGIN
        CASE Command.Action OF
            GO : ProcessGo(Command.Direction);
            INVENTORY : ProcessInventory;
            EXIT : Writeln('Goodbye!');
            LOOK : ProcessLook;
            GET : PickUp(Command.Item);
            ATTACK : ProcessAttack(Command.Character);
            USE : ProcessUse(Command.Item);
        END;
    END;


    PROCEDURE ReadWord(VAR s : String);
    VAR
        c : CHAR; i, j : INTEGER;
    BEGIN
        Read(c);
        i := 1;
        WHILE c <> ' ' DO BEGIN
            s[i] := c;
            Read(c);
            i := i + 1;
        END;
        FOR j := i TO StringSize DO
            s[j] := ' ';
    END;
```

```
PROCEDURE GetCommand(VAR Command : CommandRecord);
VAR
    s : String;
BEGIN
    Write('Command> ');
    ReadWord(s);
    Command.Action := StringToCommand(s);
    CASE Command.Action OF
        GO : BEGIN
            ReadWord(s); Command.Direction := StringToDirection(s);
            END;
        GET, USE : BEGIN
            ReadWord(s); Command.Item := GetItemNumber(s);
        END;
        ATTACK : BEGIN
            ReadWord(s); Command.Character := GetCharacterNumber(s);
        END;
        LOOK, EXIT, INVENTORY : BEGIN END;
    END;
END;

PROCEDURE RunAdventure;
VAR
    Command : CommandRecord;
BEGIN
        PrintRoomDescription(CurrentLocation);
    REPEAT
        GetCommand(Command);
        ProcessCommand(Command);
    UNTIL (Command.Action = EXIT) OR (Characters[PLAYER].health <= 0);
END;

{==============================}
{==== Game Specific Procedures ===}
{==============================}

FUNCTION CanEnter(room : RoomNumber) : BOOLEAN;
VAR
    pass : BOOLEAN;
```

```
BEGIN
    pass := TRUE;
    IF room = BEDROOM THEN
        IF NOT (KEY IN Characters[PLAYER].Items) THEN BEGIN
            WriteIn('You need a key!');
            pass := FALSE;
        END;
    CanEnter := pass;
END;


PROCEDURE InitialAction(room : RoomNumber);
BEGIN
{
    No action required in the sample game.
}
END;


PROCEDURE SetUpAdventure;
BEGIN
    InitRoom(HALLWAY,'Hallway');
    InitRoom(STUDY,'Study');
    InitRoom(BEDROOM,'Bedroom');
    InitRoom(DINING_ROOM, 'Dining Room');

    EstablishConnection(HALLWAY, DINING_ROOM, NORTH);
    EstablishConnection(DINING_ROOM, HALLWAY, SOUTH);

    EstablishConnection(HALLWAY, STUDY, EAST);
    EstablishConnection(STUDY, HALLWAY, WEST);

    EstablishConnection(STUDY, BEDROOM, EAST);
    EstablishConnection(BEDROOM, STUDY, WEST);

    InitWeapon(PLAYER_SWORD,'Sword',10);
    InitWeapon(BORIS_SWORD, 'Sword', 10);
    InitItem(KEY, 'Key');

    InitCharacter(BORIS,'Boris', 20);
    InitCharacter(PLAYER, 'The Player', 20);
```

```
        AddItemToRoom(HALLWAY,PLAYER_SWORD);
        AddCharacterToRoom(DINING_ROOM, BORIS);
        AddItemToCharacter(BORIS, BORIS_SWORD);
        AddItemToCharacter(BORIS, KEY);
        SetWeapon(BORIS, BORIS_SWORD);

        CurrentLocation := HALLWAY;
END;


{==================}
{=== Main Program ===}
{==================}


PROCEDURE InitalizeTables;
BEGIN
        CommandStringTable[GO] := 'GO';
        CommandStringTable[GET] := 'GET';
        CommandStringTable[ATTACK] := 'ATTACK';
        CommandStringTable[INVENTORY] := 'INVENTORY';
        CommandStringTable[LOOK] := 'LOOK';
        CommandStringTable[EXIT] := 'EXIT';
        CommandStringTable[USE] := 'USE';
END;


BEGIN
        seed := 0.5;
        InitializeTables;
        SetUpAdventure;
        RunAdventure;
END.
```

Glossary

GLOSSARY

ACCESS TIME — (1) The time interval between the instant at which data are called for from a storage device and the instant delivery begins. (2) The time interval between the instant at which data are requested to be stored and the instant at which storage is started.

ALGORITHM — A prescribed set of well defined rules or processes for the solution of a problem in a finite number of steps, e.g., a full statement of an arithmetic procedure for evaluating sin x to a stated precision.

ALPHANUMERIC — Pertaining to a character set that contains letters, digits, and usually other characters such as punctuation marks.

AND — A logic operator having the property that if P is a statement, Q is a statement, R is a statement ..., then the AND of P, Q, R..., is true if all statements are true, false if any statement is false.

ARRAY — An arrangement of elements in one or more dimensions.

ASSEMBLER — A computer program that prepares a machine language program from a symbolic language program by substituting absolute operation codes for symbolic operation codes and absolute or relocatable addresses for symbolic addresses.

BATCH PROCESSING — (1) Pertaining to the technique of executing a set of computer programs such that each is completed before the next program of the set is started. (2) Pertaining to the sequential input of computer programs or data. (3) Loosely, the execution of computer programs serially.

BIG O NOTATION — A way to represent the running time (T(n)) of a program based on the input size (n),

It is often used for comparisons of different sorts and searches.

	type	worst case	average case
sorts:	quick	n	n log (n)
	heap	n log (n)	n log (n)
	merge	n log (n)	n log (n)
	bucket	n	n
	bubble	n	n

	type	worst case	average case
	insertion	n	n
	selection	n	n
	shell	n	n
searches:	binary	n	log (n)
	sequential	n	n/2
	hash	n	n

BINARY — (1) Pertaining to a characteristic or property involving a selection, choice, or condition in which there are two possibilities. (2) Pertaining to the number representation system with a base of two.

BIT — A binary digit.

BOOLEAN OPERATOR — A logic operator each of whose operands and whose result have one of two values.

BYTE — A sequence of adjacent binary digits operated upon as a unit and usually shorter than a computer word.

CENTRAL PROCESSING UNIT (CPU) — A unit of a computer that includes the circuits controlling the interpretation and execution of instructions.

COMPILER — This is a program that creates a machine language program from a computer program written in another programming language by making use of the overall logic structure of the program, or generating more than one machine instruction for each symbolic statement, or both, as well as performing the function of an assembler.

COMPUTER NETWORK — A complex system consisting of two or more interconnected computers.

COMPUTER PROGRAM — A series of instructions or statements, in a form acceptable to a computer, prepared in order to achieve a certain result.

DIRECT ACCESS — (1) Pertaining to the process of obtaining data from, or placing data into, storage where the time required for such access is independent of the location of the data most recently obtained or placed in storage. (2) Pertaining to a storage device in which the access time is effectively independent of the location of the data. Synonymous with random access (1).

DOCUMENTATION — (1) The creating, collecting, organizing, storing, citing, and disseminating of documents or the information recorded in documents. (2) A collection of documents or information on a given subject.

DYNAMIC STORAGE — A device storing data in a manner that permits the data to move or vary with time such that the specified data are not always available for recovery. Magnetic-drum and disc storage are dynamic storage.

HARDWARE — Physical equipment, as opposed to the computer program or method of use, e.g., mechanical, magnetic, electrical, or electronic devices. Contrast with software.

INPUT — Pertaining to a device process, or channel involved in the insertion of data or states, or to the data or states involved.

INPUT DEVICE — The device or collective set of devices used for conveying data into another device.

INSTRUCTION — A statement that specifies an operation and the values or locations of its operands.

INTERFACE — A shared boundary. An interface might be a hardware component to link two devices or it might be a portion of storage or registers accessed by two or more computer programs.

INTERNAL STORAGE — Addressable storage directly controlled by the CPU.

INTERPRETER — A computer program that translates and executes each source language statement before translating and executing the next one.

LANGUAGE — A set of representations, conventions, and rules used to convey information.

LOCAL VARIABLE — A variable whose scope and accessibility are limited to a specific portion of a program (i.e. a subroutine).

MACHINE CODE — An operation code that a machine is designed to recognize.

MACHINE LANGUAGE — A language that is directly used by a machine.

MAGNETIC STORAGE — A storage device that utilizes the magnetic properties of materials to store data, e.g., magnetic cores, tapes, and films.

MASS STORAGE DEVICE — A device having a large storage capacity, e.g., magnetic disc.

MONITOR — Software or hardware that observes, supervises, controls, or verifies the operations of a system.

MULTIPROCESSING — Pertaining to the simultaneous execution of two or more computer programs or sequences of instructions by a computer or computer network.

OBJECT CODE — Output from a compiler or assembler which is itself executable machine code or is suitable for processing to produce executable machine language.

OBJECT PROGRAM — A fully compiled or assembled program that is ready to be loaded into the compiler.

OPERATING SYSTEM — Software which controls the execution of computer programs and which may provide scheduling, debugging, input/output control, accounting, compilation, storage assignment, data management, and related services.

OUTPUT — Pertaining to a device, process, or channel involved in an output process, or to the data or states involved.

OUTPUT DEVICE — The device or collective set of devices used for conveying data out of another device.

PROCESSOR — (1) In hardware, a data processor. (2) In software, a computer program that includes the compiling, assembling, translating, and related functions for a specific programming language.

PROGRAMMING MODULE — A discrete identifiable set of instructions, usually handled as a unit, by an assembler, a compiler, a linkage editor, a loading routine, or other type of routine or subroutine.

RANDOM ACCESS — An access mode in which specific logical records are obtained from or placed into a mass storage file in a nonsequential manner.

SCOPE — The part of the program during which a particular variable may be accessed.

SEARCH — To examine a set of items for one or more having a desired property.

SOFTWARE — A set of computer programs, procedures, and possibly associated documentation concerned with the operation of a data processing system, e.g., compilers, library routines, manuals, circuit diagrams.

SORT — To segregate items into groups according to some definite rules.

STORAGE CAPACITY — The amount of data that can be continued in a storage device.

SYNTAX — (1) The structure of expressions in a language. (2) The rules governing the structure of a language.

TERMINAL — A point in a system or communication network at which data either enter or leave.

TIME SHARING — Pertaining to the interleaved use of the time of a device.

REA's Test Preps
The Best in Test Preparation